Personal Provision of Retirement Income

Personal Provision of Retirement Income

Meeting the Needs of Older People?

Edited by

Jim Stewart

Senior Lecturer in Finance, Trinity College Dublin, Ireland

Gerard Hughes

Visiting Professor, Trinity College Dublin, Ireland

Edward Elgar

Cheltenham, UK • Northampton, MA, USA

Published by
Edward Elgar Publishing Limited
The Lypiatts
15 Lansdown Road
Cheltenham
Glos GL50 2JA
UK

Edward Elgar Publishing, Inc.
William Pratt House
9 Dewey Court
Northampton
Massachusetts 01060
USA

A catalogue record for this book
is available from the British Library

Library of Congress Control Number: 2009930850

ISBN 978 1 84720 927 6

Printed and bound by MPG Books Group, UK

Contents

PART II PUBLIC POLICY AND PRIVATE PROVISION

PART III OTHER ISSUES WITH INDIVIDUAL PENSION PROVISION

Figures

Tables

Contributors

Lucy apRoberts is an economist and she lectures on pension issues at IDHE, Université de Paris X – Nanterre.

Pierre Concialdi is an economist at the Institut de Recherches Économiques et Sociales (IRES) (Institute for Social and Economic Research) in Paris, France. He is the author of a number of studies on income distribution, social protection and the financing of social security, and tax progressivity and low-wage employment

Bryn Davies is an independent consulting actuary working mainly for trade unions, providing support for their collective bargaining on occupational pension schemes. He has been a partner and research actuary for a major firm of consulting actuaries, the pensions officer for the Trade Union Congress and has written a number of books and pamphlets on the reform of State pensions.

Kim De Witte is a researcher and associate lecturer in the Law Faculty of the Katholieke Universiteit Leuven. His research and teaching focuses on pension law.

Gerard Hughes is an economist and a Visiting Professor at Trinity College Dublin. His current research interests include pension reform, the cost and distribution of tax expenditures on private pensions, and the effectiveness of public and private pension systems in delivering pensions.

Dana Muir is Arthur F. Thurnau Professor of Business Law at the Ross School of Business at the University of Michigan in Ann Arbor, Michigan, US. She has published numerous articles on policy matters related to employee benefits. She is particularly interested in investment, fiduciary, and dispute resolution issues.

Finn Ostrup is Professor in Capital Markets, Center for Financial Law, Copenhagen Business School, Copenhagen, where he teaches courses in finance and in financial law. His current research interests include financial institutions, financial crises and international monetary economics. He has written a number of books and articles on Danish and international financial institutions and on monetary theory. He is a Doctor of Economics.

Felice Roberto Pizzuti is Professor of Economic Policy and Director of the Master in Public Economics, 'Sapienza' University of Rome, Faculty ofEconomics. He teaches courses also on welfare economics and has written a number of essays on economic theory and policy, especially on the welfare state and pensions. He is the editor of the *'Rapporto annuale sullo stato sociale'* (Annual Report on the Welfare State).

Michele Raitano is Lecturer of Economic Policy at 'Sapienza' University of Rome. In past years he has collaborated with ISAE (Istituto Studi Analisi Economica) and, as adviser for pension policies, with the Italian government. His main research topics are inequality and welfare state systems, with a special focus on pensions, areas on which he has published many papers. He teaches courses on welfare and pension economics and is a contributing author of the 'Rapporto annuale sullo stato sociale' (Annual Report on the Welfare State) edited by F.R. Pizzuti.

Paul Roels is an associate lecturer at the Law Faculty of the Katholieke Universiteit Leuven and an independent consultant. He works and publishes mainly on a broad range of pension and insurance issues. He is appointed as an expert on the Occupational Pension Board, an advisory commission to the Belgian government.

Ann-Charlotte Ståhlberg, works in the Swedish Institute for Social Research, Stockholm University, SE-106 91 Stockholm, Sweden.

Yves Stevens is an associate professor at the Law Faculty of the Katholieke Universiteit Leuven. His research and teaching focuses on pension law. He is coordinator of specialised studies in Pension Law. As a pension expert he has worked and lectured in over 20 countries. He is currently the president of the Occupational Pension Board, an advisory commission to the Belgian government.

Heinz-Dietrich Steinmeyer is a professor for Civil Law, Labor Law, and Social Security Law at the University of Münster in Germany. He served as an expert for the European Commission on social security and supplementary pensions and has been a pension consultant in a number of European countries as well as in Latin America. His research focuses on social security, labour law, European law and comparative studies. He is chairman of the European Network for Research on Supplementary Pensions and a member of the board of the German-American Lawyers Association.

Jim Stewart is a Senior Lecturer in Finance, School of Business, Trinity College, Dublin, where he teaches courses in finance. His current research interests include corporate finance, corporate taxation, low tax financial centres and financial aspects of pension policy. He has co-edited and contributed to five books on pension systems and has published a number of papers on financial aspects of pension policy.

Marek Szczepański works at Poznan University of Technology, Department of Economic Science, Poland.

John Turner is Director of the Pension Policy Center. Formerly he was Deputy Director of the Office of Research and Economic Analysis, Pension and Welfare Benefits Administration, US Department of Labor and he has also worked for the International Labour Office in Geneva. He has written and edited twelve books on pensions and employer-provided benefits, and has recently written *Pension Policy: The Search for Better Solutions* (W.E. Upjohn Institute for Employment Research, 2009). He has a PhD in economics from the University of Chicago.

Barbara Waine is an Honorary Senior Research Fellow in the Institute of Social Studies, University of Birmingham and Honorary Visitor in the School of Social Sciences, University of Manchester. Her published work in the field of pensions includes articles on personal pensions, occupational pension schemes and executive pensions.

Acknowledgements

The contributions to this book are based on papers presented at the European Network for Research on Supplementary Pensions (ENRSP) and l'Institut de Recherches Économiques et Sociales (IRES) conference 'Personal Choice in the Provision of Retirement Income: Meeting the Needs of Older People?' which was organised by IRES and held in Paris, France on 17–18 December 2007. The conference was made possible by support from IRES and the l'Observatoire des Retraite. The conference was organised by Pierre Concialdi of IRES. The members of the scientific committee for the conference were Heinz-Dietrich Steinmeyer (President, ENRSP), Lucy apRoberts, Pierre Concialdi, Bryn Davies, Gerard Hughes, and Jim Stewart.

The editors are grateful to the School of Business, Trinity College Dublin for its support during the preparation of the book for publication

Jim Stewart,
Gerard Hughes,
Trinity College, Dublin

1. Overview and Summary of Key Issues

Jim Stewart and Gerard Hughes

1. INTRODUCTION

In response to long-term demographic projections which show a significant increase in older people's share of the population many countries in the European Union have reformed their public pension systems by increasing the retirement age and indexing pensions in payment in line with prices rather than wages. These changes have resulted, or will result, in significant reductions in the percentage of pre-retirement income that is replaced by public pay-as-you-go pension schemes. The weakening of the public schemes has, therefore, opened up a gap between expected and projected income in retirement. The main option for filling this gap for most employees is to start contributing to either a group occupational pension scheme or to a personal pension account. Occupational schemes presuppose a long-term attachment to the labour force and the income capacity to save. Consequently, they have great difficulty in providing an adequate retirement income for the low paid, for many women who take responsibility for caring for children and elderly relatives, for workers who are subject to unemployment from time to time and for atypical workers. In the past personal pension plans were generally only available to self-employed workers but they have now been extended to allow employees and other individuals to start saving for their retirement in tax-advantaged personal pension plans. These personal pension products are generally sold by financial institutions such as banks and insurance companies but they are also marketed in some countries through retail outlets such as supermarkets and department stores.

During the last two decades or so personal pension plans have been introduced in France, Italy, Germany, Sweden, Denmark, the UK, Poland, Belgium and Ireland. The chapters in this book describe the objectives of the pension reforms in these countries, the results of the reforms, and how employees and other individuals have responded to the opportunities to make their own provision for retirement through tax-advantaged long-term personal pension plans.

2. PAY-AS-YOU-GO VERSUS FUNDED PENSION SCHEMES

A recurring criticism of State pension schemes financed on a pay-as-you-go basis is that they allow politicians to promise pension benefits which have little likelihood of being delivered because the costs become apparent only after a considerable period of time. Advocates of privately funded pension schemes argue that the pension promise is more secure because the amount paid out in pensions has to be equal to the contributions paid in plus the accumulated value of the return on the contributions invested over the lifetime of the scheme. However, this argument is true only if the accumulated value of the fund continues to increase until the time comes to draw down the fund to start paying pensions. If the value of the fund falls because of a collapse in the value of the assets in which it is invested, contributors will end up with pensions lower than they expected. The historical evidence from France, reviewed in the paper by apRoberts and Concialdi, and the collapse in stock market values in recent years show that this is not just a theoretical possibility.

For most of the period following World War II, policy makers in France resisted the introduction of funded pension schemes. Attempts to provide funded public and private pension schemes during the interwar period had foundered as inflation decimated the value of the schemes' assets and the funded schemes proved unable to guarantee adequate pensions for private sector workers. This negative experience was reflected for a long time in the terms used in France to describe pay-as-you-go and funded schemes. The French equivalent of 'pay-as-you-go' is *répartition* which means sharing out of contributions from the working generation to the retirement generation. The French word for 'funding' is *capitalisation* and it is associated with 'capital' or 'capitalist'. These words have negative connotations in France given its cultural and political traditions.

The collapse of the funded schemes set up in the interwar period resulted in both the Social Security General Scheme and supplementary schemes for private sector employees established in France after World War II being operated on a PAYG basis until the reforms that were undertaken during the 1990s. These reforms included replacement rates offered by the social security and supplementary schemes being cut back in response to demographic pressures, the number of years required for a full social security pension being increased from 37.5 to 40 years and pensions in payment being indexed to prices rather than wages. Long-term replacement rate projections for the period 2003–2050 show that the reforms are expected to result in a reduction of a third for managers and highly skilled technical staff (*cadres*) and almost a quarter for other staff (non-*cadres*). In order to allow groups of employees and individuals to compensate for the reductions in the benefits provided by the public pension system, France has legislated for a range of funded group and individual pension plans that operate on a defined contribution basis. For example, optional employee retirement savings plans (PERCOs), similar to individual pension plans in the US referred to as 401(k) plans, have replaced the long-term employee savings plans (PPESV) set up by the Socialist government in 2001. Optional individual retirement savings plans (PERPs) facilitate saving by individuals through an insurance contract. Nevertheless, the take-up of funded pension schemes in France has been low and they are expected to continue to have a minor role in the provision of retirement income in the future.

Other countries such as Germany have introduced personal pensions on a funded basis but with guaranteed returns, while at the same time reducing replacement rates from PAYG systems and introducing other reforms such as increasing the retirement age.

3. FROM PAYG-DEFINED BENEFIT TO PAYG NOTIONAL DEFINED CONTRIBUTION STATE PENSIONS AND FUNDED PERSONAL PENSIONS

In the face of demographic projections of ageing populations which appear to threaten the sustainability of their pay-as-you-go public pension systems, Italy, Sweden and Poland have taken similar action to tighten the link between social insurance contributions and pension benefits by replacing pay-as-you-go defined benefit State pension schemes with pay-as-you-go notional defined contribution State schemes. Pizzuti and Raitano argue that the Italian pension reform transformed the public sector and sought to promote private pension provision. It changed the pension benefit formula for the public pension scheme from a defined benefit basis to a notional defined contribution basis, shifted the indexation rule from wages to prices, increased the retirement age and linked benefits to the retirement age and to economic and demographic developments. The reforms in Sweden and Poland, described in the papers by Stahlberg and Szczepański, have the same emphasis on notional defined contribution arrangements and funded personal pension plans as the reform in Italy. In particular, these countries have opted to provide incentives for personal pension provision by diverting contributions from the end of service lump sum benefit (the TFR) in Italy and from the State social insurance scheme in Sweden and Poland to funded personal pension accounts.

As in France, the reforms in Italy, Sweden and Poland resulted in significant reductions in the replacement rates provided by the public pension schemes especially for those taking early retirement.

The most significant change affecting private pensions in Italy was the introduction of a choice for employees for the disposition of the end of service lump sum benefit, the Trattamento di Fine Rapporto (TFR). This is an arrangement which is unique to Italy. It is not a pension scheme but a type of deferred wage retained by the firm until the employment relationship ends due to redundancy, firing or retirement. Every year 6.91 per cent of the gross wage is retained by firms for the TFR. A return on the deferred wage of 1.5 per cent plus three-quarters of the inflation rate is paid annually. After eight years in employment an employee can draw down up to 70 per cent of the TFR to buy a home or for medical expenses. This facility is extensively used so that the average duration of a TFR is around ten years.

The reforms implemented in Italy in January 2007 offered employees a choice between continuing to have their deferred wage paid into a TFR or being automatically enrolled in an occupational pension fund or a personal pension plan. Although the TFR reform did not permit transfer of the accumulated fund into a pension scheme it can be considered as an experiment for analysing individual choice of the allocation of current TFR flows to long-term pension schemes with different characteristics in terms of liquidity, risk and rate of return or to a medium-term fund offering some protection against the contingencies of unemployment, dismissal or retirement. Workers are able to withdraw all of the TFR as a lump sum on retirement whereas they can only withdraw up to half of the value of the pension as a lump sum and workers with a TFR who lose their jobs can draw down the TFR as a sort of unemployment benefit whereas workers who have opted for a pension fund cannot access the fund until retirement. Largely for these reasons the great majority of employees appear to have decided to continue having their deferred wage paid into a TFR. This suggests that the private pension option has a limited appeal for Italian workers.

In Sweden the overall contribution rate for the State notional defined contribution plan is 18.5 per cent of covered earnings. Of this, 16 per cent is credited to the notional defined contribution plan and 2.5 per cent is diverted to the premium personal pension. The rate of return on the notional accounts is determined by average wage growth. An automatic mechanism comes into operation to balance the system if pension expenditure threatens to exceed contributions. The rate of return for the premium pension depends on the participants' investment choices from about 800 funds. The government provides a default fund for those who do not choose a fund. It mirrors the asset allocation of the average investor and its management cost is significantly less than for the majority of the premium pension funds.

The pension system in Poland was reformed in 1999. Employees born before 1 January 1949 remained in the old PAYG defined benefit State pension system while those born afterwards were automatically covered by the new PAYG notional defined contribution State system and by the new mandatory funded defined contribution privately managed system. In addition a voluntary funded defined contribution system offering Employee Pension Plans (PPE) and Individual Pension Schemes (IKE) were put in place. Both of the State pension schemes are managed by ZUS, the Social Insurance Institution. Employers and employees both contribute 9.76 per cent of earnings to the mandatory schemes and the contribution rate of 7.36 per cent for the funded scheme is diverted from the total contribution of 19.52 per cent. Because of the diversion to the mandatory funded scheme there will be a deficit on the old pension system until it is phased out in 2034 and approximately 1 per cent per annum of GDP will have to be allocated to the old system until then to close the gap.

The reform has resulted in a significant reduction in the replacement rate for the new State pension compared to the old State pension. Some estimates indicate that the replacement rate for the new system will fall below the international standard stipulated in ILO conventions. Consequently, the main objective of the new State pension in Poland is to provide protection against poverty in old age.

Employees who wish to have a higher pension than that provided by the State must contribute either to the group Employee Pension Plans or individual pension accounts. The voluntary occupational Employee Pension Plans have not been successful in Poland so the only alternative for most employees is to contribute to the Personal Pension Scheme (IKE) which was introduced in 2004.

Although the Personal Pension Scheme benefits from relief of capital gains tax, it has not realised the expectation that between 1.5 to 3.5 million people would join. At the end of 2006 the scheme had only 840,000 contributors, or about 6 per cent of the working population, most of whom had incomes above the national average. This compares with 13.1 million members of the mandatory funded defined contribution scheme.

4. USE OF PERSONAL PENSION ACCOUNTS TO CLOSE THE INCOME GAP AND THE MIS-SELLING SCANDAL

The papers by Steinmeyer, Ostrup and Waine note that in Germany, Denmark, and the United Kingdom long-term demographic projections have also been used to justify reductions in the percentage of earnings that will be replaced by State pensions and to argue that individuals ought to take more responsibility for providing an income in retirement by increasing their saving in personal pension accounts. In Ireland the long-term projections have been used to argue that public expenditure on pensions as a percentage of GDP should be capped and that there should be greater reliance on privately funded personal pension accounts. These personal pension accounts allow contributors to participate in stock markets and possibly reap the gains of increases in equity prices. Employees have been willing to buy these high risk products because some of them appear to have developed a stronger preference for risk in recent years and because the reductions in State pension benefits have left them with little option but to make their own arrangements if they wish to increase their retirement income. In addition, the opportunity to pursue these riskier strategies has been generally welcomed by commissions of inquiry into the pensions system. In Denmark, for example, the 'Bremer Committee', which was asked by the Danish government in 2002 to evaluate the private pension system, recommended that people should be offered greater freedom in making their own investment choices.

Reform of the public pension system in Germany in 2001, as Steinmeyer notes, was intended to keep the public pension contribution rate below 20 per cent in the face of long-term projections which indicated it would rise well above that level. This resulted in big reductions in replacement rates offered by the public system.

Thus, a gap opened up between projected benefits from the public system and desired benefits. The Federal Minister for Labour and Social Order, Walter Riester, introduced a tax-advantaged private pension called the Riester pension, to encourage individuals to save for their own retirement. In 2008 the tax deduction for a Riester pension amounted to €2,100 per annum; the amount contributed out of the wage was exempt from social security contributions and cash subsidies were provided of €154 for a single person, €308 for a married person and €185 for a child. To qualify for the maximum subsidy, at least 4 per cent of the previous year's gross wage has to be contributed to a pension plan. A unique feature of the Riester pensions is that the financial institutions which provide them are obliged to guarantee the capital sum invested. The providers, therefore, bear the investment risk and this results in a conservative investment strategy.

Initially the take-up of the Riester pension was low partly because of complicated rules which created difficulties for banks and insurance companies. Relaxation of the rules and provision for contributors to use their accumulated fund to purchase a house or apartment rather than receive an annuity has resulted in an increase in the take-up of the Riester pension. Between 2001 and 2007 the number of those contributing to a Riester pension increased from 1.4 million to 10.8 million. Most of these contributors are medium to high income earners. Low income earners generally cannot afford the contributions required for a Riester pension.

The public pension system in Denmark, as Ostrup points out, provides all residents with a basic pension at the age of 65 which is equal to about 30 per cent of the average wage earners' disposable income. It also provides additional benefits of up to 30 per cent for those who have no supplementary pension cover. All Danish wage earners are covered by occupational pension schemes financed by contributions based on wage income. Individuals can establish their own personal pension plans before the age of 60. These personal plans benefit from a special tax regime and they are provided by banks and life assurance companies. There are three different types of private personal pension plan. The first type pays benefits as an annuity, the second type pays benefits in equal instalments over a period of more than ten years and the third type pays benefits as a lump sum.

Pension savings in traditional life assurance company products are currently guaranteed that the rate of return will not fall below 1.5 per cent. Legislation requires that at least 30 per cent of retirement savings in life assurance companies is invested in low risk assets such as bonds and deposits. New pension savings products introduced by the life companies since 1999 do not offer a guaranteed rate of return although they may offer a guarantee that the value of the accumulated contributions will be protected. No limits are placed on pension saving in banks in relation to the allocation of the investment portfolio between equities, bonds and deposits.

The take-up of personal pension plans in Denmark has been very limited. During the period 1990–2005 contributions to personal pension plans increased marginally from 1.9 per cent to 2.4 per cent of personal income in spite of the efforts of policy makers to raise personal savings in order to reduce the deficit on the balance of payments current account. Among the reasons why personal pension plans have failed to expand in Denmark in this period are the fact that occupational pension plans increased their coverage, asset prices and especially the price of houses, showed large increases, and there were some reductions in the tax advantages available for personal pension plans.

The drive for individual pension accounts in the UK has taken three forms: the Personal Pension developed by the Conservative government in the mid-1980s; the Stakeholder Pension introduced by the Labour government in 2001; and the soft mandatory Personal Accounts recommended by the Pensions Commission. The latter is to come into effect from 2012 onwards.

As the paper by Barbara Waine points out, the decision by the Thatcher government in the 1980s to index pension benefits in line with prices rather than earnings was not reversed by the Labour government when it came to power in 1997 although it has now committed itself to restoring the link sometime between 2012 and 2015. Over time the change from wage to price indexation has resulted in a serious deterioration in the percentage of income replaced by the public pension. Consequently, private pension providers have been encouraged by both Conservative and Labour governments to provide personal pension products which are intended to increase saving and eventually to result in an increase in pension income. The vehicle favoured for this purpose by the Conservative government following the pension reforms in 1986 was the Personal Pension while the vehicle favoured by the Labour government was the Stakeholder Pension. Both of these are individual money purchase schemes.

In order to encourage take-up of the Personal Pension, the Conservative government offered age-related tax incentives and other subsides to encourage older workers to leave their occupational schemes and take out a Personal Pension. Initially the Personal Pension appeared to be successful as it had about 5 million contributors by the end of 1992/93. However, within a few years the insurance companies were accused of 'mis-selling' Personal Pensions to people who it was established would have been better off remaining in their occupational pension schemes. The Securities and Investment Board, for example, estimated in 1993 that half of those who had taken out a Personal Pension as an alternative to remaining in an occupational scheme had been 'missold' this product. It took until 2002 to provide compensation for the 1.6 million people affected at a cost of €12 billion pounds to the pension providers.

The Stakeholder Pension in the UK and the Personal Retirement Savings Account (PRSA) in Ireland have had only a limited impact. The main problem in the UK appears to be the lack of trust in financial institutions engendered in potential customers by the 'mis-selling' scandal. In Ireland the introduction of PRSAs occurred after the launch of Special Saving Investment Accounts (SSIA). These accounts, as Hughes and Stewart point out, made a short-term savings plan available which was far more attractive than a PRSA. The Government provided an explicit matching contribution of €1 for every €4 contributed. The money invested could be withdrawn after five years rather than at the age of 60 or over. There were no charges for deposit account PRSAs and the banks and building societies paid interest on the deposits.

5. GENDER ISSUES

Sweden has paid particular attention to the way in which pay-as-you-go and funded pension schemes can disadvantage women. It has designed some crucial features of its notional defined contribution public system to redistribute pension income in favour of women. Although women on average are projected to receive lower pension benefits than men, because of their lower lifetime earnings and other reasons, women in Sweden are projected to have higher replacement rates and higher rates of return on their lifetime contributions than men. The use of unisex life tables largely explains these positive outcomes for women.

The Personal Accounts proposed by the Turner Commission for the UK have some features which could improve women's pension entitlements. However, insurers in the UK are not obliged to provide unisex annuities and the vagaries of the market will still have more of an effect on the final pension of a woman than of a man in a Personal Account. Research in the UK indicates that the majority of women are unlikely to achieve the government's target replacement rate of 45 per cent of median earnings from the State and private pension schemes.

6. INFORMATION REQUIREMENTS FOR PERSONAL PENSIONS

The shift from a defined benefit to a defined contribution pension system increases the need for individuals to understand the pension system, financial markets and the principles of investment. The need to educate the public about pension issues and to provide information about pension entitlements has been recognised as an important issue in many EU countries. The Swedish public pension system, for example, addresses the demand for information by sending an annual statement to every income earner explaining how the system works, the value of contributions and accrued interest to date and the expected annual amount of pension benefit at 61, 65 and 70. In addition, the National Social Insurance Board, the Premium Pension Agency and the private insurance companies operate a website which enables people to ascertain what their total annual pension is likely to be from public, occupational and private pension plans.

In Denmark a special website has been created to provide a complete picture of the pensions which individuals can expect to receive from public, occupational and personal pension schemes. In Ireland the Pensions Board, the government's advisory body on pensions, has an annual pensions week to provide information on pension issues and the Board also has a pensions calculator on its website which can be used by individuals to estimate how much they would need to contribute to a pension to end up with the retirement income they expect.

Despite these efforts to educate the public about pensions, it appears that the information provided has a limited impact. Surveys in Sweden, Ireland, the UK and other countries show that most people know very little about the pension system and that the information campaigns have not increased the public's knowledge very much over time. People usually know more about the private pension system than about the public system even though only a minor part of their retirement income is likely to be provided by the private pension system. The people who know least about the pension system are blue collar workers, low income earners, the less well educated and women. These groups generally overestimate the size of their future pension. Consequently, they are likely to end up with a much lower pension than they expect.

7. RISK AND PERSONAL CHOICE

A key issue for individual account systems is whether investors are diversifying their portfolios to achieve a suitable balance between risk and return. Research in Sweden shows that people at the bottom of the income distribution are taking the same level of risk as people at the top. Consequently, poorer people are not diversifying their portfolios to provide a desirable balance between the risks of investing in equities and other assets and the rates of return on such investments. Furthermore, the investment choices which people make in Sweden appear to be inhibited by the fact that there are far too many funds (around 800) from which they have to choose five to invest their contributions in a premium pension plan. Rather than making active choices from this range of funds most people do nothing. Consequently, they end up in the default fund. Currently 90 per cent of new entrants to the labour market in Sweden fail to make an active choice. Of those who do make a choice, very few subsequently change their investment allocation. Similar outcomes have been found in other EU countries and they are in line with the findings of behavioural economics which show that offering a large number of options is likely to paralyse decision making.

8. FEES AND CHARGES

Individual pension accounts are more expensive to operate than group and national pension schemes which have the advantage of economies of scale. In Denmark, for example, the Bremer Committee criticised the high cost of changing a pension plan from one life assurance company to another. It found that it could cost up to 14 per cent of the accumulated fund to make such a change.

In Poland the structure of fees and charges for Personal Pension Scheme accounts is not transparent and the Financial Supervising Authority does not collect information about fees and charges. The information which is available indicates the investment funds charge 4 per cent for managing assets, while the life insurance companies charge 1.5 per cent and the banks have no handling charges.

In the United Kingdom the annual management charge for a Stakeholder Pension is 1 per cent of the contribution. In Ireland the annual charge for a Personal Retirement Savings Account is 5 per cent of the contribution and 1 per cent per annum of the value of the fund. The charges for personal pension accounts in the UK compare with a cost of 0.1 per cent for the State pension scheme and between 0.1 and 0.3 per cent for large company schemes according to the second report of the UK Pensions Commission. The Commission has recommended that there should be an independent central authority with responsibility for investing contributions and that it should aim for an Annual Management Charge of 0.3 per cent. However, many of those working in the private pensions industry argue that this is unrealistic.

9. EXPLOITATION OF TAX ADVANTAGES

The tax reliefs available for retirement saving open up a number of opportunities for some taxpayers to minimise their tax liabilities including the possibility of moving on retirement to other EU countries with low taxation of pension benefits. The Danish government has been able to conclude double taxation agreements with some EU countries to close this loophole but it has not proved possible to conclude a double taxation agreement with France and Spain.

In contrast, individual pensions are popular in Belgium because of tax reliefs. However the exact size of the tax incentive is not transparent for most people. Kim De Witte, Paul Roels and Yves Stevens examine these and other issues in Chapter 9 and conclude that even though individual voluntary pension provision can be considered a ‘social good’ most of the tax reliefs in Belgium, as in

Ireland and other countries, accrues to those with the highest income; an effect these authors describe as 'the Matthew effect'.

10. OTHER ISSUES WITH PERSONAL PENSION PROVISION

The last section of the book deals with two key issues in personal pension provision, that is the issue of annuitisation and the problem of regulation. In Chapter 11 Turner gives a comparative summary of the differences and implications of different annuitisation policies in three countries, the UK, Sweden and Chile. He points out that it is the requirement to annuitise that distinguishes personal pensions from a tax favoured savings scheme. A key issue that emerges is the wide variety in annuity terms and the lack of transparency in annuity charges.

Chapter 12 by Muir deals with issue of regulation by an examination of policy issues and conceptual problems in the regulation of pensions in the UK and the US. The author argues that the experiences of the UK and the US with personal pension schemes provide evidence that their regulatory approaches have not been entirely successful in encouraging take-up, contributions and the building of wealth in those schemes. Regulating individual pension accounts presents particular difficulties and in particular this chapter notes difficulties that may follow from regulation of individual pension accounts by multiple regulatory authorities.

Pensions terminology is difficult but as discussed in the last chapter by Davies, language is often used to bias discussions of reform and the introduction of personal pensions in a particular way. He examines the debate between the two main alternative views of pension provision in terms of 'promises' (PAYG) versus 'saving' (funded pensions). He notes the widespread use of positive concepts such as saving for retirement which may be juxtaposed with negative concepts such as the burden of taxation in financing pensions. Because the debate on pension reform is framed in this way, there is an inherent bias in favour of reforms that emphasise funding.

11. WILL PERSONAL PENSIONS CLOSE THE INCOME GAP?

Two decades after personal choice was introduced into the pension system there is little evidence that individual pension accounts have improved, or will improve the pension entitlements of most contributors. The reasons for this are not hard to find. A significant proportion of participants make only minimum contributions and consequently the fund values remain low. In Poland, for example, the average contribution to a Personal Pension Scheme is quite low amounting as it did in 2006 to around €12 per week. Keeping up the payments into a personal pension plan poses major difficulties for many contributors. Research has shown that up to one third of those participating in a Stakeholder Pension in the UK discontinued their contributions within one year of starting. In 2004 the UK Pensions Commission recognised that for these and other reasons personal pensions are not an effective form of pension provision for the low paid, those who have to take time out of the labour market to care for children or elderly relatives (mainly women) and atypical workers.

There is one feature of many of the proposals for greater reliance on the private pension system which it is argued will solve the problem of low private pension coverage and increase saving for retirement. This is that there should be automatic enrolment for all employees who are not covered by other pension schemes with an option to opt out of the personal pension arrangements. Advocates of personal pension plans argue that automatic enrolment, minimum pension contributions and low management charges will go a long way to solving the problems of low private pension cover, lapsed contracts and inadequate retirement saving.

However, automatic enrolment in personal pension accounts does not change the fact that these accounts share certain features with the voluntary personal pension plans which preceded them which will make it difficult for the new plans to succeed where the previous ones have failed. The personal accounts will be run on a defined contribution basis for which governments are unwilling to provide any guarantees that the value of the funds will be greater than the value of the contributions and returns on the amounts invested.

PART I

Individual Countries' Experience

2. Pension Reform and Personal Provision of Retirement Income in France

Lucy apRoberts and Pierre Concialdi

1. INTRODUCTION

As in most European countries, there have been major changes in the French retirement system over the past twenty years. However, despite these changes, the French system mainly relies on current earnings for paying pension benefits. In other words, the share of funded schemes remains marginal. In this chapter, we analyze this situation and highlight the factors that explain why saving explicitly for retirement is not common practice among French workers.

The French language itself reflects a rather positive attitude towards pay-as-you-go financing and a rather negative attitude towards funding (apRoberts 1993). The French equivalent to 'pay-as-you-go' is *répartition*.[1] It comes from the verb *répartir*, which means 'to share,' in reference to the practice of sharing out contributions from those currently working among those who are retired. The French equivalent to 'funding' is *capitalisation*, a term associated with 'capital' or 'capitalist,' words that do not have particularly positive connotations given French cultural and political traditions. In contrast, the English term 'funding' suggests sound practice with a solid foundation. We shall see that other more positive terms for funding have come into use in the French language since the 1980s.

The rest of this chapter is organized as follows. We begin with a brief history of the French pension system. We show that almost all retirement pensions, including supplementary pensions, are financed on a pay-as-you-go basis. We also highlight the fact that the minor role of funded schemes does not seem to have discouraged household savings. The next section describes the various types of funded schemes that exist in France and the changes that have taken place over time, especially since 2003 when legislation established new types of retirement savings plans. We then examine the scope of funded schemes and current trends in the provision of retirement benefits. A concluding section briefly explores prospects for funded schemes in the near future.

2. RETIREMENT INCOMES IN FRANCE: PAY-AS-YOU-GO PENSIONS PLUS HOUSEHOLD SAVINGS

The Predominance of Pay-As-You-Go Financing since the Second World War

Before the creation of today's Social Security system in 1945, there were two main attempts to establish retirement schemes for private sector employees in France. The first dates back to 1910 when legislation set up a scheme for manual workers in industry and farm laborers (Retraites ouvrières et paysannes). This scheme was funded. Financing came from employee and employer contributions. However, many workers were opposed to paying contributions and the mandate was not effectively enforced. Hence, many eligible workers never contributed and benefits were very low. This scheme virtually disappeared during the 1920s.

German social security concepts inspired much interest among the French after the Alsace-Lorraine region was reunited with France following the First World War. As a consequence, legislation established a new social insurance scheme in the 1930s. As in the 1910 scheme, pensions were to be funded. Social insurance was made compulsory for all employees with earnings below a ceiling.[2] At the same time, some companies set up occupational pension schemes for employees with earnings above the ceiling, these being mostly managerial staff and engineers. These higher paid employees are often referred to as *cadres*, a term which to this day refers to managers and highly skilled technical staff. In 1937, a collective agreement for the metallurgy and mining sector created the first industry-wide occupational scheme for *cadres*. Similar agreements were signed in other sectors soon after. All of these occupational schemes were funded.[3]

During the Second World War, inflation caused drastic depreciation of the assets of both occupational schemes for *cadres* and social insurance. The social insurance pension scheme was disbanded in 1941 and its funds were used to finance a means-tested benefit,[4] which is now part of the minimum income guaranteed to people aged 65 and over.

Funded schemes hence proved unable to guarantee adequate pensions for private sector workers. Rejection of funding explains why the Social Security General Scheme for private sector employees, established in 1945, was designed to operate on a pay-as-you-go basis, like social insurance general pension schemes in most countries. What is distinctive about the French retirement system is that the supplementary pension schemes created subsequently for private sector workers were also established on a pay-as-you-go basis. Supplementary schemes were set up by employers' associations and trade unions through collective bargaining agreements covering the whole private sector, starting in 1947 for *cadres* and in the late 1950s and early 1960s for other employees (non-*cadres*). In 1972, legislation made these supplementary schemes mandatory for all private sector employees covered by the Social Security General Scheme. Today, these mandatory supplementary schemes play an important role in the French retirement system. The pensions they pay out represent around one third of total pay-as-you-go pensions for an average worker, and much more for *cadres*.

Although it is always difficult to ascertain the causes of historical developments, certain factors help to explain why French employers and employees have chosen this particular path to develop supplementary pensions.[5]

One reason is that, just after the Second World War, the French had a very negative opinion of funded schemes since they had experienced the failure of funded social insurance schemes and funded occupational schemes to provide adequate pensions. Because of the failure of their earlier occupational schemes, a whole generation of *cadres*, both those who were already retired and those approaching retirement, faced a future without any prospect of an adequate pension. The creation of new funded schemes could not solve this problem. From its inception in 1947, the scheme for *cadres* paid out pensions to current retirees and paid out pensions to new retirees based on completed previous employment.

Another reason for the success of *répartition* was that the scheme for *cadres* benefited from favourable economic conditions in its first decades of existence. The ratio of contributors to pensioners was high because the proportion of the labour force classified as *cadres* increased greatly over the 1950s and 1960s. In addition, many of the new entrants to the scheme were young. Furthermore, up to the end of the 1950s, employers and employees successfully pressured the government to keep the Social Security ceiling relatively low, which meant that the wage base for contributions to the scheme, which consisted of wages above the Social Security ceiling, expanded during this period.[6]

Another factor behind the success of pay-as-you-go supplementary schemes, which still holds true today, was their sheer scale. This enabled them to keep administrative costs very low, much lower than for schemes restricted to the personnel of single companies.

A further advantage of pay-as-you-go supplementary schemes lay in the fact that they allowed employers and employees who wanted to obtain higher pensions to make extra voluntary contributions, above the minimum obligatory rate. For example, the minimum contribution rate in the scheme for *cadres* was initially 8 per cent of salary above the Social Security ceiling (of which 6 per cent was paid by the employer and 2 per cent by the employee). With the agreement of their *cadres*, employers could choose to contribute at a higher rate, up to a maximum of 16 per cent.[7] Hence, employers and employees could increase pensions within a company without resorting to a company pension scheme, which would have had to be funded in order to be viable. This possibility was phased out in the 1990s.

French mandatory supplementary pension schemes provide for greater flexibility in benefit levels than is usually the case in pay-as-you-go schemes. Pensions are not computed as a percentage of a reference wage with a formula based on an accrual rate for each year of contributions. Instead, each employee's pension depends on the number of 'points' he or she has accumulated in an individual account over his or her working life. There are two key parameters in this system: the amount of contributions necessary to acquire one point (the 'cost' of a point) and the value ascribed to each point once employees retire (the 'value' of a point). The pension is equal to the number of points accumulated multiplied by the value of one point. Both of these parameters vary from year to year in such a way as to balance scheme finances in each period. In addition, supplementary schemes may adjust effective contribution rates without changing the 'contractual' contribution rate, which is used to calculate benefits. In the first years of existence of the schemes, effective contribution rates were lower than contractual rates. Effective contribution rates were gradually increased in relation to contractual rates, a policy which has allowed supplementary schemes to stabilize replacement rates.[8]

Overall, French supplementary pension schemes have distinct advantages both for employers and employees. Until the 1990s, they offered employers the option of making additional contributions to raise benefit levels. They offer employees fairly secure pensions. While workers are not completely sure of the future value of their pensions, pension levels vary according to rules that are transparent and negotiated. In any case, fluctuations in the value of pensions are never as drastic as the changes that affect the level of benefits paid out by funded defined contribution schemes when financial markets collapse or when inflation rises.

The Importance of Income from Savings for Older People

Because French employers and employees have chosen this particular way of providing supplementary pensions, there is virtually no space in the French pension system for funded schemes. Funded schemes account for less than 2 per cent of all pensions paid out every year. According to standard economic theory, this feature of the French pension system should discourage private sector savings. This is far from being the case as shown in Table 2.1.

Care is needed in comparing savings rates across countries. Despite the problems associated with inter-country comparisons, it is widely acknowledged that France is among the countries wher the household savings rate is high. Data collected by the European Commission show that the household savings rate

Table 2.1 Household saving rates, 2006 (percentage of gross disposable income)

Germany	16.2
France	15.3
Italy	14.9
Austria	14.1
Switzerland*	14.2
Belgium	12.5
Netherlands	12.5
Ireland	11.0
European Union (27)	10.9
Spain	10.5
Sweden	9.8
Portugal*	8.9
Norway	5.6
Finland	5.6
United Kingdom	5.0
Denmark	4.0

Note: *Data refers to year 2005

Source: European Commission.

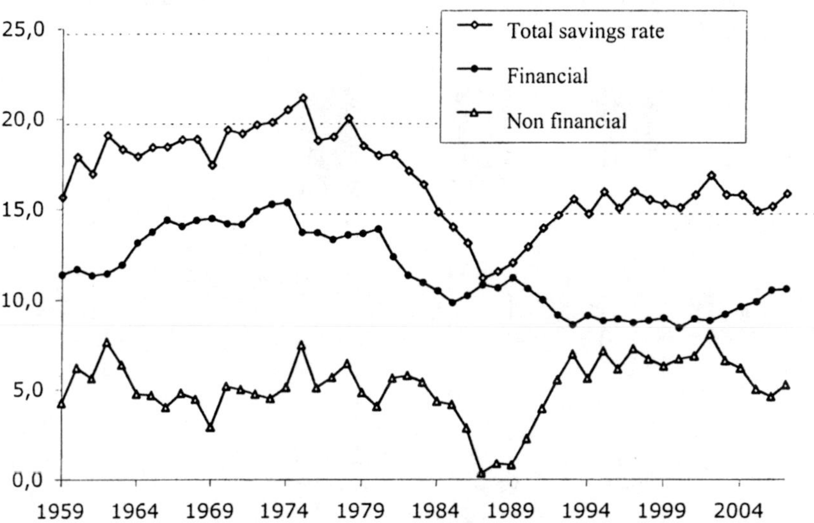

Total Savings Rate: Gross savings/Gross disposable income; Financial: Net lending/ Gross disposable income; Non financial: Gross fixed capital formation/ Gross disposable income.

Source: INSEE, national accounts.

Figure 2.1 French household savings rate 1959–2007

in France is one of the highest among developed countries (see Table 2.1).

Long-term series from French national accounts show that the household savings rate has been high for a long time. It was around 20 per cent until the end of the 1970s and then dropped sharply in the 1980s. There has been a slight upswing since the beginning of the 1990s. The savings rate of French households has been around 15 per cent since then. The main difference between household savings today and in the 1960s and 1970s lies, not in the savings rate, but in the structure of savings. Today, financial savings and non-financial savings account for approximately the same share of total savings. Thirty years ago, the share of financial savings was much lower than the share of non-financial savings because of the predominance of real estate in household portfolios (see Figure 2.1).

As a consequence of the high savings rate of households, overall income of French pensioners is considerably higher than their pension income. Income other than pensions accounts for 40 per cent of the gross disposable income of the population age 65 to 74 (Figure 2.2). A little more than 10 per cent comes from earnings and about 30 per cent comes from property. Overall, income from property (as defined in the National Accounts) is equivalent to about 45 per cent of income from pensions. Despite the fact that their pensions are financed almost exclusively on a pay-as-you-go basis, French people save a great deal, and they derive substantial amounts of income in addition to their pensions from their savings after they retire.

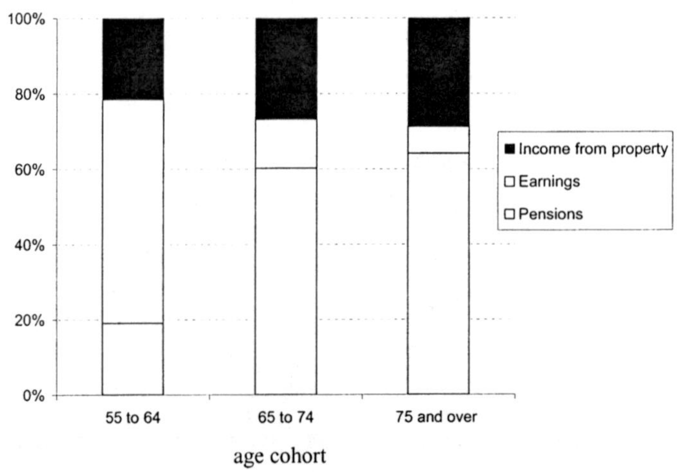

Note: * Households are classified by the age of the individual for a person living alone or a lone parent and by the age of the man for a couple.

Source: INSEE, authors' calculations.

Figure 2.2 Structure of incomes for households aged 55 and over, 2003*

Since many French pensioners own their homes, a large proportion of their property income takes the form of imputed rents. This raises the question of what we mean by 'saving for retirement'. Should we define 'saving for retirement' as holdings of purely financial assets which could be used to purchase an annuity on retirement? Or should we consider any form of savings that provides people with supplementary incomes when they are retired to be a kind of 'saving for retirement'? The French example shows that buying a home is probably the main – and most secure – form of saving for retirement because it meets people's basic need for housing.

3. FUNDED PENSIONS BEFORE 1993

Despite the predominance of pay-as-you-go financing in France, some funding existed within the French retirement system before the 2003 law on retirement. The 1990s witnessed much debate over whether or not funding for pensions should be expanded. Developments in regulations concerning funding over the 1990s pointed to the future shape of new funded schemes set up by the 2003 legislation.

Funded Schemes up to 1993

The mandatory supplementary schemes for private sector employees have long had some reserves, generally equivalent to about one year of benefits, even though these schemes operate mostly on a pay-as-you-go basis. Since the 1950s, optional tax-favoured retirement savings plans have been available to civil servants. Some companies have also offered long-term schemes to their employees, financed either directly by the company or through group insurance contracts.

Optional plans for civil servants

Since 1949, civil servants have had access to optional supplementary retirement savings plans set up by their trade unions, with their contributions entirely deductible from their taxable income. The *raison d'être* for these plans stems from the fact that many civil servants receive part of their remuneration in the form of bonuses, which are not included in pensionable salary. On average, civil servants receive about 20 per cent of their remuneration in the form of bonuses. The proportion varies greatly between different groups; higher paid civil servants tend to receive a larger share of their remuneration in the form of bonuses. The State compensates for the exclusion of bonuses from pensionable salary by allowing civil servants to contribute to tax-favoured retirement savings plans.

Employers do not contribute to such plans, but participants' contributions and returns on investments are deducted from their taxable incomes. This arrangement allows those civil servants who choose to participate, to accumulate retirement savings free of tax during their careers. Participants choose their contribution rate. Withdrawals are exclusively in the form of retirement pensions, which are taxed like other pensions. Funds are run collectively, with no individual choice as to investments. Although these plans are intended to compensate for exclusion of bonuses in the calculation of civil service pensions, access is not limited to those who have bonuses, and contribution levels are not linked to the amount of bonuses.[9]

Company pension schemes

Funded or partially funded pension schemes existed for some time for personnel in some private firms. A few such schemes were non-insured, that is, they were financed directly by sponsoring companies; in the late 1990s, only liabilities concerning currently retired beneficiaries had to be recorded in company balance sheets. Some company pension schemes were financed by company pension funds that were jointly administered by employer and employee representatives; these schemes are referred to as 'Supplementary Retirement Institutions' (*Institutions de retraite supplémentaire*).

Most company pension schemes were and still are financed through group insurance contracts, with employer and employee contributions paid directly to an insurer. These schemes do not pay out lump sums but only retirement pensions. Employers can deduct their premiums from taxable company revenues. Like any tax qualified employee benefit scheme (invalidity insurance, death benefits, and so on), such contracts must apply to all members of an objectively defined category of personnel (that is all employees, all managerial staff, all manual workers, and so on), and the employer must participate in financing. Because regulations concerning tax exemptions play a great role in determining scheme rules, the different types of schemes are generally referred to by the number of the article of the tax code that concerns them.

Insured defined benefit schemes ('article 39') are financed entirely by the employer. Tax regulations do not allow such schemes to offer vested rights. Hence, employees who are members of such a scheme qualify for a pension only if they work for the company continuously until retirement. Tax exemptions are granted based on the fact that members are not certain to receive a benefit until they actually retire. On this basis, employer contributions are not considered part of wages and hence they are exempt from employee income tax and from social contributions.

Insured defined contribution money purchase schemes ('article 83') are also common. Annuity amounts depend on investment returns, which are undertaken for the insured group as a whole without any individual choice concerning investments.

Public Policy and Funding over the 1990s: Hesitation and Compromise

Protracted political debates took place throughout the 1990s about the possibility of expanding the role of funding within the French retirement system. Advocates argued that such a change would be beneficial for the economy for a number of reasons. One was that funding would purportedly enhance economic growth by increasing demand for company equity shares. Proponents of this idea pointed to foreign countries – particularly, the United States, the United Kingdom, the Netherlands and Germany – where they claimed occupational pension plans gave companies access to capital that they could use to finance investments. Another idea that was often evoked was that, if France had pension funds, French companies would not be easy prey for foreign institutional investors, particularly foreign pension funds. It was also claimed that pension funds would enhance industrial democracy, since employees and their unions would have a say in investment policies and thereby acquire a new tool with which to influence employer practices.

Over the 1990s, there was hesitation even among proponents of funding as to the form it should take in France. Should funding be organized on an individual basis or within an occupational framework? Should participation be compulsory or optional? Should companies be allowed to finance plans using book reserves? Should funded pension schemes be defined benefit, guaranteeing a certain replacement rate, or defined contribution, with benefit amounts depending on investment returns? Should schemes pay out only pensions or annuities or should they also be allowed to pay out lump sums at the time of retirement? All of these questions were openly debated. Over the decade of the 1990s answers gradually emerged and these answers shaped legislation in 2003.

Policy makers implicitly rejected defined benefit company schemes, with little public debate on the question. Regulations concerning insured defined benefit schemes ('article 39') do not allow vesting and this requirement has not been lifted. Hence, this form of company retirement scheme has not expanded. Employees who think they might not want to stay on in the same company or who they do not have a good chance of being kept on until retirement see no benefit from these arrangements. The refusal to authorize vesting contrasts sharply with regulations in other countries, where company defined benefit schemes have, on the contrary, been required to vest rights and to shorten waiting periods for vesting.

Non-insured company-defined benefit schemes were actively discouraged over the 1990s (apRoberts and Reynaud 1998). Legislation passed in 1994 required companies to register book reserves in their balance sheets to cover any new liabilities contracted through a non-insured company pension scheme.[10] Above all, this legislation forbade creation of new non-insured company pension schemes financed by company pension funds ('Supplementary Retirement Institutions'). Given that most such schemes were already closed to newly hired personnel, this type of retirement scheme, which closely resembles defined benefit company schemes in the United States or the United Kingdom, became doomed to extinction.

Shortly before the legislation forbidding new non-insured defined benefit company schemes, a new type of optional retirement savings plan was created for self-employed workers. It is called the 'Madelin' plan, after the minister who sponsored the law.[11] These plans were designed to offer the self-employed tax advantages similar to those enjoyed by private sector salaried workers and civil servants, allowing them to contribute tax free to a defined contribution pension scheme. Plans for the self-employed take the form of group insurance contracts, with each group having at least one thousand participants. As a rule, withdrawals take the form of annuities upon retirement. Savings may, however, be withdrawn as a lump sum in the event of death, total invalidity or bankruptcy.

At the time of their creation, these optional retirement savings plans were perceived by many commentators as heralding the shape of things to come for private sector salaried workers. The fact that relatively few self-employed workers subscribed to these plans was subsequently thought to bode ill for further development of optional retirement savings. Many of the self-employed were apparently reluctant to contribute to a plan that imposes withdrawal in the form of an annuity. This feature was generally felt to be unattractive.

No fewer than four bills proposing funded pension schemes for private sector employees were tabled in Parliament between March 1993 and May 1994, under a right wing government. Legislation that was finally passed in March 1997 was designed to make available to all private sector employees a new type of occupational retirement savings plan, called the *Plan épargne retraite* (PER) or 'Retirement Savings Plan'.[12] The law was referred to as the 'Thomas' law, after the member of parliament who sponsored the bill. It never came into force and was finally repealed several years later.

The PER was to consist of a group contract signed by the employer on behalf of employees with a specialized insurer. A plan could be part of a company or industry-wide collective agreement but, if an occupational group failed to reach an agreement, an employer could set up a plan unilaterally. By the end of a one-year period following application of the law, employees who did not have access to a retirement savings plan set up for their own company or industry, would be able to join an existing plan set up for another occupational group. Employees were to be free to participate or not and to choose their contribution rate. Employers could match employee contributions within the limit of 4 times employee contributions. Employer and employee contributions were to be exempt from employee income tax within certain limits.[13] Employer contributions were also to be exempt from contributions to mandatory retirement schemes within certain limits.[14] Withdrawals were to take the form of retirement annuities, with the possibility of a lump sum equivalent to no more than 20 per cent of the individual's savings, capped at 75 per cent of the annual Social Security ceiling.[15] In order to encourage holding of equities, legislation stipulated that the maximum investment in fixed-return bonds was 65 per cent.

The 'Thomas' law was hotly contested by the left opposition parties and by labour unions. One of their main objections was the fact that employer contributions were to be exempt from contributions to mandatory retirement schemes, that is, both the General Scheme and supplementary schemes. Under this provision, expansion of retirement savings plans would deprive pay-as-you-go schemes of resources, leading to partial replacement of pay-as-you-go financing by funding. When the left came to power after the June 1997 legislative elections, the Socialists pledged to repeal the March 1997 law and they finally did so in January 2002.

In 2001, shortly before the 'Thomas' law was repealed, the Socialist government set up a new type of savings plan for private sector employees[16]. This type of plan was called the 'Optional Employee Partnership Savings Plan' (*Plan Partenarial d'Epargne Salariale Volontaire* or PPESV). The term 'partnership' indicated that there was a role for trade unions. Unlike the savings plans of the 'Thomas' law, these optional employee plans were not explicitly designed to finance retirement: participants could withdraw their savings after only ten years and they could choose a lump sum or phased withdrawals.

Right wing members of parliament, bitter over the fact that the 'Thomas' law had been blocked, protested adamantly. They declared that it was high time that France create what had come to be known as *fonds de pension*. This expression, which appeared in the French language in the 1990s, is a word-for-word translation of 'pension fund.' It does not carry the negative connotations of *capitalisation*. Since it came from a foreign language, its meaning was rather vague and so it quickly came to be widely used by those who favoured funding (apRoberts 1993).

In 1999, the Socialist government set up a reserve fund to be invested on financial markets in order to contribute to the financing of the General Scheme for retirement. The fund is called the 'Retirement Reserve Fund' (*Fonds de reserve des retraites* or FRR). It is designed to help finance pensions for the baby-boom generation and thereby contain increases in contribution rates. Its main source of financing is a fraction (65 per cent) of a 2 per cent tax on capital gains. It also collects surpluses from the budget of the General Scheme, which, however, has been in deficit for several years. Originally, gains on proceeds from sales of publicly held companies were to be turned over the fund, but in reality this was not done. The Retirement Reserve Fund is expected to grow until 2020 and then gradually draw down its reserves until they are exhausted in 2040. Reserves are invested on financial markets, both abroad and in France, by private fund managers selected by the board of the fund, with the majority of investments currently in company shares. As of the end of 2006, the fund had received allocations of €21.0 billion and its total assets were worth €27.5 billion[17]. Unlike some reserve funds, the French one is not intended to finance a certain proportion of pensions. It is intended to smooth the increase in the contribution rate due to retirement of the baby-boom generation. It is therefore a temporary fund that is expected to disappear.

The decision to partially fund a scheme that is basically pay-as-you-go helped to disarm proponents of funded retirement schemes, at least temporarily. It showed that funding could be applied within a broad nation-wide collective framework, instead of being used only for individual savings plans or retirement schemes for narrow occupational groups.[18]

4. RETIREMENT SAVINGS SINCE THE 2003 LAW ON RETIREMENT

The political right had to wait until the 2003 law on the retirement system for legislation giving all private sector employees and indeed all French people, access to funded pension plans in the form of optional retirement savings plans.[19] The new legislation enabled private sector employers and unions to voluntarily set up plans similar to those of the defunct 'Thomas' law. These must be established for groups of employees by collective agreement. The 2003 law also allowed any adult below retirement age to subscribe to an individual retirement savings plan.

The expression for the funded pension plan that came into vogue around this time was *épargne retraite* or 'retirement savings.' It is now used as equivalent to *capitalisation*, even for company-defined benefit plans to which employees do not contribute and, under which, employees do not have a claim on funds. This language reflects the choice that has been made regarding the form of funding. It is to consist primarily of individual savings plans, with no guarantee on returns to savings. Such defined contribution plans may be subscribed outside an occupational framework or through employee savings plans. In either case, participation is optional and the individual may choose their contribution rate and types of investment.

Cutbacks in Mandatory Retirement Scheme Replacement Rates

The arguments put forward in favour of funding at the time of the 2003 law differed from those used during the 1990s. The question of the impact of funding on the French economy was no longer at the forefront of the debate. Rather, the main idea invoked was that pensions from pay-as-you-go schemes were decreasing in relation to wages and would continue to do so as a result of changes in the retirement system.

General Scheme pensions for private sector employees were lowered considerably by a 1993 law on retirement. Several clauses of the 1993 law have resulted in lower replacement rates: the reference salary for calculating a pension was changed from the highest 10 years of salary to the highest 25 years; past wages used in the calculation of the reference salary were indexed to prices instead of wages; increases in pensions in payment were pegged to prices instead of wages; and the number of years of contributions required for a full pension was increased from 37.5 to 40 years.

Supplementary pension schemes have been gradually reducing replacement rates since the mid-1990s.

The 2003 law reduced replacement rates for civil servants, whose schemes had been untouched in the 1993 reforms. Prior to 2003, civil service pensions were calculated by multiplying the number of years of service by a 2 per cent accrual rate, with a full pension equal to 75 per cent of final salary for 37.5 years of service. Pensions in payment increased in line with civil service salaries. Civil service pensions continue to be calculated on the basis of career end salaries, but other features of the scheme were aligned with the General Scheme. The 2003 reform reduced the accrual rate by increasing the number of years of service required for a full pension to 40. Pensions in payment are now pegged to prices instead of wages.

The text introducing the 2003 bill, in a section on how the proposed law would give individuals more choice concerning their retirement, set out the rationale for new retirement savings plans. Individual choice was to be enhanced in two ways. Firstly, people would be able to choose to get a higher or lower pension depending on the age at which they decide to retire, an idea based on the assumption that workers decide individually when to stop working. Secondly, they would be able to choose whether to put aside savings for their retirement or not and to choose how much to save (Assemblée nationale 2003, pp. 8–9). This change is based on the assumption that workers have the capacity to save more or to transfer assets from other types of savings.

Table 2.2 shows the expected decline in replacement rates for private sector employees, assuming that current legislation continues to apply and that supplementary schemes continue to follow their current rules. Results are given separately for *cadres* and non-*cadres* for hypothetical full-time careers beginning at age of 25 and ending with retirement at age the age of 65 (Table 2.2).

Table 2.2 Replacement rates under current legislation: 2003, 2020, 2050

		2030	2040	2050
Non-*cadre*	General Scheme	56%	52%	50%
	Supplementary schemes	28%	24%	14%
	Total	84%	76%	64%
Cadre	General Scheme	27%	24%	23%
	Supplementary schemes	37%	32%	20%
	Total	64%	56%	43%

Source: Conseil d'orientation des retraites 2006, p. 144

The figures in Table 2.2 reflect the importance of supplementary schemes. For the hypothetical career profile used in the projections, supplementary pensions account for 33 per cent of the total pension of a non-*cadre* and 58 per cent of the total pension for a *cadre*.

Projections point to a drop of almost 10 per cent in the replacement rate for non-*cadre* between 2003 and 2020 (from 84 per cent to 76 per cent) and a 13 per cent drop over the same period for a *cadre* (from 64 per cent to 56 per cent). The reduction between 2003 and 2050 would be 23 per cent for a non-*cadre* and 33 per cent for a *cadre*.

These projections are based on the assumption that current legislation will continue to apply to the General Scheme and that supplementary schemes will not change their collective agreements, especially concerning the way pensions are indexed. Since 2003, supplementary schemes have indexed the 'cost' of a point to wages, whereas the 'value' of a point has been indexed to prices (the pension is equal to the number of points accumulated by each employee multiplied by the value of a point). This policy results in a continual drop in replacement rates. If supplementary schemes were to start indexing both parameters to prices, replacement rates would drop less rapidly. Projections based on such a change in formula as of 2008, when the collective agreements on supplementary schemes are due for new negotiations, indicate a 9 per cent drop in total replacement rate for a non-*cadre* between 2003 and 2020 and a 12 per cent drop over the same period for a *cadre*. The reduction between 2003 and 2050 would be 12 per cent for a non-*cadre* and 28 per cent for a *cadre*.

In sum, whatever decision is taken for supplementary plans, French employees face a substantial reduction in pensions. This cutback has become the main argument used to encourage individuals to save more for their retirement.

New Funded Arrangements Set Up by the 2003 Law

The 2003 law on retirement changed the types of retirement savings plans available to French people and the groups that could use such plans. One provision is not actually a new type of retirement savings plan; it allows employees to make voluntary contributions to a company defined contribution plan ('article 83'). It is referred to as a 'Company Retirement Savings Plan' (PERE: *Plan d'épargne retraite d'entreprise*). This measure has attracted little interest so far.

The law created two new types of retirement savings plans: one available to anyone below retirement age and one available to private sector employees whose companies negotiated a collective agreement. Both arrangements are optional and have a defined contribution. Individuals choose whether or not to contribute and they choose the level of their contributions and the types of investments of their savings. The amount of the benefit varies with returns on investments.

Participants' contributions can be deducted from their taxable income within certain limits. Contributions by employers to their employees' plans are deductible from taxable company revenues within certain limits and employer contributions are exempt from contributions to mandatory social security schemes.

The law defines the form of funding that is to be encouraged. Defined benefit plans are excluded. Priority has been given to optional retirement savings plans, with individual choice on several levels. For example, individuals choose to contribute or not; they choose how much to contribute; and they choose the types of investments. Plans can be subscribed individually or within an occupational framework. Money may not be withdrawn before retirement, except under certain specified circumstances. Individually subscribed plans must pay out annuities. Occupational plans must offer an annuity but they may allow lump sum withdrawals. This provision is in keeping with the European Directive on Institutions for Occupational Retirement Provision, adopted 3 June 2003, a few months before the French law on retirement of 21 August 2003. The Directive defines occupational retirement provision as any funded arrangement concerning an occupational group (employees, the self employed) that pays out benefits at retirement in the form of life time pensions or lump sums.

The 2003 law set up a funded pension scheme for civil servants that does not adhere to all of these principles. This scheme is defined contribution, but participation is mandatory and reserves are invested collectively, with no individual choice. It corresponds to what in the UK is referred to as a money purchase scheme.

A Mandatory Money Purchase Scheme for Civil Servants (RAFP)

The 2003 law will reduce replacement rates for civil servants who do not contribute the full forty years required for a full pension. In order to make these cutbacks more palatable, the government set up a system to include bonuses as part of pay on which pensions would be based. This was a longstanding demand of civil service unions. Simply integrating bonuses directly as part of salaries would have resulted in a large immediate increase in civil service pensions, since they are based on final salaries. Instead, a new defined contribution scheme financed by contributions on bonuses was introduced.

This scheme, called the RAFP (*Régime additionel de la Fonction publique*, – 'Additional Scheme for the Civil Service'), is financed by employer and employee contributions of 5 per cent each, levied on bonuses up to a limit equal to 20 per cent of salary. Withdrawals take the form of pensions. The RAFP is a money purchase scheme, with benefits calculated to be fully financed by reserves. Investments are collective and there is no individual choice as to types of investments. Since the scheme does not recognize past service, benefits will be low for several decades. For a civil servant retiring at 65 after 40 years of service with bonuses equal to 20 per cent of salary (about the average in the civil service), projections forecast a RAFP pension equal to 1.4 per cent of final salary in 2020 and 2.9 per cent in 2050 (COR 2006).

Optional Employee Retirement Savings Plans (PERCOs)

The PERCO (*Plan épargne* retraite collectif or 'Collective Retirement Savings Plan') replaced the long-term employee savings plans (PPESV) set up in 2001 under the Socialist government. Within the framework of a PERCO, withdrawal of each employee's assets from the scheme are blocked until retirement, instead of ten years under the older formula.

Under certain circumstances, a participant may withdraw assets before retirement: death of a partner, invalidity of the employee or a partner or a child, purchase of a home or repairs to a home for damage due to a natural catastrophe, excessive debt of the employee, or if the participant is unemployed and no longer has a right to unemployment benefits. If a participant dies before reaching retirement, his or her assets are distributed to designated beneficiaries.

A PERCO must be set up by a collective agreement, either within a single company or for employees in several companies. Only employees who have access to an employee savings plan may participate in a PERCO, since it is felt that employees should be able to choose between long-term savings (that is, retirement savings) and short-term savings. Individual participation is optional. Employees may arrange to contribute up to 25 per cent of their wages. They may also contribute using remuneration from a mandatory profit sharing plan (*participation*) or a profit sharing plan set up voluntarily by the company (*intéressement*). The employer may make matching contributions worth up to three times the amount of employee contributions, under an annual limit of €4,600 (as of 2006). Participating employees must be offered a choice between at least three investment funds.

According to the law, each investment fund must be governed by a committee half of whose members are participating employees and the other half representing the employer or employers.

Participants must be offered withdrawal in the form of an annuity, but the collective agreement may authorize employees to choose other forms of withdrawal: a lump sum, phased withdrawals or a mix of these formulas and an annuity. Annuities are taxed and subject to the same social contributions as pensions. Lump sums are also subject to social contributions, but they are exempt from income tax. This arrangement favours lump sums over annuities (COR 2007, p. 143).

PERCO plans bears a close resemblance to 401(k) plans, a type of individual retirement savings plan that is widespread in the private sector in the United States.[20] The main differences between the two types of plans are the following: employees cannot invest in employer stock through a PERCO, whereas American employees are generally free to invest as much as they want in employer stock through a 401(k) plan, if that option exists. In the US, employees may withdraw all their assets from a 401(k) plan when they leave their employer, whatever their age; fiscal rules encourage them to transfer their savings to another 401(k) plan with a new employer or to an individual retirement account (IRA). French employees cannot withdraw assets from a PERCO before retirement except under certain circumstances. When a French employee leaves an employer, he or she must either keep their retirement savings account with the old employer or transfer their savings to a PERCO with a new employer. Lastly, French employee representatives are involved in decisions about investments, which is rarely the case for US 401(k) plans.

Optional Individual Retirement Savings Plans (PERPs)

Any individual may open this type of plan, which consists of an insurance contract. Withdrawals may only take the form of annuities except in the event of invalidity or purchase of a first residence. In the event of death, the participant may designate a beneficiary to receive an annuity or choose a temporary annuity for a child or children. Contributions are deducted from taxable income up to a limit.

Financing of Retirement Income in 2006

Pay-as-you-go plans continue of course, to predominate in the French retirement system. The following table shows contributions and benefits to retirement plans, broken down by plan type (Table 2.3).

Table 2.3 Financing of retirement pensions in France, 2006 (€ billions)*

	Contributions	Benefits
Basic schemes	142.4	159.5
Mandatory supplementary schemes	52.3	56.0
Non-mandatory supplementary schemes	9.3	4.2

**Note*: In addition to contributions levied on earnings, mandatory retirement schemes derive some revenues from other sources: general taxes and earmarked taxes for basic schemes, returns on assets in the case of mandatory supplementary schemes. Total contributions for 'non mandatory supplementary schemes' published by the DREES (Ministry in charge of social affairs) do not precisely match total contributions in Table 2.4.

Source: DREES 2008.

In 2006, mandatory schemes paid out a total €215.5 billion in pensions, while non-mandatory schemes (retirement savings plans and company retirement schemes) paid out only €4.2 billion, that is, less than 2 per cent of total benefits. The contributions collected by non-mandatory schemes came to 4.8 per cent of total contributions, a figure that reflects the fact that these schemes are funded and have been operating for a short period.

More detailed data by type of scheme is shown in Table 2.4 on the contributions collected by non-mandatory supplementary schemes.

The total amount of contributions was €9.65 billion in 2006. In comparison, the same year, net flows to life insurance contracts came to €88.2 billion and net flows of all financial savings, including life insurance, came to €138.5 billion. These sums dwarf the amounts involved in funded pension plans or retirement savings accounts. A key question is whether this will continue to be the case or whether retirement savings plans will come to play a greater role in retirees' income in future.

Table 2.4 Contributions collected by supplementary retirement savings schemes, 2005 and 2006 (€ millions)

Type of Plan	Contributions	
	2005	2006
Optional plans for individuals outside a company framework	3,777	4,129
Anyone under retirement age (PERP)	853	943
Civil servants and local elected officials (PREFON, etc.)	815	794
Self-employed ('Madelin' plans)	1,848	1,922
Self-employed farmers	200	202
Other	61	217
Private sector employee benefit schemes	4,772	5,523
Optional for employee		
Retirement savings plans (PERCO)	209	387
Optional employee contributions to a DC plan (PERE)	ns	46
Company group insurance contracts		
Defined benefit ('article 39')	2,713	2,820
Defined contribution ('article 83')	1,850	2,270
Total	8,549	9,652

Source: DREES 2008.

Table 2.5 shows the number of individual participants for different types of plans in the years 2004, 2005 and 2007. Data on the number of employees covered are difficult to obtain for group company contracts. At the end of 2006, 348,000 private sector employees and 816,000 civil servants had made voluntary contributions to an occupational retirement savings account. These numbers are small compared to the total of 5 million civil servants and still smaller compared to the total of 18 million private sector employees.

Company retirement schemes that are obligatory for all employees who belong to covered categories collected a total of €4,563 million in 2005; €1,850 million for defined contribution schemes and €2,713 million for defined benefit schemes (see Table 2.4). For the moment, these relatively old schemes collect much more in contributions than optional individual retirement savings plans (PERPs or PERCOs), but of course the latter could expand. PERPs and PERCOs date only from 2004, when the 2003 law came into force and PERE were authorized only in 2005.

Table 2.5 Number of participants in non-mandatory funded retirement schemes, 2004, 2005, 2006 (in thousands)

Type of plan	Participants end 2004	Participants end 2005	Participants end 2006
Optional plans for individuals outside a company framework			
Anyone under retirement age (PERP)	1,235	1,672	1,876
Civil servants and local elected officials (PREFON, etc.)	819	818	816
Self-employed ('Madelin' plans)	740	808	940
Self-employed farmers	254	261	264
Other	157	149	226
Private sector employee benefit schemes			
Optional for employee			
Retirement savings plans (PERCO)	38	102	201
Employee contributions to a DC plan (PERE)	ns	1	147
Company group insurance contracts			
Defined benefit ('article 39')	na	est. 2,300 to 2,500	est. 2,700 to 2,800
Defined contribution ('article 83')	na	na	na

Source: DREES 2008 and DREES 2007.

Table 2.6 shows the value of assets for the different types of funded schemes. This mainly illustrates the fact that older type schemes have more assets than newer ones.

5. CONCLUSION: THE FUTURE OUTLOOK FOR RETIREMENT SAVINGS

What factors might boost or hamper expansion of savings specifically devoted to retirement in France? It is always very difficult to answer such questions about the future. The French retirement system has long followed a path in which funding played a very minor role. However, as has been argued by Bruno Palier (2007), a series of minor changes made year after year may change the 'path' of a social protection system, even if no single change alters the structure or rationale of the system in the short run.

Nonetheless, in the case of France, there exist several obstacles to the development of funded retirement pension schemes.

Firstly, in France, as shown at the beginning of this chapter, savings already play an important role in providing resources to the older population. Life insurance contracts account for a large share of households' financial assets and this proportion has increased greatly inrecent years, even after the 2003 law on

Table 2.6 Reserves of funded retirement schemes by type of scheme, end 2006 € millions

Type of plan	Reserves End 2006
Optional plans open to individuals outside a company framework	
Anyone under retirement age (PERP)	2,373
Civil servants and local elected officials (PREFON, etc.)	11,009
Self-employed ('Madelin' plans)	1,036
Self-employed farmers	1,964
Other	2,022
Private sector employee benefit schemes	
Optional for employee	
Retirement savings plans (PERCO)	769
Employee contributions to a DC plan (PERE)	na
Company group insurance contracts	
Defined benefit ('article 39')	21,361
Defined contribution ('article 83')	34,872

Source: DREES 2008.

retirement offered greater access to retirement savings accounts. Because the savings rate of French households is already quite high, the most plausible scenario for development of savings specifically devoted to financing retirement would be a transfer from purchases of life insurance. In order for such a transfer to occur, tax exemptions on retirement savings would have to be enhanced.

Secondly, while public policy appears to favour retirement savings, certain government decisions actually work against the development of retirement savings. New measures adopted by the government following the June 2007 legislative elections do not seem to favour saving specifically for retirement. One of the first measures was designed to favour investment in real estate through tax exemptions on interest on mortgages for people who buy their own homes. Later the same year, in November, the government enacted other measures to encourage people to purchase homes.

Yet another measure introduced by the government in 2007 does not favour savings. There has been a good deal of controversy about the purchasing power of French households. In order to boost household consumption, the government decided to allow some employee savings that were previously frozen in special accounts to be withdrawn. The measure came into force at the beginning of 2008. According to professionals in the finance industry, between 5 and 8 billion euros could be withdrawn from these savings plans.

Generally speaking, French workers have experienced poor wage growth for a long time. The national statistical institute recently issued a study showing that the average annual wage has stagnated in real terms over the past thirty years (INSEE 2007). Of course, this is not true for all workers. However, it shows that it might be very difficult for low wage households to save more, be it for retirement or for other purposes.

Finally, it should be stressed that financial markets have become more volatile and hence more risky. Over the past twenty years, volatility has become one of their structural features. French households are increasingly aware of this fact and it might dampen their enthusiasm for the expansion of savings, especially savings invested on stock markets.

It could be argued that, even today, 'paying for pensions', to quote the title of Tony Lynes's seminal study on the French retirement system (Lynes 1985), remains a more secure choice for French workers than saving for retirement.

NOTES

1. Terms in French are written in italics throughout this chapter.
2. The ceiling for membership was roughly equivalent to a skilled worker's wage.
3. Members were free to choose whether their contributions should be paid to an insurance company, a mutual benefit society, an employer's pension fund or a government fund.
4. The benefit is called AVTS, *Allocation aux vieux travailleurs salaries* or 'Allowance for old salaried workers'.
5 For a detailed analysis of the history of mandatory supplementary schemes, see Tony Lynes (1985). A more recent description of the retirement system as a whole may be found in Moore (2001).
6 In theory, the Social Security ceiling, which is the cut-off point for General Scheme contributions and benefit calculation, was to increase in line with average manual workers' wages. Over the 1950s, the ceiling increased more slowly.

7. Employers who chose to contribute at a rate above the minimum could not go back down to a lower rate, a rule that was necessary to ensure payment of accrued rights because the schemes used pay-as-you-go financing.
8. Effective contribution rates are adjusted by applying a 'call-up' rate (*taux d'appel*) which may be lower than, equal to or higher than 100 per cent. Initially, call-up rates were below 100 per cent. Today, 'call-up' rates are set at 125 per cent.
9. There exist three such schemes. COREM was set up in 1949 for elementary school teachers; today, this scheme is open to any salaried worker whose employer has subscribed to a group contract. CRH was created in 1962 for civil servants employed by public hospitals. PREFON was set up in 1967 for any civil servant or ex-civil servant. Of the three, only PREFON is fully funded, with liabilities covered by reserves at all times. COREM and CRH are partially funded, but they are in the process of moving to full funding (Marini 2006, pp. 70–99).
10. Law of 8 August 1994.
11. Law of 11 February 1994.
12. Law of 25 March 1997.
13. Income tax exempt employee and employer contributions were to be capped either at 20 per cent of the annual Social Security ceiling or 5 per cent of the employee's total remuneration, whichever was higher.
14. Employer contributions were to be exempt from contributions to mandatory retirement schemes within the same limits as those defined by regulations for insured employee benefit schemes in general (notably invalidity and death benefits). The limit was equal to 85 per cent of the annual Social Security ceiling.
15. The Social Security ceiling defines the level of wages subject to contributions to the General Scheme and the wages taken into account in the calculation of General Scheme pensions. Today, it is indexed to the average wage of private sector employees and is equal to about 1.3 times the average wage. In 2008, the ceiling is 33,276 euros per year.
16. Law of 19 February 2001.
17. At the end of 2007, the Retirement Reserve Fund had received total allocations of 25.8 billion euros and held total assets of 34.5 billion euros. According to official projections, the fund should finance at least 22 per cent of the projected shortfall between schemes' revenues and total expenditures.
18. The creation of the French Retirement Reserve Fund is similar to proposals put forward in the United States at the end of the 1990s to invest Social Security reserves collectively in financial markets, rather than set up individual savings accounts as part of the mandatory retirement system.
19. Law of 21 August 2003.
20. For a detailed comparison of PERCOs and 401(k) plans, see Delahousse (2006).

ABBREVIATIONS FOR INSTITUTIONS USED IN LIST OF REFERENCES

COR: Conseil d'orientation des retraites, French national advisory council on retirement policy

DGTPE: Direction générale du trésor et de la politique économique, French Ministry of the economy, finance and industry

DREES: Direction de la recherche, des études, de l'évaluation et des statistiques, French Ministry in charge of social affairs

INSEE: Institut National de la Statistique et des Etudes Economiques, French national statistical institute

MIRE: Research organisation of the Ministry in charge of social affairs

REFERENCES

apRoberts, Lucy (1993), 'Complementary retirement pensions: Towards a definition of terms', *International Social Security Review*, **46** (4), pp. 51–66

apRoberts, Lucy and Emmanuel Reynaud (1998), *Un panorama de la protection sociale complémentaire*, Report for the MIRE, February, Paris: MIRE

Assemblée Nationale (2003), 'Projet de loi portant réforme des retraites', Exposé des motifs, Presented by François Fillon, Minister of social affairs, labour and solidarity, on behalf of Jean-Pierre Raffarin, Prime Minister, 28 May 2003, Paris: Assemblée National

COR (2007), *Retraites: questions et orientations pour 2008*, Fourth Report of the COR, 10 January 2007, Paris: COR

COR (2006), *Retraites: perspectives 2002 et 2050*, Third Report of the COR, 29 March 2006.

Delahousse, Laure (2006), 'Les retraites d'entreprise aux Etats-Unis : Peut-on prévoir l'avenir du PERCO à partir du parcours du 401(k)?', Association française de la gestion financière, www.afg.asso.fr/Etudes et rapports/Epargne retraite, accessed June 2006.

DGTPE (2007), 'Panorama de la fiscalité des produits d'épargne', Document presented to the COR, 31 January 2007, Paris: COR

DREES (2007), Yannick Croguennec in collaboration with Nathalie Augris, 'L'épargne retraite en 2006', *Etudes et résultats*, No. 626, February 2007.

DREES (2008), Yannick Croguennec in collaboration with Nathalie Augris, 'L'épargne retraite en 2006', *Etudes et résultats*, No. 626, February 2008.

INSEE (2007), Romain Aeberhardt, Julien Pouget and Anne Skalitz, 'Le revenu salarial et ses composantes, évolutions et inégalités de 1978 à 2005', Les salaires en France - édition 2007, Paris: INSEE, pp. 27–49.

Lynes, Tony (1985), *Paying for Pensions: The French Experience*, STICERD Occasional Papers, no. 9.

Marini, Philippe, Senator (2006), Rapport d'information du Sénat, presented on behalf of the French Senate's Commission on finance, budget control and national accounts, report on retirement savings, 21 September 2006.

Moore, Kathryn L. (2001), 'The Best of Times and the Worst of Times: Lessons from the Recent Reforms of the French Retirement System', *Georgia Journal of International and Comparative Law*, **29** (3), pp. 441–490.

Palier, Bruno (2007), 'Tracking the Evolution of a Single Instrument Can Reveal Profound Changes: The Case of Funded Pensions in France,' *Governance: An International Journal of Policy, Administration and Institutions*, **20** (1), January 2007, pp. 85–107.

3. The Development of Private Pension Pillars in Italy: An Assessment of Recent Reforms

Felice Roberto Pizzuti and Michele Raitano

1. INTRODUCTION

During the last 15 years Italy has undertaken a deep pension reform process of both public and private pillars. After the reforms[1] the Italian pension system is still public and pay-as-you-go, even if many of the measures aimed at increasing the role of the funded private sector have been introduced since 1993.

The main objective of the reform process has been the financial sustainability of the public scheme (to fulfil the constraints to the public finances fixed by the EU), which has been pursued by extending the retirement age, changing the pension benefit formula (from defined benefit to Notional Defined Contribution – NDC[2] and the indexation rule (from wages to prices), and linking benefits to the retirement age and to economic and demographic developments. The latter has been done in an actuarially fair way by using the NDC method. However, in order to achieve sustainability, the reforms have hugely reduced the replacement rates provided by the public scheme (especially for early retirees).[3]

In order to keep the old replacement rates constant and, in some cases not to be exposed to social exclusion risks,[4] workers will have to work longer (because benefits depend on the retirement age) or will have to pay contributions to supplementary private pension schemes, as often suggested in the political economy debate.

However, participation in private schemes (both occupational and personal) is voluntary, recently (they were regulated in 1993) and their take up is still low. At the end of 2006, the membership of pension funds was about 14 per cent of private sector employees; in order to increase it the 2005 reform, phased in from January 2007, has sought to induce workers to devolve to pension funds the TFR (*trattamento di fine rapporto*),[5] a deferred part of the salary which is retained by firms and is paid as a lump sum to employees when the job relationship ends (for firing, dismissal, retirement).

This chapter analyses the role of Italian private pension schemes, focusing, in particular, on the choice – induced by the 2005 reform – between maintaining TFR in firms or moving it to pension funds. These choices are treated as two different investment options in our appraisal of the development of private pensions in Italy. In the second section we will describe the main features of private schemes and we will define the TFR, presenting also some data on enrolment in pension funds after the 2005 reform. In the third section we will analyze the many elements which can affect individual choice between retaining TFR in firms or devolving it to a pension fund, showing that these two options are not at all perfect substitutes. In the fourth section we will assess the main features of the Italian private schemes development, focusing especially on their risk–return profile, on the administrative costs they impose on members and on the effects on the Italian economic system of their asset allocation strategy. Our conclusions, outlined in the fifth section, will provide an overall evaluation of the reforms in the 1990s, focusing on the possible auspicious role of private pension schemes within the Italian pension system.

2. THE ITALIAN PRIVATE PENSION SCHEMES AND THE TFR AFTER THE 2005 REFORM

The Private Pillar

After the 1993 reform that regulated the supply of supplementary pensions in Italy,[6] the private pillar was organized through three different kinds of pension funds: closed (contractual) funds, open funds, and personal pension plans (*piani pensionistici individuali* – PIPs – introduced in 2000).

Private pension schemes are fully funded and benefits are based on a defined contribution method, without any redistributive feature. Contributions paid earn a market return, which (of course, together with its risk) depends on the kind of capital market investment chosen.[7] Worker enrolment in pension funds is always voluntary (even for employees whose job sector manages a pension fund).

Pension funds provide two different kinds of benefits: old age pensions, when the worker has at least 5 years of seniority in the fund and has reached the age required for the old age pension in the public scheme (65 years old if male, 60 if female); seniority pensions, when the worker retires at an age no more than 10 years lower than the one required for the old age pension in the public scheme and has at least 15 years of seniority in the fund.

The fiscal regime is a sort of hybrid in terms of tax relief: contributions are exempted until a threshold of 5,165 euros each year; investment returns are taxed at an 11 per cent proportional rate; benefits were taxed before 2007 by personal income tax rates and after that date by a proportional rate between 9 per cent and 15 per cent, depending on the seniority in the fund. This can be described as exempt, taxed and taxed (ETT). However, the share on which the tax on investment returns has already been paid is exempt. The tax regime of the three different private pension schemes (closed and open funds and PIPs) is the same. However, among these schemes there are several relevant differences.[8]

Closed funds are set up within the frame of collective bargaining between employer and employee associations (trade unions, whose representatives participate in the fund's board) and are not-for-profit enterprises. They can be created at several levels: company or group of companies, industrial or economic sectors, and geographical areas; the self-employed associations can organize a closed pension fund too. They are independent legal entities: a separation between the closed fund and the sponsoring employer is envisaged. They are not allowed to manage directly their assets: the governing board must therefore delegate such activity to professional managers (banks, insurance companies, investment firms or asset management companies).

Open funds are promoted and managed by banks, insurance and investment companies. They can offer occupational (that is, based on a collective enrolment) and personal plans; however only if a closed fund does not exist for a certain category of worker, collective agreements can foresee the group adhesion to schemes offered by open pension funds. They do have not an independent legal status; however their assets have to be separated from those of the financial company managing them.

Since 2000, personal pension plans can be offered also through life insurance policies (PIPs), under the condition that the benefits have to be paid according to the same rules applied to pension funds. They receive the same tax treatment and incentives as pension funds. The 2005 reform introduced some new rules for PIPs, mainly concerning the kind of administrative costs they can impose on buyers.

However it must be pointed out that, before the main 1993 reform, several hundred pension funds (so called pre-existing funds) were already operating; they were usually sponsored by banks and insurance companies in favour of their employees (they are a sort of fringe benefit for their employees). At present, around 450 pre-existing funds are still in operation, with about 650,000 members in total. They can continue to operate in their original forms, without following the 1993 rules; they have different investment limits to the new kinds of funds and can also offer defined benefits, but after the 1993 reform the defined benefit plans have been closed to new members.

It has to be stressed that in Italy a true difference between occupational and personal schemes, that is, second and third pillar) does not depend on the kind of closed or open pension fund, but on the kind of personal or collective worker enrolment. In a collective way an employee can enrol only in closed funds, except where a firm or sector does not provide such a fund; in this case, collective participation in an open fund is allowed. Acting individually, everyone (independently of job status) can enrol in an open fund or can buy a personal pension plan.

The TFR

In Italy, when the labour relationship ends, employees receive the TFR *(Trattamento di Fine Rapporto)*, a lump sum paid by employers. The sum paid as TFR is a deferred part of the salary; every year 6.91 per cent of gross wage is retained by firms as TFR and a fixed return (1.5 per cent plus 75 per cent of the inflation rate) is guaranteed on such amount.

TFR cannot be considered as a sort of mandatory occupational plan; in fact, it is a lump sum (never an annuity) paid to workers by firms for any reason ending the employment relationship (firing, job dismissal or retirement). Moreover, after eight years of employment an employee can receive 70 per cent of the capitalized TFR, if needed for buying a home or for medical expenses. Consequently, the average length of the TFR accumulation does not exceed ten years.

In other terms, TFR retained by firms cannot be considered a pension arrangement because its main aim is to provide a lump sum amount to ease liquidity constraints in phases of the life cycle (at retirement or after having lost a job), rather than to correct individual myopia by providing an annuity in old age.

Nonetheless, since the 1993 systematization of the private pension sector, the payments for TFR have usually been considered the main source for financing private pension schemes and the 2005 reform (in force since 2007) is really seeking to foster the pension funds development using the annual flows of TFR.[9]

Since 1993, private pension sector regulation has tried to encourage workers to transfer their TFR to pension funds and employees were obliged to pay part or all of the TFR (if they began to work after 1993) to the collective fund if they enrolled in it. Besides, until the 2005 reform employers and employees contributions to a private pension fund were exempted only if an equal amount of the TFR was paid to the fund.

Aiming at fostering private pillar development by carving out the TFR, the 2005 reform did not oblige workers to enrol in the private pillar but it introduced a requirement for workers to assent to the TFR arrangement. The reform stated that, if workers do not explicitly disagree, TFR flows but (never the stock already accumulated) are transferred away from firms and paid into pension funds.[10]

In a six-month period (before 30 June 2007, or within six months after their hiring) workers had to decide if they wished to retain TFR annual flows in the firm.[11] However, only the choice to devolve it to a fund is irreversible. After six months a worker can decide to devolve TFR flows to a private pension scheme.

However, the reform tries to encourage early transfers to private pension funds as it decreases the tax rate on private pension benefits with seniority in the fund.

The reform has therefore changed the default option for the TFR and has also established that individuals who began to work before 1993 can pay all of the TFR to private pension schemes.[12] Further, it has stated that TFR can be allocated to any kind of fund (closed, open and PIP, that is, even in cases of individual participation in funds), but, if the worker does not clearly declare to which fund it should be paid, it is automatically transferred to the closed fund specified in the collective agreement.[13]

The Sources of Contributions to Pension Funds and the Fiscal Rules

Pension fund contributions come from three different sources: employees, employers and the sum not retained as TFR. Regarding these sources, until the enforcement of the 2005 reform on 1 January 2007 there existed a clear hierarchy between pension funds, depending on whether membership was occupational or personal.

In fact, only if employees were enrolled in a fund in a collective way (that is, on the basis of social partners agreement) the employers had to pay private pension contributions and had to devolve a TFR share. On the contrary, if employees were members of a personal plan (open fund or PIP) the employer was not obliged to pay contributions and TFR contributions could not be transferred to such a plan. Moreover, given that fiscal deductions on contributions to private pension schemes depended on the payment of a share of TFR, a further advantage emerged for collective funds in attracting employees as members because in cases of individual membership, employee's contributions were not tax exempted.

The 2005 reform has partly changed this hierarchy by establishing that TFR can be allocated to any kind of private scheme (that is to personal open funds and PIPs which allow tax exemptions for employees), but also by keeping an advantage for collective funds by requiring that employers contributions can be paid only to them.[14]

The dimensions of contributions paid to closed funds (or in the case of a collective adhesion to open funds) are defined in the collective agreements: on average employers' and employees' contribution rates are, respectively, 1.22 per cent and 1.16 per cent of the gross wage. The TFR share depends on worker seniority; those who began to work after 1 April 1993 must pay the whole TFR (6.91 per cent of the gross wage) to the collective fund if they enrol in it, while those who were already working by that date can freely decide to either pay the whole TFR or the share established in the collective agreement (on average 2.37 per cent). Instead, an employee who enrols individually in an open fund or buys a PIP can freely choose the contribution rate (while the employer's contribution is not provided) and can decide to allocate the TFR or not.

Moreover the 2005 reform sought to encourage workers to allocate the TFR to private pension funds by generous fiscal incentives. Tax exemptions on contributions have been widened and, especially, new fiscal rules for private pension benefits have been arranged. In contrast to the TFR which is paid as a lump sum by firms and is taxed at the average personal income tax rates, benefits provided by pension funds (either lump sum or by annuities) will be taxed at a low 15 per cent proportional rate which is further reduced each year by 0.3 percentage points for every enrolment year after the 15th year, until a minimum rate of 9 per cent is reached.

The Private Pillar Development and the First Effects of the 2007 Reform

In this section the private pillar development is discussed showing first some quantitative data at the end of 2006 (that is, before the TFR reform phasing in) and then observing the changes which happened during 2007.

At the end of 2006 in Italy, 42 closed pension funds (of which 37 are directed to employees) and 84 open pension funds had been authorized (Table 3.1). Nevertheless the enrolment rate was still limited.

Only 1.2 million workers or 14.1 per cent of individuals working in a sector managing a fund (pension funds for public employees are still not operating[15]) were enrolled in a closed fund, while less than 450,000 individuals were members of an open fund. Nearly all those enrolled in open funds adhered to them in person (only the 14 per cent are collective members) and 81 per cent of their members were self-employed (COVIP 2007). Notwithstanding, two-thirds of the new funds are open, closed funds account for 75 per cent of members and of financial assets of the sector. PIPs seem more appealing given that in the period 2001–2006 about 960,000 policies were issued.

Until 2003 every closed fund provided only one kind of investment (generally with a low risk profile); in the following years most of the closed funds began to provide different options (equity, balanced, bonds, mixed bonds) from which the worker can freely choose his preferred one. Since their introduction, open funds have provided many investment options to their members.

Perhaps due to binding liquidity constraints and high discount rates for future pension benefits, the enrolment rate was very low among younger generations, despite their future replacement rates having been hugely reduced by the 1995 reform of the public scheme (which introduced the notional defined contribution method, so called *contributivo*)[16] and pension funds are usually considered the main tool available to younger people for increasing pension replacement rates.[17] Pension funds members' average age is in fact very high (approximately 44 years old); only 16 per cent and 18 per cent, respectively, of closed and open funds members are younger than 35, while among private employees and the self-employed aged less than 35 years old individuals' shares are 38 per cent and 28 per cent (COVIP 2007). Thus it seems that most of the members are not young workers who intend to increase their future pension; rather they are older workers who could invest in funds for speculation or a shorter term investment perspective.

However the entolment rate in closed pension funds is not homogeneous in the different kinds of funds; at the end of 2006 it was much higher in the company funds, 43.6 per cent, than in the category funds at 12.2 per cent (which have a much greater number of potential members). In companies' funds, enrolment is higher because pension fund membership is usually considered a sort of fringe benefit provided by the employer.

Table 3.1 Pension funds on 31 December 2006

	Funds	members[a]	% change from 31/12/2005	potential members	Enrol - ment rate[b]	net assets[c]	% change from 31/12/2005
closed fund	42	1,219,372	5.6	11,831,600	n. a.	9,257	21.6
for emplys.	37	1,205,667	n. a.	9,573,600	14.1	9,201	n. a.
category funds	28	991,048	n. a.	9,261,600	12.2	7	n. a.
Comp. funds	9	214,619	n. a.	492,000	43.6	2,174	n. a.
For self-Employed	5	13,705	n. a.	2,078,000	n. a.	n. a.	n. a.
Open funds	84	440,486	8.2	n. a.	n. a.	3,257	19.4
Total new (closed and open) funds	126	1,659,858	6.3	n. a.	n. a.	12784	21.0
Pre-existing funds	448	649,519	n. a.	n. a.	n. a.	34,148	n. a.
Personal Pension plans (PIPs)	-	959,867	16.7	-	-	4,546	36.0

Notes

a For PIPs we refer to the number of issued policies;

b Due to some duplications enrolment rate is different from the ratio of the third and the fifth column; [3] Millions of euro; for PIPs we refer to premiums collected.

c Millions of euro; for PIPs we refer to premiums collected.

Source: COVIP (2007)

Highlighting the role played by the kind of productive system (that is, of firms' size and sector) in fostering pension fund membership, it has to be stressed that at the end of 2006 among category funds the enrolment rate was higher (more than 30 per cent) in those covering chemical and metal mechanical workers, that is, in sectors with larger firms (more than 250 employees), while it was very low (less than 1 per cent) in the funds covering individuals working in trade and services sectors, that is, where there is a wide fragmentation in the productive system with mostly small and medium-sized firms. Confirming the influence of firm size, about 25 per cent of closed fund members came from firms employing less than 50 employees, while half of the labour force works in such firms. The different role played by trade unions in these sectors, and also the different firm size, can partly explain the enrolment rate differences.

The crucial role played by firm sized and sector of activity (mediated by the trade union role) in influencing employees' enrolment is confirmed by the observation of the geographical distribution of pension funds membership. It is higher in the north than in the south, where, comparatively, sectors (services and construction) where many small-sized firms prevail. About 61 per cent and 15 per cent of closed funds members live, respectively, in the north and in the south while their shares in the employees labour force are 52 per cent and 28 per cent.

Finally, it has to be stressed that the reduced role of private pension schemes in Italy until the end of 2006, is not due to a low contribution rate nor to pension funds availability (almost all private employees have an occupational reference fund), but to the very low enrolment rate.

Table 3.2 Open funds structure on 3 December 2006[a]

	Values			%		
Funds issued by	No. of funds	Members	assets[b]	Number of funds	Members	assets[b]
Insurance comp.	47	113,508	1,011	63.5	25.8	28.7
Banks	3	81,321	377	4.1	18.5	10.7
Saving management comps. (SGR)	18	139,626	1,330	24.3	31.7	37.7
Movable intermediation comps. (SIM)	6	106,031	809	8.1	24.1	22.9
Total funds	74	440,486	3,527	100.0	100.0	100.0
Sections						
Equity	72	156,410	1,365	22.8	35.5	38.7
Balanced	95	148,826	1,150	30.1	33.8	32.6
Bond	149	135,250	1,012	47.2	30.7	28.7
Total sections	316	440,486	3,527	100.0	100.0	100.0

Notes
a Only operative funds – with at least one member – are considered;
b Millions of euro.

Source: COVIP (2007)

At the end of 2006 the number of individuals enrolled in open funds was much more limited than in closed funds (Table 3.2) compared to the number of potential members (self-employed, professionals and employees without a reference closed fund). Most of the funds are managed by insurance companies, but savings management companies (SGR) have the biggest share of assets. Every open fund provides many investment options, with different risk profiles; the biggest share of members and assets are in the equity section.

As stressed, since January 2007 the new rules about the allocation of TFR have been enforced. Workers had until June to decide the destination of their TFR, otherwise it would have automatically transferred to their collective fund.[18]

However, the first results about the new memberships of funds seem to confirm the limited appeal that Italian employees feel towards private pension schemes although the reform does not apply to employees in the public sector). The large majority of workers has in fact preferred to retain the TFR in the firm; however about 1.4 million of private employees chose to devolve the TFR to private pension funds and the enrolment rate in closed funds grew up to 25 per cent (Table 3.3). The new members of closed funds (777,350) are about three times as much the number of employees new members of open funds (242,905), while about 200,000 private employees have paid their TFR to a PIP.

The increased participation in private pension schemes has not changed in a very significant way the socio-demographic features of funds' members, even though 40 per cent of new members are aged less than 40.

Table 3.3 Changes in pension fund membership 31 December 2006–31 December 2007

	2006	2007	Absolute change	Change ratio
Closed Funds	1,219,372	1,996,722	777,350	63.8
for employees in private sector	1,095,546	1,859,051	763,505	69.7
Enrolment rate for employees in private sector	15.0	24.9	9.9	66.0
Open Funds	440,486	745,389	304,903	69.2
for employees in private sector	83,585	326,490	242,905	290.6
«New» PIP	n. a.	483,210	n. a.	n. a.
for employees in private sector	n. a.	296,740	n. a.	n. a.
«Old» PIP	959,867	800,000	n. a.	n. a.
for employees in private sector	100,000	n. a.	n. a.	n. a.
Total members of new funds	2,619,725	4,025,321	1.405.596	53.7
for employees in private sector	1,279,131	2,482,281	1,203,150	94.1
Pre-existing funds	649,519	650,000	n. a.	n. a.
Total members of pension funds	3,269,725	4,675,321	1,405,596	43.0

Source: COVIP (2008).

Notwithstanding the great emphasis in the debate on the allocation of TFR to pension funds for increasing future pensions, it seems that Italian workers prefer retaining it in firms. It is necessary, therefore, to analyse the features of the two different possible destinations of the TFR, firm or pension funds, and also to understand which elements affect individual choices.

3. TFR INTO FIRMS OR PENSION FUNDS: TWO IMPERFECT SUBSTITUTES

As noted in the last section, the 2005 reform gave workers the opportunity to choose where to allocate the whole annual flow of TFR but made pension funds the default option. In relation to this choice, transferring the TFR to private schemes or retaining it in the firm are alternative kinds of investment.[19] These alternatives have different features concerning the services they offer, the fiscal rules and the risk–return profile. Consequently, they are not perfect substitutes (see Cozzolino, Di Nicola and Raitano 2006).

The disbursement provisions and the fiscal rules governing the TFR in firms and in pension funds are shown in Table 3.4. The sums accumulated in firms and in pension funds can be paid, at least partially, on retirement, unemployment, resignation and as an advance for specific needs. As stressed in Section 2, pension funds are subject to a favourable tax system compared to TFR in firms.

However, whatever the reason for disbursement, firms always pay a lump sum amount and the fiscal rules do not differ for pension fund disbursements. The method of payment and tax rates differ according to when the worker asks for the amount accumulated by pension funds.

In particular, at retirement, firms pay a lump sum capital amount, while a worker cannot receive a lump sum of more than half of the capitalized value of the pension fund. Consequently, a worker who needs cash at retirement (or with a high inter-temporal discount rate) should prefer lump sum to an annuity. *Ceteris paribus*, he or she should prefer to keep the TFR in firms in order to receive a bigger lump sum amount to use for immediate or future consumption.

Moreover, in case of making employees redundant, the TFR in the firm is a form of unemployment benefit, because it is wholly and immediately reimbursed to the worker. Only after one year of unemployment can a redundant individual receive some money from the pension fund.

In addition, and consistent with the willingness of the 2005 reform to increase pension benefits using the TFR contributions, the amount accumulated in a pension fund is less liquid than the amount retained by the firm because the whole lump sum is not reimbursed except in the case of a very long unemployment.

However, the TFR and pension fund investment returns have different risks. With the TFR, firms generally guarantee a sort of defined benefit while pension funds do not cover workers for financial market risks as the Italian private pension scheme operates on a defined contribution basis. Hence, employees have to choose between a defined benefit investment, with a low but safe return, and a defined contribution plan, where the return may be higher but it is much more uncertain. Given the safer return and, consequently, a higher degree of liquidity, the TFR in firms also has important buffer stock features for workers. For example, when an employee is fired they will receive a much more certain sum from the firm than from a pension fund.

Table 3.4 Disbursement provisions and fiscal rules of TFR in firms and pension funds

Moment of disbursement	Firms	Pension funds
Retirement	The whole accumulated amount is paid lump sum. Separate taxation (net of returns already taxed)*.	Maximum 50 per cent paid lump sum. On lump sum and annuity (net of returns already taxed) a 15 per cent proportional tax rate is levied (reduced by 0.3 per cent points after the 15th year of fund membership, until a minimum 9 per cent tax rate).
Firing	The whole accumulated amount is paid lump sum. Separate taxation (net of returns already taxed)*.	Partial lump sum payment (50 per cent) in case of unemployment lasting 1 to 4 years. The whole amount is paid for unemployment lasting more than 4 years or permanent disability. Separate taxation with the same rules applying for retirement.
Resignation	The whole accumulated amount is paid lump sum. Separate taxation (net of returns already taxed)*.	Transfer to the new reference fund. Otherwise partial disbursement (50 per cent), but taxed by a proportional 23 per cent tax rate.
Advance	Lump sum disbursement <=70 per cent of the accumulated amount after 8 years of job relationship for buying home or sustaining health expenses. Separate taxation (net of returns already taxed)*.	Lump sum disbursement <=75 per cent in case of health expenses, independently form from? the length of job relationship (and the same tax rates of retirement apply). Lump sum disbursement <=75 per cent for buying home or <=30 per cent for other needs, but after 8 years of fund membership and separate taxation through a 23 per cent tax rate.

**Note*
Separate taxation is based on the average personal income tax rate during the 5 years prior the disbursement.

In addition to increasing living standard in old age (the social security target), TFR savings in firms can also be used as a buffer in case of contingencies such as firing or sickness or as a reserve of liquidity that lessens constraints in another phase of working life (see Castellino and Fornero 2000). Considering the drawbacks of the Italian unemployment benefit system and of financial markets, these two additional roles that the TFR can play should not be overlooked when analysing individual choices to allocate the TFR to firms or pension funds.

Hence, because of these different features, the two options for the TFR cannot be considered as perfect substitutes. Workers' choices will depend on a large set of individual elements including the expected risk–return profile (net of taxes and administrative costs), their risk aversion and their opportunities to receive advance reimbursement.[20]

Finally, from the point of view of risk and social exclusion, it has to be noticed that the TFR applies only to employees. Atypical workers, of whom there are about 1,000,000 individuals (Raitano 2007a), and whose contribution rate and wages are usually lower than those paid to employees, do not receive TFR contributions. They are, therefore, socially segmented and less protected by the private pension system (see Raitano 2007b). In addition, these workers are very often liquidity constrained so that they cannot save for retirement in personal pension funds.

4. THE DEVELOPMENT OF PRIVATE PENSION SCHEMES: AN APPRAISAL

We have described in the previous sections the main features of the Italian pension schemes and the basic elements which can affect individual choices about the allocation of the TFR. In this section we intend to assess the private pillar experience from different points of view. In particular: the risk–return profile, administrative costs, competition between different kinds of funds, fiscal rules and asset allocation strategies.

Italian private pension schemes are financed by the accumulation of funds. They invest contributions on capital markets, and benefits depend on the defined contribution principle under which the investment risk is completely borne by the individual. Consequently, supplementary pensions wholly depend on market returns, even if, as seen in Section 2, the individual can choose among different investment options depending on his or her degree of risk aversion.

In the pension literature those who favour private funded schemes[21] argue that in the long run market returns are usually higher than the GDP growth rate which is approximately the rate of return that a PAYG system can guarantee in a steady state.[22] However, the empirical evidence on the long-term relationship between GDP growth rates and bond returns does not confirm the superiority of private sources, while the comparison between GDP growth rates and equity returns highlights the much wider volatility of the latter.[23]

Burtless (2000) studied the effect of the volatility of market returns on private pension benefits. Using historical data on USA share returns, he computed pension replacement rates that would have been paid to hypothetical workers who retired in the period 1911–1999 if the USA social security system had been fully funded and contributions had been invested only in equities. Then, he compared 89 hypothetical individuals (working from the age of 22 to the age of 62 and retiring after 40 years) with the same wage, working career, contribution rate and life expectancy and differing only in relation to the yearly returns earned on contributions paid to the funded scheme. He found that the average replacement rate for these 89 hypothetical individuals was 52 per cent. However Burtless (2000) stresses the individuals' exposure to risk in a funded defined contribution system and shows the huge dispersion of the replacement rate series; for example, a worker who retired in 1921 would have received a pension amounting to less than 20 per cent of his or her last wage; the replacement rate would instead have been 100 per cent for those who retired in 1969, but it would have decreased to 39 per cent in 1975, only 6 years later.

Considering the performance of the Italian private pension pillar it is necessary to compare the returns earned by pension funds with the rate guaranteed by firms on TFR because many policy makers and economists suggest allocating the TFR to pension funds in order to earn a higher rate of return.[24]

Table 3.5 Nominal yearly returns net of taxes and administrative costs

	1999	2000	2001	2002	2003	2004	2005	2006	2007
closed funds	11.29	3.31	−1.43	−4.43	5.00	4.50	7.50	3.80	2.10
open funds	23.95	2.99	−5.64	−13.15	5.70	4.30	11.50	2.40	−0.30
TFR	2.26	3.56	3.19	3.50	2.80	2.50	2.60	2.40	3.10

Source: Marano and Raitano (2008)

Private pensions were introduced recently in Italy; consequently a long time series needed to assess pensions fund returns is unavailable. However, observing private pension fund real returns since their introduction in different time spans (Figure 3.1), the superiority of private schemes with respect to TFR is not evident, while annual nominal returns show very high volatility (Table 3.5).[25]

Figure 3.1, shows that in many cases the cumulative return on TFR retained by firms is still higher than the one paid by closed or open funds. In particular most individuals, especially if members of open funds who invest in equities much more than closed funds, enrolled in funds in the period 2000–2002 (characterised by the crisis of financial markets, following the bubble of the end of the 20th century) until the end of 2007 were earning on their contributions a return lower than the safer yield guaranteed on TFR; the same is true for individuals entered into funds in 2007 (and also in 2006 if enrolled in open funds). Only those who entered the private pillar sector between 2003 and 2005 are, at the moment, earning a return much higher than TFR.

Moreover, observing the funds returns split by investment section, some stylized facts emerge (Marano and Raitano 2008): returns earned on safer investment options such as bonds are usually similar to the yield provided by firms on TFR; the riskier options (equities and balanced funds) are the only ones that provide, but only in some periods, much higher returns than TFR. However, they show considerable volatility with negative real yearly average return in many periods. In addition, funds returns are usually significantly lower than their benchmark perhaps due to inefficient and costly management.

In the light of recent pension fund experience, it appears that private pension schemes could offer higher (but very uncertain and volatile) returns than the fixed yield paid by firms on the TFR only in cases where workers are willing to accept a much higher exposure to risk.

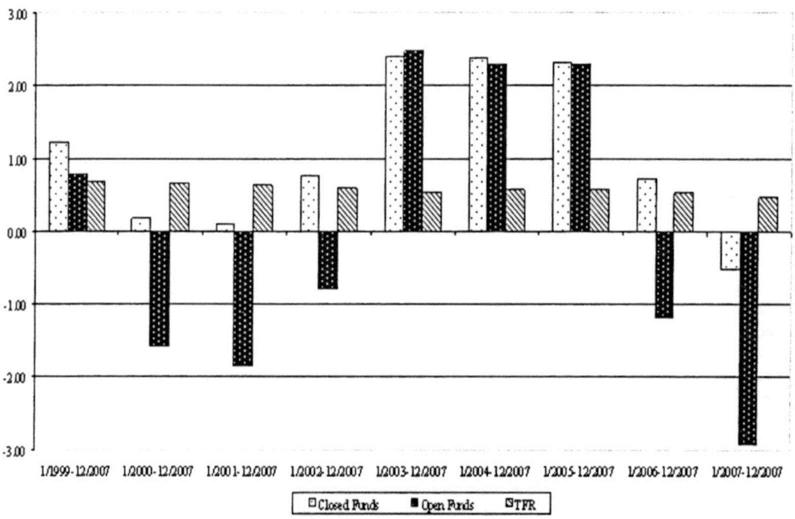

Source: Marano and Raitano (2008)

Figure 3.1 Annual average returns of pension funds and TFR net of taxes and administrative costs for different periods

Apart from financial market performance, net returns on pension fund investments depend on the level of administrative costs.[26] In the literature three different kinds of administrative costs are identified (Murthi, Orszag and Orszag 1999): accumulation costs (the usual costs paid to the fund management when contributions are invested in the market), alteration costs (paid if an individual quits the fund or stops and then starts to contribute again, for example after an unemployment period) and annuity costs (the price for managing the phase of benefits payment).

Other studies point out that occupational plans have usually much lower costs than personal ones.[27] In fact, where the membership of funds is constrained by belonging to a specific firm or category, the competition among funds to attract members is lower and this significantly reduces marketing expenses and administrative costs compared to a situation where workers are completely free to choose in which plans to enrol.

This stylized fact is confirmed observing administrative costs of Italian pension funds (Table 3.6).[28] Since 2005, open and closed funds (and PIPs issued after that date) are obliged to publish their cost indicator (*Indicatore Sintetico dei Costi* – ISC), that is defined as share of pension fund's assets. Such indicator is computed for a representative individual who pays yearly €2,500 into the plan each year, earning 4 per cent gross nominal return; that is, an ISC equal to 1.5 per cent means a 2.5 per cent net of administrative costs return.

Closed funds administrative cost are significantly lower than those of open funds and PIPs (the most expensive plans), although there is a wide dispersion in the funds performances.[29] However, for all kinds of funds, given the significant presence of alteration costs (often fixed costs), the ISC decreases when the period of membership of the fund increases.[30]

The 2005 reform has increased competition between the different kinds of fund as it allows the TFR to be allocated to personal plans, although it prevents the transfer of employers' contributions to personal plans. Hence, the effects of the increased competition on closed funds marketing costs will have to be carefully monitored in the future.

Table 3.6 Costs Synthetic Indicator (Indicatore Sintetico dei Costi – ISC) of pension funds for length of membership in the fund; values as percentage of funds' assets

	2 years	5 years	10 years	35 years
Closed funds	1.1	0.6	0.4	0.3
Minimum	0.4	0.3	0.2	0.1
Maximum	4.2	2.2	1.2	0.8
Open funds	2.0	1.3	1.2	1.1
Minimum	0.6	0.6	0.5	0.5
Maximum	4.1	3.6	2.0	1.8
PIPs issued after 2005 reform	3.6	2.4	1.9	1.5
Minimum	2.1	1.5	1.3	0.7
Maximum	5.4	3.8	3.0	2.5
PIPs issued before 2005 reform	5.6	3.4	2.6	2.0

Source: COVIP (2007) and COVIP (2008)

Apart from the impact on administrative costs, the effect of portability between the different funds has been debated for a long time. Those who favoured full portability argued that it would provide the individual with freedom of choice and that it would increase competition among funds and improve their efficiency.

However, information about the plans' features (mostly the risk profile of each investment option and the structure of administrative costs) is limited, asymmetric between buyers and sellers and very complex to understand. Although the 2005 reform does not guarantee full competition (limiting employers, contributions portability), it does not seem to limit individual freedom of choice and market efficiency too much.[29] On the other hand increasing competition in a highly imperfect market could worsen the starting point as we know from the theory of the second best.

Further, from an equity perspective administrative costs are usually regressive because fixed costs and alteration costs (for example, commencing contributions after unemployment) are relatively larger for disadvantaged persons than for well-off ones. At the same time the rich are usually better informed than the poor and so they are less exposed to the risk of missing pension investment opportunities.

A controversial point of the recent reform, especially on equity grounds, concerns the new tax rates on private pension benefits. As seen in Section 2.3, the reform has changed the tax rates on benefits from a progressive income tax system to a low and flat rate one. Apart from the cost to the public budget of such tax expenditure (that will materialize only in the future, given that such incentives concern the far benefits payment phase), it creates a policy incoherence between a public pension scheme whose benefits are progressively taxed and a private one whose benefits are proportionally taxed. Moreover, such fiscal rules are substantially regressive because the proportional rate applies to a system whose membership increases with income.[31] Consequently, such tax rate differences could induce in the long run a strong demand by better-off groups to reduce contributions to the public system in order to increase private pension savings (that is, a demand of opting out from public to private schemes).

Usually fiscal incentives alone are not able to increase membership by less advantaged workers as they are more likely to be liquidity constrained.[32] Hence, tax expenditures linked to such fiscal incentives for poorer workers could be a deadweight loss. This loss would occur whenever the tax incentives did not change the behaviour of these workers but reduced the fiscal burden for individuals who would have saved enough for their old age in any case.

Apart from considerations based on a micro perspective, in the literature the development of the private pillar is often suggested as a tool for increasing financial market efficiency and boosting economic growth (the so called thick market externalities).[33] It is argued that because pension funds are inclined to invest in shares with the best long-term rates of return, they would contribute to improving credit allocation and increasing growth.

The effective asset allocation strategy chosen by pension funds (see Figures 3.2 and 3.3) shows that about three quarters of closed funds' assets are invested in debt securities (almost entirely in Italy and other EU countries). Because of the safer risk–return profile usually chosen by members, only a quarter of the assets are invested in equities and only 2.2 per cent of the assets are invested in the shares of Italian firms. Because of a higher weight of riskier options, nearly half of the open funds' assets (46.2 per cent) are invested in debt securities. However, the appeal of Italian firms is still very limited given that about one tenth of equity assets of open funds (4.6 per cent of total) are invested in Italian firms' stocks.[34].

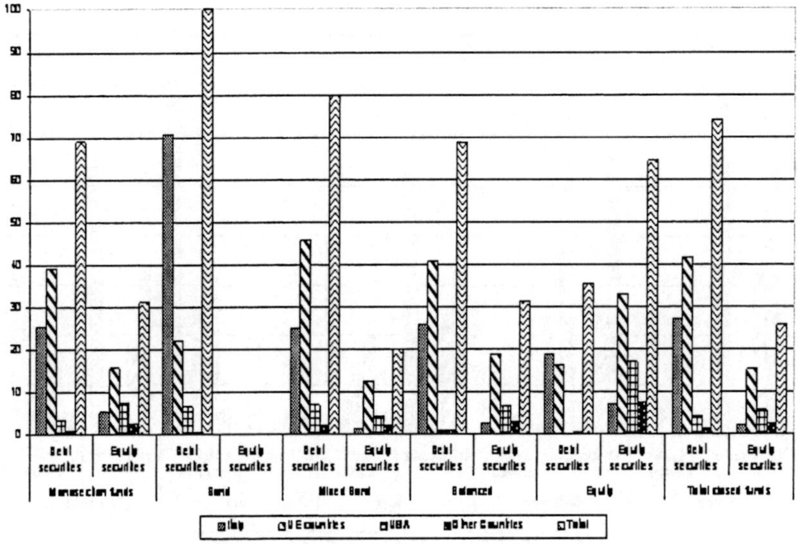

Source: elaborations on Covip (2008)

Figure 3.2 Closed funds: managed assets by geographical area on 31 December 2007 (in percentage terms)

This evidence confirms the weakness of Italian capital markets and highlights the very limited role played so far by pension funds in financing the domestic productive system (Pizzuti 2004).[35] It also casts some doubt on the opportunity to replace an imperfect form of financing, such as the TFR, with a more market-oriented financing source, such as pension funds, given financial market failures.

5. CONCLUSIONS

The debate preceding the 1995 'Dini reform' was not totally aware of the changes it was bringing about and of their effects. Specifically, looking back at things from the present perspective, little attention was given to the importance of the reduction in replacement rates or to the almost total elimination of the solidaristic effects that the reform allowed.

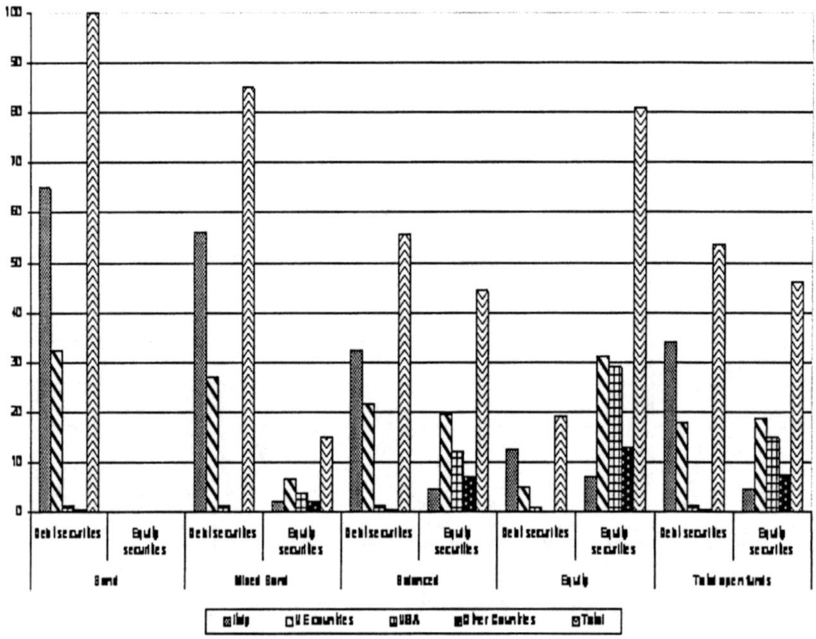

Source: elaborations on Covip (2008)

Figure 3.3 *Open funds: managed assets by geographical area on 31 December 2007 (in percentage terms)*

From a financial point of view, the results of the 1990s reforms were very efficacious and went far beyond all expectations.[36] In spite of a slow income growth, since 1997, the pension expenditure related to GDP – previously significantly increasing – has substantially stabilised to around 13.5 per cent. Moreover, such a rate (about 2 per cent) also includes assistance-oriented benefits (that is, benefits not depending on the actuarial calculation connected to paid contributions) that the public pension system distributes on behalf of the State. Contribution receipts, on the contrary, constantly increased, especially after 1995.

The balance between contributions and pensions expenses (net of assistance-oriented benefits) recorded in the statistics is still negative (about €17.5 billion), but in the expenditures about €29 billion of taxation burden on pensions are also included and they remain, on the contrary, in the State Treasury. Hence, the real balance related to the compulsory pension system is positive for public finance, that is, for a total of 0.8 per cent of GDP.

The Government Commission entrusted with assessing the 1990s reform effects, verified that during the decade 1996–2005, public finance improvements had exceeded the legislator's initial expectations of €11 billion.

Future improvements are even more encouraging. Before the 1990s it was estimated that there would be a maximum value of the expected relationship between pension expenditure and GDP of 25.3 per cent, that is, more than 10 points over the maximum value of 15.2 per cent, officially foreseen after the reforms. This latter result was achieved, however, on the assumption of a net balance of immigrants (115,000–124,000 per year) much lower than the actual one (267,000 in 2005). In the prudential assumption that in the next decade – with a home population decrease exceeding 6 million individuals – the net balance will fluctuate between 145,000 and 190,000 individuals, the trend of the relationship between pension expenditure and GDP will achieve the maximum value of 14.5 per cent (Tancioni 2007).

All these financial improvements produced, of course, effects going beyond all expectations on the degree of the pension system coverage.

Before the 1995 reform, workers in the private sector calculated their pension, as a general rule, doubling the contribution years: for instance, 35 years seniority gave a pension close to 70 per cent of final salary; 40 years seniority close to 80 per cent. In the public sector, treatments were – on an average – 10 points higher.

After the 1995 reform, in the new system – progressively adjusting the performance calculation to the expected demographic ageing, as foreseen in the reform – an employee with 35 years of contributions and retiring at 60, will rteceive a pension of 48 per cent, that is, about 20–30 points less than before. An atypical salaried worker (that is, with irregular contribution history), retiring at 60 with 35 years of contribution (hard to accumulate), will get a pension of about 37 per cent (Pizzuti and Raitano 2005).

Since the pension adjustment to the real salary dynamic was abolished in 1992, the income of a retired person, compared with the income of a worker, is tending towards a constant reduction. The 48 per cent of the last salary of an employee at the age of 60, after 10 years of retirement, will fall to about 40 per cent of the salary of those who at work and will fall to 33 per cent after 20 years (Pizzuti and Raitano 2005). The relative impoverishment of atypical salaried workers with irregular contribution history will follow a corresponding lower trend.

On the basis of these data, it should be clear that the major problem of our pension system is not its financial sustainability but the social disequilibria and the economic effects caused by its lack of coverage.

It has to be stressed that private pension funds can play a positive role, provided that their 'complementary' – not 'substitutive' – role is clear. In the social security debate, on the contrary, the reference is to life expectancy increase and demographic ageing in order to back the need – not at all justified – of a significant social security privatization. In this chapter we have argued that, despite the many reforms introduced in the last 15 years for boosting the private pension pillar, the extent of supplementary pensions in Italy is still quite limited. Furthermore, the way in which this pillar has so far been built is highly questionable, both on efficiency and equity grounds.

Given the significant decrease of public pension coverage caused by the 1995 reform, the participation in private supplementary pensions through the TFR allocation is the only available tool for increasing replacement rates. But, as previously discussed, it seems that workers do not like this option so much. In spite of young workers experiencing the greatest fall in replacement rates, most of them do not choose to enrol in private pension schemes.

In particular, enrolment rates in occupational and personal plans are low; the great majority of workers seems to prefer retaining the TFR in firms rather than transferring it into private pension funds.

Workers perceive that a significant feature of private funded pension schemes is the uncertainty of their benefit because of the variability of the returns on investments in financial markets. The experience with financial markets generally confirms this perception. To entrust too large a share of the pension insurance cover to the volatility of financial markets is contrary to the requirement for social security. Private pension schemes can complement, but not substitute for PAYG schemes in the primary function of ensuring a sufficient income in old age.

The fact that the Italian economic system is based mostly on small firms not quoted on the Stock Exchange is an additional reason to limit the quantitative development of private pension funds. The risk is that the financial resources available for domestic firms (the flow of TFR) will be reduced to increase financial investments in foreign markets.

Private pension funds – especially if they are well regulated, from a taxation point of view – can have a positive role, but it has to be a supplementary one, that is, additional to a 60–70 per cent replacement rate provided by the cheaper and safer public system.

So far, using TFR to increase future pensions is only possible by allocating it to private pension schemes; using TFR flows as additional voluntary contributions in the public NDC scheme is forbidden. However, this prohibition seems very questionable. It is unfair not to give workers the option to allocate the TFR to the safer public scheme whose rate of return is linked to the GDP growth rate which is less volatile than financial market returns. At present, workers can only choose between the two private sources to supplement their pension by maintaining TFR in the firm or moving it to a private pension fund.

Voluntary additional contributions to the public pension scheme would increase public revenues and improve the sustainability of the Italian public finances.[37]

The Budget law for 2007, in section 760, explicitly provided that by 30 September 2007 the Government should discuss in Parliament the possibility of voluntarily increasing the contribution to the public NDC scheme using TFR shares, but at the moment such measures are still not debated. However, we think that this possibility could be a useful measure for increasing pension coverage, meeting workers' preferences and improving the stance of the public finances.

NOTES

1. The last reform of the requirements for early retirement has been approved by the Parliament in December 2007.
2. However, the introduction of the new NDC scheme (in the 1995 reform) has been very gradual. Individuals working in 1995 for more than 18 years will continue to be included in the previous earnings-related scheme, while those working at that date for less than 18 years will have a mixed benefit (earnings-related for the contribution years up to 1995 and NDC thereafter). Only individuals who entered the labour market after 1995 will receive pensions entirely based on the new formula.
3. For an analysis of the replacement rates expected decrease, see Pizzuti and Raitano (2005) and Mazzaferro (2005).
4. The new notional defined contribution (NDC) public scheme is almost completely redistributively neutral. Pension benefits depend proportionally, in an actuarial way, on the contributions paid during the whole working life. Consequently, the public pension scheme will reproduce the same inequalities and the same risks of the labour market. In the NDC scheme risks of social exclusion in old age will mainly depend on the risks deriving from individual working history and labour market features, and such risks will not be corrected by the public pension system . A public means-tested benefit (*assegno sociale*) will top up only the income of the very poor elderly, without further changing the income distribution.
5. In the 2005 reforms, workers were not obliged to enrol in the private pillar as was intended in the first draft of the reform.
6. Before 1993 there was no comprehensive private pillar covering most workers. Nonetheless some firms, especially banks and insurance companies, provided an occupational plan for their employees.
7. Workers can freely choose among many different investment sections managed by pension funds according to their risk profile (that is, equity, balanced or bond sections).
8. For an in-depth analysis of the features of the Italian pension funds, see Fornero and Fugazza (2002), Forni (2003), Cesari (2007).
9. Many authors (Fornero and Castellino 2001; Amato and Marè 2007) state that the low participation rate in the private pillar is due to the high contribution rate paid to the public pillar (33 per cent), and on a shortage of additional savings that can be set apart for old age consumption.
10. As the rate of return guaranteed by firms on TFR, 1.5 per cent plus 3/4 of the inflation rate, is usually much lower than the interest rate on debt (especially for small and medium size enterprises, that are often credit constrained in Italy) TFR has usually been considered by firms as a very cheap financing source. Therefore, in order to secure the firms agreement, the 2005 reform provided compensation for firms giving up their TFR. See Pammolli and Salerno (2006) for an assessment.
11. The 2007 Budget Law stated that for firms with more than 50 employees, TFR flows not devolved by workers to pension funds have to be transferred to an account managed by INPS (the public social security institute). This measure does not change workers' options because INPS provides the same rules guaranteed by firms (which were compensated for allocating

TFR to a pension fund).
12. Given that for public sector employees there is no supplementary pension scheme the TFR reform does not apply for such workers.
13. In the few cases in which a collective fund does not exist and the worker does not declare to which fund he or she wishes to allocate the TFR, it is retained by a specific fund managed by the Italian Public Social Security Institute (INPS).
14. The reform has eased the portability of private contributions by reducing the minimum membership period to 2 years before it becomes possible to move to another fund; however in cases of movement from a collective to a personal plan the portability of employers' contributions is forbidden.
15. In 2004 the first pension funds directed to public employees (Espero, directed to school personnel) has been authorized to collect adhesion, but it has not yet begun to invest contributions.
16. For an assessment of the decrease of replacement rates induced by the 1995 reform see Pizzuti and Raitano (2005).
17. According to the limited role so far played by pension funds almost all the members already retired prefer, when possible, a lump sum payment rather than an annuity stream.
18. In case of silent adhesion to the pension fund, the employer contribution is not paid to the fund. Otherwise, the worker can choose to which kind of fund the TFR should be paid (including also the employer contribution if he or she chooses the contractual fund) or to retain the TFR in firms (and it is transferred to INPS for firms with more than 50 employees).
19. From the worker perspective the fact that for firms with more than 50 employees, TFR not opted to funds, is transferred to INPS is irrelevant, given that INPS guarantees the same features provided by firms.
20. Given the positive probability of receiving advance reimbursement, the individual has to assess the risk–return profile of his investment during the whole period rather than the average return in a given period (for example, 30 years).
21. See Feldstein (1997), Modigliani, Ceprini and Muralidhar (2000),
22. See Aaron (1966) and Samuelson (1958).
23. See Fornero (1999) and Jorion and Goetzmann (2000). From a theoretical point of view Pizzuti (2000) argues that in the long run the profit returns rate cannot be higher than GDP growth rates, unless a continuous increase in profit share is assumed.
24. See Brugiavini (2007) and Boeri (2007).
25. For a comparison of pension funds and TFR returns see Marano and Raitano (2008).
26 The international evidence shows a very high level of administrative costs of funded schemes; see Orszag (1999), Whitehouse (2000), Queisser (1999).
27. See Whitehouse (2000) and James, Smallhout and Vittas (2000).
28. In the table the costs for advance redemption and for receiving annuities are not considered. So far Italian policy makers have not devoted much attention to the rules concerning the annuity phase.
29. For an in depth study of administrative costs of open funds and PIPs see Cesari, Grande and Panetta (2007) and Fornero, Fugazza and Ponzetto (2004) who argue that open fund costs are in line with international standards, while PIPs costs are higher.
30. In 2005 PIPs were prohibited from imposing an extra cost on the first contribution instalment. Before the ISC reform, the cost for a 2 years membership exceeded 10 per cent (COVIP 2007).
31. For example, too much competition could stimulate funds to invest in shares with higher short term returns in order to attract members with limited information (that is, unable to understand the true long-term perspectives of their investment) rather than, in line with their role of institutional investor, in activities with the best long-term perspectives. On this point, see Atkinson (1999).
32. It has also to be remarked that the payment phase (being contributions deductible from fiscal income taxed by the progressive system) relatively favours richer individuals; in addition capital gains on contributions invested are taxed by a proportional (11 per cent) rate. Further, the same 0.3 percentage points tax rate decrease for each year of enrolment to the fund exceeding the 15th – mainly introduced in order to encourage an early devolution of TFR to funds – relatively favours those who, for income levels and stability of working life, can continuously contribute to the fund for many years.
33. See Giannini and Guerra (2006).

34. On this point, see Walker and Lefort (2001), Musalem and Catalan (1999) and Amato and Marè (2001).
35. Besides, very few Italian firms are quoted on the Stock Exchange because of their relatively small size.
36. For financial aspects of Italian pension reforms see Pizzuti and Antichi (2000) and Pizzuti (2007).
37. For the option to pay the TFR voluntarily to the NDC scheme see Pizzuti, Raitano and Tancioni (2006).

REFERENCES

Aaron H. (1966), 'The social insurance paradox', *Canadian Journal of Economics*, **32** (3) 371–4.

Amato G. and Marè M. (2001), *Le pensioni: il pilastro mancante*, Il Mulino, Bologna.

Amato G. and Marè M. (2007), *Il gioco delle pensioni: rien ne va plus?* Il Mulino, Bologna.

Atkinson A.B. (1999), *The Economic Consequences of Rolling Back the Welfare State*, Boston: The MIT Press.

Boeri T. (2007), 'Il TFR da ammortizzatore sociale a pilastro previdenziale', www.lavoce.info.

Brugiavini A. (2007), 'TFR o fondo pensione? Una scelta di convenienza', www.lavoce.info.

Burtless G. (2000) 'Financial Market Risks of Individual Retirement Accounts: The U.S. Record in the Twentieth Century,' *L'Assistenza Sociale*, Winter.

Castellino O. and Fornero E. (2000), 'Il TFR: una coperta troppo stretta', *Rivista di politica economica*, **90**, (9).

Cesari R. (2007), *TFR e fondi pensione*, Il Mulino, Bologna.

Cesari R., Grande G. and Panetta F. (2007), 'La previdenza complementare in Italia: caratteristiche, sviluppo e opportunità per i lavoratori', Working Paper MEFOP, n. 16.

COVIP Commissione di Vigilanza sui Fondi Pensione (2007), Relazione per l'anno 2006, Rome, www.covip.it.

COVIP Commissione di Vigilanza sui Fondi Pensione (2008), I fondi pensione: principali aspetti quantitativi, aggiornamento al 29 February 2008, Rome, www.covip.it.

Cozzolino M., Di Nicola F. and Raitano M. (2006), 'Il futuro dei fondi pensione: opportunità e scelte sulla destinazione del TFR', ISAE Working Paper, n. 64, Rome.

Feldstein M. (1997), 'Transition To a Fully Funded Pension System: Five Economic Issues', NBER Working Paper Series, n. 6149.

Fornero E. (1999), *L'economia dei fondi pensione*, Il Mulino, Bologna.

Fornero E. and Castellino O. (eds) (2001), *La riforma del sistema previdenziale italiano*, Il Mulino, Bologna.

Fornero E. and Fugazza C. (2002), 'Un mercato troppo segmentato? Uniformità e differenze nel mercato previdenziale italiano', Working Paper MEFOP, n. 4/2002.

Fornero E., Fugazza C. and Ponzetto G. (2004), 'A Comparative Analysis of the Costs of Italian Individual Pension Plans', CERP Working Paper, n. 33.

Forni L. (2003), 'Alcune considerazioni sui provvedimenti recenti e sul dibattito in corso in tema di previdenza complementare', Argomenti di Discussione CERP, n. 3/03.

Giannini S. and Guerra M.C. (2006), 'Alla ricerca di una disciplina fiscale per la previdenza complementare', in Messori M. (ed.), *La previdenza complementare in Italia, Il Mulino*, Bologna.

James E., Smalhout J. and Vittas, D. (2000), 'Administrative Costs and the Organization of Individual Account System: A Comparative Perspective', *World Bank Pension Research Volume*, Washington D.C.

Jorion P. and Goetzmann N. (2000), 'A Century of Global Stock Market', NBER Working Paper Series, n. 7565.

Marano A. and Raitano M. (2008) 'La previdenza complementare', in Pizzuti F.R. (ed.), *Rapporto annuale sullo stato sociale*. Anno 2008, Utet, Turin.

Mazzaferro C. (2005), *Aspetti distributive del sistema pensionistico nella prospettiva del passaggio al sistema contributivo*, CAPP, Modena.

Modigliani F., Ceprini M. and Muralidhar A. (2000), 'A Solution to the Social Security Crisis', Sloan Working Paper, n. 4051.

Murthi M., Orszag J.M. and Orszag P.R. (1999), 'Administrative Costs Under a Decentralized Approach to Individual Accounts: Lessons from the United Kingdom', New Ideas About Old Age Security Conference, Washington D.C. World Bank.

Musalem A. and Catalan M. (1999), 'Contractual Savings and Capital Markets Development: An Analysis of OECD Countries' Evidence', mimeo, Washington D.C.: World Bank,.

Orszag P.R. (1999), 'Administrative Costs in Individual Accounts in the United Kingdom', mimeo, Center on Budget and Policy Priorities, Washington D.C.

Pammolli F. and Salerno N. C. (2006), Le imprese e il finanziamento del pilastro previdenziale privato: una quantificazione dei costi di smobilizzo del TFR alla luce del Testo Unico Previdenziale e del Decreto Legge n. 203-2005', Nota CERM n. 2-06.

Pizzuti F.R. (2000), 'A Political Economy Approach to Pension Financing', in Hughes G. and Stewart J. (eds), *Pensions in the European Union: Adapting to Economic and Social Change*, Kluwer Acedemic Publishers, London.

Pizzuti F.R. (2004), 'Labour Cost, Social Security and Employee Severance Funds', in Hughes G. and Stewart J. (eds), *Reforming Pensions in Europe*, Edward Elgar, Cheltenham, UK and Northampton, MA, USA.

Pizzuti F.R. (ed.) (2007), *Rapporto annuale sullo stato sociale*. Anno 2007, Utet Università, Turin.

Pizzuti F.R and Antichi M. (2000), 'The Public Pension System in Italy. Observations on the Recent Reforms, Methods of Control, and their Application', in Reynaud E. (ed.), *Social Dialogue and Pension Reform*, International Labour Office, Geneva.

Pizzuti F.R. and Raitano M. (2005), 'La copertura pensionistica delle diverse figure di lavoratori', in Pizzuti F.R. (ed.), *Rapporto annuale sullo stato sociale*. Anno 2005, Utet, Turin.

Pizzuti F.R., Raitano M. and Tancioni M. (2006), Le principali questioni che si pongono in campo previdenziale: alcune proposte e la simulazione dei loro effetti', in Pizzuti F.R. (ed.), *Rapporto annuale sullo stato sociale. Anno 2006*, Utet, Turin.

Queisser M. (1999), 'Pension Reform: Lessons from Latin America', Policy Brief, n. 15, OECD Development Centre, Paris.

Raitano M. (2007a) 'I lavoratori parasubordinati: dimensioni, caratteristiche e rischi', *Economia e Lavoro*, n. 3/07.

Raitano M. (2007b) 'Le prospettive previdenziali dei lavoratori dipendenti e parasubordinati: carriere a confronto in Pizzuti F.R. (ed.), *Rapporto annuale sullo stato sociale. Anno 2007*, Utet, Turin.

Samuelson P. (1958), 'An exact consumption-loan model of interest with or without the social contrivance of money', *Journal of Political Economy*, **66** (6), 467–82.

Tancioni M. (2007) 'Simulazione a lungo termine della spesa e del saldo previdenziale in Pizzuti F.R. (ed.), *Rapporto annuale sullo stato sociale*'. *Anno 2007*, Utet, Turin.

Walker E. and Lefort F. (2001), 'Pension Reform and Capital Markets: Are There Any (Hard) Links?', *Pension Reform Primer Series*, Washington D.C.: World Bank.

Whitehouse E. (*2000*), 'Administrative Charges for Funded Pensions: An International Comparison and Assessment', *Pension Reform Primer Series*, Washington D.C.: World Bank.

4. Personal Provision of Retirement Income in Germany

Heinz-Dietrich Steinmeyer

1. INTRODUCTION

Germany has a long established pension system consisting of three tiers (or layers): the public insurance pension, supplementary pensions – usually provided by the employer – and personal savings. In the late 1980s and early 1990s reforms were introduced which led to a move towards employee-financed supplementary pensions using an instrument known as 'conversion of earnings'. This means that the employee decides to put a certain amount of his salary into the pension plan of his employer. This was attractive for the employer as well as the employee. The employer was able to reduce the risk associated with occupational pensions and the employee had a scheme protected by the law on occupational pensions and could deduct contributions allowable against tax. The employer often co-sponsored the plan by supplementing the amount the employee paid into the plan.

In 2001 there was a major pension reform in Germany which introduced subsidized private pensions and subsidized conversions of earnings.[1] The relevant acts (*Altersvermögensgesetz and Altersvermögensergänzungsgesetz*) were passed on June 26 2001 and March 21 2001 respectively and became effective January 1 2002. The reasons for the reform were as follows: it was feared that the contribution rate for public pension insurance would rise to 26 per cent by 2030 – due to demographic change. Such a high contribution rate together with expected increases in public health insurance contributions were viewed as being too high. The public pension system in Germany is a pay-as-you-go system. The viability of this system is vulnerable to demographic change (a low birth rate in the baby-boom generation), from early retirement and late entry into the job market. Reforms over recent years have made early retirement less attractive and have introduced small cuts or 'adjustments' in the benefit system; but without the reforms of 2001, the contribution rate for pension insurance would have been 26 per cent of gross salary compared with a current rate of 19.9 per cent. If the current contribution rate for health insurance of 15 per cent, of long-term care insurance of 1.7 per cent is and of unemployment insurance at 3.3 per cent is taken into account, the overall contribution rate for all public social protection systems would amount to about 40 per cent of gross salary (paid equally by employers and employees). Health care and long-term care expenditures are likely to increase further with a 'greying society'. Hence the general acceptance of reforms to reduce costs. This focus is also due to the fact that the average income tax rate is around 30 per cent of income which means that social insurance contributions plus income tax amount to half of the gross salary of a single worker.

The reform therefore was aimed at keeping the contribution rate in public pension insurance at 20 per cent until 2020 and 22 per cent until 2030 but with some reduction in the overall replacement rate. The outcome of a debate on pay-as-you-go financing compared with funding led to the introduction of some elements of capital funding in the overall system of old age protection.

2. SOME CLARIFICATIONS

In the public pension system in Germany there have been changes in the benefit formula which take into account changing demographics. One of the factors in the reform of 2001 was the relation between contributors and beneficiaries. These changes will lead to a cut in benefits and to an overall lower replacement rate of the public pension scheme.

The German public pension insurance system assumed a 'typical' person had a full working career of 45 years, earning the average wage and retiring at age 65. This person was deemed to have a net replacement rate of 70 per cent from public pension insurance prior to the 2001 reform. By 2030 this percentage is projected to be at 58.5 per cent (a decrease of 16.5. per cent). In 2040 the projected level will be at 51.5 per cent. All individuals who have a shorter working career will receive less since one of the factors in the benefit formula is the number of years of contributions. The average male worker in the former East Germany has 45 years contributions and 40 years in West Germany; the average female has 37.4 years contributions in the former East Germany and 26.1 working years in West Germany.

These changes resulted in a gap between projected benefits from the public pension system and desired pension benefits. The solution was to introduce a capital funded personal pension – named Riester-Pension after the Federal Minister for Labour and Social Order at that time. It is a system of subsidized personal pensions organised on a voluntary basis. The subsidy is via tax deductibility, cash subsidies and a reduced social insurance contribution base. When the scheme was initially developed, lawmakers were not sure if this new measure would be widely accepted and thus planned to make it mandatory if the acceptance rate was low.

An important question to consider is: have the reforms met expectations? In the period from 1988 to 1992 the German occupational pension system started to change from an almost totally employer-sponsored system to a system sponsored in part by employees and employers. In 1992 conversion of earnings – which means that the employee puts part of his salary in the pension plan of his employer – was regarded as part of occupational pensions by the Federal Labour Court which means that all the legislative rules for protection of pension rights as well as the rules for protection in case of insolvency apply to these additional employee contributions pensions as well. As of 2004, 29 per cent of all plans were exclusively financed by employees, 41 per cent financed by both employers and employees, and 38 per cent exclusively by employers.[3]

If an employee decides to convert earnings into pension entitlements in a pension plan provided by his or her employer, the employer then has to convert this into a pension right which means that they will set up an account on behalf of the employer in the employer pension scheme. This is voluntary for the employee and the employee can in principle convert as much of their current pay into pension entitlements as they want, but practically speaking will limit it to what can be afforded and what is tax deductible as expenses for pensions and other provision. The employer sometimes but not generally, will also pay a certain amount on behalf of the pension account of the employee.

The pension plans are usually defined contribution schemes and they are usually established on a funded basis, that is, direct insurance, pension funds and so on. There was a steady increase in the conversion of earnings since introduction. This is because the scheme is attractive for employees for tax reasons and attractive for employers because it lowers their risks in providing pensions. As a result 'conversion of earnings' schemes often attract additional employer payments. The 'conversion of earnings' scheme is now called the employee-sponsored occupational pension.

The Riester Reform in 2001 recognised these developments and introduced a requirement that employers are obliged to provide plans for conversion of earnings. Employees may also purchase other personal pensions which meet certain requirements set up by law.

In summary, in the period 1988–1992 a new personal pension option was introduced in Germany which enable employees to convert current earnings into pension entitlements. It is an employee-sponsored plan administered by the employer. Since the aim of the Riester Reform was to motivate people to arrange their own individual retirement provision the Riester reforms included provisions already in existence.

A combination of different approaches was used in these reforms: in the first instance any employee could require that his employer establishes a pension plan to be used for conversion of earnings of up to €212 per month. In addition a system of state subsidies was established which applies if a person establishes a pension plan or a pension contract meeting certain requirements. This pension plan can be used either for conversion of earnings – linked to an insurance-based employers pension plan – or for any other plan which can be exclusively used only for retirement and works as a lifetime annuity, that is covering longevity risks as well. These plans are offered by insurance companies, banks and investment funds. The investments chosen depends on the rules for the different providers. 'Riester Pensions' in a narrowly defined sense refer to these latter plans. The conversion of earnings in the meaning described above might be referred to as a Riester-sponsored pension or – in a broader sense a Riester Pension.

In all cases it is required by law that an amount equivalent to the contributions paid has to be guaranteed at the time of payment of the Riester pension. This means that investment risks are borne by the provider of the Riester product and result in a conservative investment approach. There has been no discussion on the effects of the credit crisis on Riester pensions.

To make Riester pensions attractive for employees a special tax subsidy was introduced (see Table 4.1). This means that up to €2,100 per annum is tax deductible from the year 2008 onwards. The subsidy was initially €525 per annum in 2002/2003, increased to €1050 in 2004/2005 and to €1,575 in 2006/2007. These subsidies apply to all Riester Pensions in the sense mentioned here. This tax deductibility means that about €8.7 billion in taxes were foregone in 2007.

Table 4.1 Tax deductions for Riester Pension, € per year

Year	Highest Deductible Amount
2002/03	525
2004/05	1,050
2006/07	1,575
Since 2008	2,100

In addition, the amount of an employee's wages used for conversion of earnings is exempt from social security contributions, which are generally based on gross wages. Table 4.1 shows the amounts that may be deducted against tax.

An alternative subsidy is not based on tax exemptions but on a cash subsidy administered by a special authority. This is specifically aimed at low income people who may be unemployed or whose income is insufficient to pay tax. In order to receive this subsidy an individual must establish and contribute to a Riester Pension. From 2008 onward the amount of the subsidy is €154 plus €185 per child (Table 4.2).[4]

In order to be eligible for the cash subsidy at least the basic amount (percentage of the previous year's income) has to be paid into the contract. For 2008, the subsidy applies if a person spends at least 4 per cent of last years gross salary on a pension plan; otherwise the subsidy is reduced pro rata. These subsidies were gradually phased in, so that the subsidies per year in 2002/2003 were €38 plus €46 per child and the minimum amount to be spent was 1 per cent of the gross salary; this was increased to €76 plus €92 per child and a minimum

Table 4.2 Cash subsidies for Riester Pension, € per year

Year	Basic Subsidy Single Person	Basic Subsidy Married Couple	Child Subsidy
2002/03	38	76	46
2004/05	76	152	92
2006/07	114	228	138
Since 2008	154	308	185 (300)

amount of 2 per cent for 2004/2005, and to €114 plus €138 per child and a minimum amount of 3 per cent for 2006/2007 (see Table 4.3).

The amount spent on this cash subsidy since its introduction amounts to €3.1 billion and the amount paid out for the period January to May 2008 was €866 million. Those who are entitled to these subsidies (tax as well as cash subsidies) – are generally all those covered by mandatory public pension insurance. The decision to give a cash subsidy or a tax subsidy is decided by the tax authority on the basis of what is more advantageous for an individual. In the case of those with higher incomes, the final tax benefit is more valuable than the cash subsidy.

Table 4.3 Amounts that must be paid into Riester Pension to attract subsidies, € per year

Year	Basic Amount (%)	Highest Amount
2002/03	1	525
Since 2004	2	1050
Since 2006	3	1575
Since 2008	4	2100

These subsidies are applicable to supplementary occupational pensions where earnings have been converted into pension entitlements such as an annuity meeting certain requirements and accepted by a special authority. The subsidies can apply to pension products sold by banks or life insurance companies.

These incentives were introduced to encourage the take up of Riester pensions so that an individual with a Riester Pension would end up with a replacement rate equivalent to the replacement rate prior to the reform. The intention was that the Riester pension would compensate for the reduction in the public pension.

3. THE FIRST YEARS

In the first years the take up of Riester pensions was low. Possible reasons for this were the lack of awareness of the need for additional pension coverage, the unattractiveness of these plans for the insurance industry since charges could not be 'front-loaded' but must be spread over a period of ten years. In addition in the first years subsidies were low as the system was phased in over a number of years. Last but not least the rules for this system were very complicated, difficult to understand and to work with – not so much for employees but for financial firms such as banks and the insurance industry. In this period it was feared that the Riester Pension would turn into a Riester flop.

From foreign experiences, for example IRAs in the US, it would appear that there is a link between simplicity of rules and the number of individual participants. Immediate acceptance could not be expected. There needed to be a learning process associated with the Riester pension reforms.

Some Reforms

Against this background there were some reforms of the Riester system in more recent years. In 2005 the rules for certification were simplified and the system of commission for financial firms selling Riester contracts was made more attractive. In 2006 a general requirement of unisex mortality tables in Riester pensions was introduced.[5] Finally from January 1 2008 Riester pension entitlements can be used for financing a house or apartment intended for one's own use instead of receiving a Riester pension as an annuity.

4. THE CURRENT POSITION

In recent years there has been an increasing awareness of the need for additional protection in old age and this has led to an increase in the take up of Riester pensions. By June 2008 about three million workers had participated in the conversion of earnings scheme and at the same time there were about eleven million Riester contracts. At the end of the year 2007 there were about 10.8 million Riester contracts. The development in coverage of Riester pensions since their introduction is shown in Table 4.4.

Further Reforms

The rule that all earnings converted into pension entitlements has the effect of reducing the amount of earnings subject to levies for social insurance purposes.

This rule was initially due to end on December 31 2008. This means that – since social security contributions are expressed as percentage of income – the contribution base was by law reduced by the amount spent on conversion of earnings. After December 31 2008, it was likely that there would be a dramatic decrease in conversion of earnings. Conversion of earnings also reduces the contribution base for social insurance payments and thus the amount paid into the state insurance system. Since pension payments from the state Social Insurance system depend on contributable earnings, reduced payments, due to 'conversion of earnings', also reduce benefits paid from the state system.

Table 4.4 The development of Riester Pensions to end 2007

Period	Insurance Contracts	Bank Contracts	Investment Fund Contracts	All
2001	1,400,000	No information	No information	1,400,000
I/2002	1,900,000	50,000	2,500	1,952,500
II/2002	*2,300,000*	*60,000*	*50,000*	*2,410,000*
III/2002	2,500,000	68,000	60,000	2,628,000
IV/2002	3,047,000	149,500	174,000	3,370,500
I/2003	3,280,000	161,600	180,000	3,621,600
II/2003	3,385,000	177,300	187,000	3,749,300
III/2003	3,480,000	180,100	194,000	3,854,100
IV/2003	3,486,000	197,440	241,000	3,924,440
I/2004	3,564,000	202,100	244,000	4,010,100
II/2004	3,633,500	207,400	256,000	4,096,900
III/2004	3,689,000	208,000	270,000	4,167,000
IV/2004	3,660,500	213,000	316,000	4,189,500
I/2005	3,753,000	218,000	338,000	4,309,000
II/2005	3,909,800	224,500	346,000	4,480,300
III/2005	4,120,400	230,000	381,000	4,731,400
IV/2005	4,796,900	260,000	574,000	5,630,900
I/2006	5,249,000	265,000	689,000	6,203,000
II/2006	5,345,000	278,000	811,000	6,434,000
III/2006	5,725,000	303,000	937,000	6,965,000
IV/2006	6,468,000	351,000	1,231,000	8,050,000
I/2007	6,776,000	368,000	1,346,000	8,490,000
II/2007	7,206,000	396,000	1,475,000	9,077,000
III/2007	7,677,000	415,000	1,621,000	9,713,000
IV/2007	8,355,000	480,000	1,922,000	10,757,000

Source: Bundesministerium für Arbeit und Soziales (Federal Ministry of Labour and Social Affairs), Berlin 2008.

Therefore there was opposition by the state system to lifting the time limit as it was argued that this would decrease the replacement rate of the public system even further. Nevertheless trade unions as well as employers associations asked for a continuation of the rule. Eventually it was decided that the time limit should be lifted which gives a further incentive for conversion of earnings since it reduces an employees contribution paid into social insurance fund.

The reasons for the increase in coverage shown in Table 4.4 are:

- Simplification of rules;
- Increased public awareness of a need of additional protection for old age;
- Increased knowledge of the subsidized available for Riester pensions.

5. AN EVALUATION

When trying to evaluate the personal pension provision[6] system in Germany it is useful to recall the history of its development. The stated purpose of introducing personal pensions was to keep the contribution rate for public pension insurance below 20 per cent of gross wages. This was done by cutting the replacement rate for pensions paid from the public pension insurance system. The new approach means that for an individual person, additional contributions to a pension plan are necessary to replace public insurance pension. If individual pension arrangements were widely adopted, amounts contributed were adequate and costs in terms of charges and returns were as expected. Then Riester pensions could compensate for the reduction in the state social security pension resulting in overall replacement rates remaining the same. But cost of old age provisions has increased considerably for individuals.

Recent findings have shown that personal pensions, that is, Riester plans and conversion of earnings, are popular among medium and high income people. But they are not popular among low income people. It could be argued that low income individuals cannot afford additional pension contribution. Although it should be noted that those on low incomes receive a cash subsidy so that in order to contribute to a Riester pension very little of their own funds must be contributed; the cash subsidy is applicable if a person contributes at least 1 per cent of the previous year's income. One possibility is that low income groups are not aware of the subsidies attached to Riester pensions. Another possibility might be that the Riester pension will be regarded as income under a means-test in the case of a means-tested benefit in old age.

Therefore a basic criticism of the reforms is that the aim of avoiding poverty in old age is only reached for people with medium and higher incomes who must contribute a greater amount now than before the reforms. So those who contribute to Riester pensions will compensate for the reduction in Social insurance-based pensions but in the end they pay more to achieve the same replacement rate as might be expected from the public insurance system alone prior to the reforms.

Those who do not participate in the Riester system will suffer a loss in replacement income, compared with the situation prior to the reforms, which could result in a situation where they are dependant on 'means-tested' social assistance in old age. At the same time the existence of a minimum pension, might result in some individuals choosing not to participate in Riester pensions. The current amount of the means-tested benefit is about €350 per person plus expenditures on housing and so on. This small amount shows that low income people need additional pension provision in addition to the basic pension. Similar situations exist in other countries such as the UK and Ireland (see Hughes and Stewart this volume). The dilemma is that low income individuals cannot afford to contribute additional amounts currently for future retirement income.

6. CONCLUSION AND SUMMARY

Will the Riester pension be made mandatory? This is very unlikely given the increased coverage of personal pensions in Germany. Making personal pensions mandatory would also mean that the State becomes more responsible for individual pension provision; the current philosophy in relation to private pension provision is to provide incentives rather than running and organizing an additional system. This might also involve providing additional information, and despite the current cost, it is possible that additional incentives might be introduced.

However despite the level of coverage and incentives provided in terms of tax reliefs and cash subsidies, it is likely that the overall replacement rate will fall. This is particularly likely to affect women because of their shorter total period spent in the workforce.

Apart from the costs in terms of tax expenditures and subsidies there are also considerable administrative costs. These can amount to as much as 10 per cent of the amounts contributed, and could be higher in some cases

In summary the result of this analysis of the German personal pensions is mixed.[5] The system works in general but increases the total costs for the same replacement rate, that is making old age provision more expensive. While costs in terms of the social protection system have been reduced, private costs of pension provision in terms of both administrative charges and contributions have increased. In addition state payments for future pension provision have been replaced by current subsidies. The system does not really help people with lower income. But for those who use Riester pensions, replacement rates should not fall compared with the pre-2001 reforms.

The reforms to the pension system introduce some capital funded elements to the German pension system and represents a move away from a pay-as-you-go system. Whether these reforms improve income security of future retirees remains to be answered given the risks and costs involved.

NOTES

1. See Steinmeyer, Private und betriebliche Altersvorsorge zwischen Sicherheit und Selbstverantwortung, Gutachten 65. Deutscher Juristentag, 2004, München 2005; See on this Veil, Germanys Pension Reform in 2001: More or Less Gender Equality?, in: Hughes G and Stewart J. (ed.), *Reforming Pensions in Europe*, 2004, p. 207.
2. For more detail see Steinmeyer, in: Erfurter Kommentar zum Arbeitsrecht, 8th ed. Munich 2008, p. 815.
3. Source: Infratest Sozialforschung, Situation und Entwicklung der betrieblichen Altersversorgung in der Privatwirtschaft und im öffentlichen Dienst 2002–2004, p. 72.
4. €300 if the child is born in 2008 or later.
5. See on this Veil, Germany's Pension Reform in 2001:More or Less Gender Equality?, in: Hughes and Stewart (ed.), *Reforming Pensions in Europe*, 2004, pp. 207–.
6. See also Sommer, Fiskalische Auswirkungen einer Erweiterung des Förderrahmens von Riesterrenten, Mannheim Research Institute fort he Economics of Aging, Mannheim 2007.

REFERENCES

Infratest Sozialforschung (2008), Situation und Entwicklung der betrieblichen Altersversorgung in der Privatwirtschaft und im öffentlichen Dienst 2002–2004, Munich 2005.

Sommer, M. (2007), *Fiskalische Auswirkungen einer Erweiterung des Förderrahmens von Riesterrenten*, Mannheim Research Institute for the Economics of Aging, Mannheim.

Steinmeyer, H. (2005), Private und betriebliche Altersvorsorge zwischen Sicherheit und Selbstverantwortung, Gutachten 6, *Deutscher Juristentag*, 2004, München 2005.

Steinmeyer, H. (2008), in: Erfurter Kommentar zum Arbeitsrecht, 8th edition, Munich.

Veil, M. (2004), 'Germany's Pension Reform in 2001: More or Less Gender Equality?', in Hughes G. and Stewart J. (ed.), (2004), *Reforming Pensions in Europe*, Cheltenham, UK and Northampton, MA, USA: Edward Elgar, pp.211-28

5. Demographic Ageing in Sweden: The Role of Defined Contribution Schemes[1]

Ann-Charlotte Ståhlberg

1. INTRODUCTION

Pension systems are being modified in many parts of the world. The growing financial pressure of ageing populations makes policies that strengthen the link between individual contributions and benefits particularly important. Many countries have swapped a defined benefit system for a defined contribution one, since ageing populations may make defined benefit pay-as-you-go schemes economically unstable. Defined contribution systems, on the other hand, are financially stable because no more can be taken out of the system than has been put into it.

The system may be politically unstable, however. In order to be politically sustainable, the pension system must retain majority support. If the citizens in general think that the pension benefits are inadequate or are unduly low, the pressure from them on politicians to change the system may become apparent.

In 1998, Sweden passed pensions legislation that specified a gradual transition from the public defined benefit scheme to a defined contribution plan. The old system was no longer financially stable, suffering as it did from a construction where incentives to work and save were weak and the redistribution unfair. The development of costs was inversely related to economic growth, there was no response to demographic change and the principle of a standard of living guarantee was weak and becoming weaker (Ståhlberg 1995b).

This chapter provides a short description of the Swedish pension reform and the reform process. It also contains estimates of the replacement rates for different cohorts and income groups, and the pension design is assessed from a gender perspective. This is followed by an examination of the individuals' needs for information enabling them to make decisions in defined contribution plans. Finally the discussion turns to whether the new system includes shortcomings which might affect the political stability of the reform.

2. CONTENTS OF THE PENSION REFORM

Defined contribution PAYG with a small funded component

The reformed pension system is a defined contribution system financed primarily on a pay-as-you-go basis (notional defined contribution) but with a small funded component (see Table 5.1). The defined contribution feature, with the close connections between contributions and benefits, rewards work, which may help to mitigate part of the strain caused by the increase in the dependency ratio. The contribution rate is 18.5 per cent of covered earnings: 16 per cent is credited to the notional account (the income pension). Each person has an individual account in which the contributions accrue. The account is notional as the system is pay-as-you-go and contributions are used for the payments of outgoing benefits to contemporary pensioners.

The remaining 2.5 per cent of covered earnings is contributed to a self-invested personal pension (the premium pension/PPM-pension). The premium pension is the type of pension system that has received significant attention and evaluation from policy makers in many other countries. The contributions to the individual accounts constitute, however, a much smaller share than the notional defined contribution system.

There is a ceiling (wage-indexed) on benefits but not on contributions.[2] However, above the ceiling contributions are halved. Since contributions on earnings above the ceiling do not result in any pension benefits, they are regarded as a pure tax on high earnings, which may reduce labour supply incentives among high income earners.

An automatic balancing mechanism

The rate of return on the notional accounts is determined by average wage growth, specifically by the change in average covered wages. Using average wage growth introduces a possible instability into the system however. For example, if the work force decreases, benefits and pension rights will grow faster than the contribution base from which benefits are paid. In order to deal with this possible instability, an automatic balancing mechanism is built into the system that will reduce the indexation of earned pension rights and outgoing pensions if the system faces a deficit.

With the self-invested personal pensions, the rate of return is determined by participants' investment allocations. Participants can choose from around 800 funds. To date the bulk of the money has gone into equities. For individuals who do not want to choose their own investments, the government provides a default option. The investment strategy of the default fund is to mirror the asset allocation of an average investor in the system. The money management fee

(0.15 per cent) is significantly less than for the majority of the funds in the premium pension system (between 0.00 to 1.87 per cent).[3]

Table 5.1 Features of the new pension

Notional defined contribution (Income Pension)

Pay-as-you-go

Individual notional accounts

- 16 per cent of covered earnings are credited to the notional account
- The rate of return is average wage growth
- Annuity divisor
- An automatic balancing mechanism
- Flexible retirement age from the age of 61

Defined contribution (Premium Pension)

Funded

Individual financial accounts

- 2.5 per cent of covered earnings are paid to a self-invested personal pension
- The rate of return is the capital rate
- About 800 funds
- Divided pension rights

- Guaranteed pension
- Defined benefit
- Financed from general tax revenues

Pension rights

Pension rights are credited from the age of 16 and for every year individuals have income that earns pension rights. Hence, lifetime contributions determine benefits. Individuals earn pension rights from labour income as well as from income from transfers, such as parental leave benefits, unemployment insurance and sickness benefit insurance. Individuals also earn additional pension rights for having young children, for military service, for years of higher education and for years with disability pension. The state pays contributions into the individual's account. Parents with young children are apportioned a fictive income for the calculation of pension credits according to one of three options, and the custodian, who may be either the mother or the father, may choose the one that is most advantageous to the child.[4] The credit is also paid when the parent continues to work in the labour market. This is an increase in work incentives compared to the old system which subsidised all kinds of non-market activities whether the time was spent caring for infants, healthy husbands or doing some other activity. Credits for having children are paid until the youngest child is four years old, with a maximum of four years per child.

Divided pension rights

The premium pension allows married individuals to transfer pension rights between spouses. This means, for example, that if one spouse has low earnings while the other has high earnings, the spouses can equalize expected pension benefits by transferring credits from the high-income spouse to the low-income spouse. This option is for married people only, and not for co-habiters. The transference is voluntary and is stopped at the request of either spouse or automatically upon divorce. Transferring pension credits to a spouse has not turned out to be very popular, however. So far very few have done so. It is not free of charge, which might be an explanation. When dividing pension points an adjustment is made regarding the difference in life expectancy between men and women.

Annuity divisor

The retirement age is flexible and benefits can be drawn from the age of 61. Upon retirement, annual benefits are calculated by dividing the balance in the notional account by an annuity divisor. This divisor is determined by average life expectancy at retirement for a given cohort and an imputed real rate of return of 1.6 per cent. Since the annual pension benefit is equal to the net present value of benefits using a real interest rate of 1.6, the initial benefit upon retirement is higher than if benefits were adjusted for economic growth each year. The divisor is the same for men and women. Benefits are price-indexed plus/minus the deviation from this 1.6 per cent growth norm. Under the new scheme, it is the pensioners themselves who bear the cost resulting from increases in longevity, since the individual's accumulated capital, up to retirement, is divided by the number of years a particular age group is expected to have left to live. The way of calculating annual benefits neutralises the strain caused by increases in longevity. The implication is that the higher the life expectancy, the lower the pension benefit. Hence, the 'burden' of a longer life does not fall on the working generation.

The account balance in the premium pension is converted into either a fixed or a variable annuity using standard insurance practices. This annuity is nominal and not indexed for inflation, and unisex life tables are used.

Thus, no specific outcome is promised in the new Swedish system. The benefit will depend on the notional and financial capital balance at the time of retirement and the annuity divisor. To some extent the individual can influence the outcome, for example, by postponing retirement.

The Swedish legislation on job security was changed in 2003 so that mandatory retirement agreements at an age lower than 67 years are now prohibited. This aims at raising the actual retirement age by counteracting early exit.

A guaranteed pension

In addition to the earnings-related benefits, the pension system includes a guaranteed minimum pension. The guaranteed pension pays a supplement on top of the annuities from the notional and funded accounts if their sum falls below a certain level. Individuals without any earnings-related benefits in the national scheme are eligible for the full guaranteed benefit.[5] In 2007, the lowest pension benefit a person could receive was SEK 6,380 (€683) per month if married (each partner has a separate pension entitlement) and just over SEK 7,000 (€749) if unmarried. With such a low pension, housing allowances up to 90 per cent of the rent could be granted. The lowest pension in relation to the average wage is about 30 per cent of that wage if unmarried.

The minimum pension is payable from the age of 65, is financed from general tax revenues and is indexed to the consumer price index. With continued price indexation, the guaranteed pension becomes less and less important. It is doubtful, however, that the value of the guaranteed pension in real terms will be permitted to wither away forever. Sweden's economic history tells us that the politicians sooner or later will increase these benefits.

The new pension system is autonomous from the state budget although the guaranteed pension is financed by general revenues.

Income redistributions

The pension reform in Sweden tightens the link between payroll contributions and benefits. Low lifetime incomes result in low annual pensions and vice versa. However, there are certain features in the new pension that redistribute income. The new system contains important elements that are financed from the state budget. First, the state pays the expenses for the (pension-tested) guaranteed pension, which means that income is redistributed in favour of low earners. Second, contributions on transfer payments and disability pensions and amounts credited for child rearing, for study and compulsory national service are paid from the central government budget. Third, the ceiling on benefits but not on contributions redistributes income from high-income earners to low-income earners.

Choosing to index the system with the change in average covered wages supplemented by an automatic balancing mechanism has implications for the distribution of benefits among cohorts. Some cohorts are likely to bear a larger share of the burden of adjustment.

Occupational pension

Retirement income in Sweden comes mainly from two sources: public national pensions covering all individuals, and occupational pensions building on collective bargaining agreements between labour unions and employers' associations and covering practically all employees. There are four main schemes covering private sector white-collar workers, private sector blue-collar workers, state employees and local authority and county council employees.

Everyone working for an employer who has signed a collective agreement – and thus not only union members – automatically has the coverage that has been agreed upon. Less than 10 per cent of the total workforce work in companies that do not have such an agreement. Even most temporary and part-time employees have the right to collective agreement benefits. The occupational pensions raise the level of compensation and are important to high earners in particular, since most of the plans replace earnings above the capped ceiling in the national scheme.[6]

The reform of the social insurance pension is presumably the one best known outside of Sweden, but pension reforms have continued, albeit in other social insurance areas. The occupational pension systems have been fundamentally changed in recent years. They have followed the path taken by the public pension, and have been changed from defined benefit to defined contribution plans.[7] About 3.5–4.5 per cent of earnings are contributed to a self-invested personal pension. This means that an average Swede pays 22–23 per cent of his or her earnings in order to receive pension benefits. On top of this come the costs (financed through general tax revenues) of the guaranteed pension, the pension rights for periods of sickness, disability, unemployment and parental leave, insurance and the non-contributory rights for young children.[8]

Survivors' pension

In 1988 Parliament passed a government proposal for the reform of family pensions, and new regulations were brought into force in 1990. The widow's pension was gradually repealed and replaced by a re-adjustment pension, given to both men and women for a very short period. The reasons for this vast structural change in the pension schemes for survivors were partly to adapt the schemes to changes in family and income patterns, and partly to reduce the strongly increasing costs of supplementary pensions in the future. The proportion of gainfully employed women has greatly increased, and families have become smaller due to a reduced birth rate. Divorces have become more frequent, and co-habitation has become a more common way of starting up a family. That the growing demand for equality between men and women required a gender-neutral survivors' pension was also evoked as a means to bring about the demise of the widow's pension. Eventually, though, reduction of rapidly growing future costs was probably the most important motive.[9]

The new regulations apply to deaths occurring in 1990 or later. For widows the new system entails substantial limitations compared to the previous regulations. However, there is a long transitional period in consideration of women who were already widowed when the new system was brought into being, as well as of elderly and middle-aged women who have not grown up in the kind of society and with the family patterns on which the reform is based.

Under the new regulations, both widows and widowers under the age of 65 have equal rights to re-adjustment pensions from the public scheme. Those entitled to pensions are legally married spouses and registered partners who had either been living uninterruptedly with the deceased for at least the previous five years or had children at home under the age of 18 that either one or both had custody of.[10] Those equivalent to legally married spouses and registered partners are men and women living permanently together and who have or have had children together or are expecting a child. Divorced couples are on an equal footing if they – in spite of the divorce – co-habit permanently.

A re-adjustment pension offers temporary aid to the surviving man or woman to overcome any immediate economic difficulties due to the change in the family situation after the death of a spouse. This pension is paid for one year with a possibility of continued support in special cases. If there are children under the age of 18 the pension is paid for an additional year or until the youngest child reaches the age of 12. The amount is set at 55 per cent of the deceased person's hypothetical old age pension. The right to the re-adjustment pension is forfeited upon remarriage, nor is it paid to those who become widows/widowers after 65, who then have to wholly rely upon their own pensions.

The 1990 regulations concentrate on child support, since the new benefits for adults are more time-limited than the previous widows' pensions. Children receive a child pension from the social insurance system if either one or both parents are deceased. This is paid until the child is 18, or, if still a student, until the age of 20. Child pension amounts to 35 per cent of the deceased parent's old-age pension (actual or hypothetical) for the first child. Each additional child receives 25 per cent.

Most collective agreement schemes contain both widows' and widowers' pensions as well as supplementary children's pensions and constitute a substantial part of total income security. However, there are large differences in survivors' pensions between different sectors.

3. THE REFORM PROCESS

Reform proposals in several countries have been met with fierce resistance and large demonstrations by the 'grey panthers'. How is it that Sweden was successful in reforming its pension system?

During the 1980s a parliamentary pensions commission worked for six years without coming up with an acceptable solution, but it demonstrated that the system desperately needed reform. Either the old system would require large increases in the contribution rate (with a low rate of growth) or it would turn into a flat rate pension system (with normal growth). Moreover, the design gave rise to 'perverse' income redistribution and incentives to retire early, detrimental to a pay-as-you-go system.

During the late 1980s, people's trust in the pension system had begun to erode and the view that the system would not be able to meet its promises started to become widespread, in particular among young entrants into the labour force.

In the early 1990s, Sweden experienced an economic crisis with a negative growth rate three years in a row. This made the Swedish people aware of economic necessities and underlined the urgency to reform the pension system.

Politically the reform was facilitated by not forming a large parliamentary committee. Accordingly, a small parliamentary group was set up in 1991. It was headed by the responsible Minister for Health and Social Insurance in the non-Socialist government, and included high-ranking members of the political parties then in the Riksdag (Könberg et al. 2006).[11]

The group proposed a pension alternative that met the requirements of being practical and the interests of particular lobby groups. By adapting pensions to current economic and demographic trends, the group solved the most important problem. The Swedish Trade Union Confederation supported the commission's incorporation of the life-income principle into the reform.[12] The former Swedish pension system favoured white-collar workers over blue-collar workers, as the average ratio between expected lifetime benefits and contributions was higher for white-collar workers than for blue-collar workers, that is, white-collar workers had a higher rate of return on lifetime contributions than blue-collar workers (Ståhlberg 1989, 1995a).

Political decision makers' awareness of the problem and the need for a solution drove the initiative forward. Five of the seven parties, representing 85 per cent of parliamentary votes, signed the agreement.[13] The existence of a fairly large buffer fund from the former pension system (ATP fund) would help cover the post-war baby-boomers and ease the transition. In addition, the transition rules made it possible to form a majority in favour of the new system. Disability pensions and guarantee pensions were removed from the old age pension system (Kruse and Palmer 2006).[14]

Selén and Ståhlberg (2007) explain the transition to a defined contribution system in Sweden in terms of age structure of the population and the age of the median voter. They demonstrate that most voters are winners in a notional defined contribution reform by comparing the net effects (the present value of expected benefits minus the present value of remaining contributions) of the new and old systems. That the contributions of the working generations (age < 53) are reduced by more than their expected pensions might explain the success of the reform. If Sweden had retained the old pension scheme, the contribution would have had to be significantly greater than it is in the new system. For example, the official report of the parliamentary group on pensions (SOU 1994 p. 20) estimated that in certain scenarios the contribution would have amounted to more than 35 per cent of wages.

One objection to the Selén and Ståhlberg analysis is whether people in general know if they are the winners or losers in a pension reform. (However, a survey by Boeri, Boersch-Supan, and Tabellini (2001) in France, Germany, Italy and Spain shows that the rate of acceptance of a pension reform decreases with age, which is what one would expect.) The Swedish reform is not the outcome of a referendum but of an agreement of five of the seven parties in the Riksdag, representing about 85 per cent of the voters; in a representative democracy, we might expect decision makers to be well-informed.

Income Security

Often, comparisons are made between the promised benefits in the old system and the expected benefits in the new system, and as often the new system comes out badly in this comparison. But what is forgotten here is that the old one was unsustainable, that is, that piecemeal changes are unavoidable, and in the absence of these the system might reach a point where a generation will have to face the fact that it belongs to the last generation that could be covered by the existing system.

One of the most common indicators used in pension policy analysis is the replacement rate. It provides information regarding well-being during retirement years relative to well-being during working years. In Flood et al. (2006) the replacement rate has been simulated for Swedish pensioners born between 1937 and 1955. They use a dynamic microsimulation model to simulate individual lifecycle incomes and to calculate pensions for different cohorts and income groups. A growth in yearly real earnings of 2 per cent is assumed, and the real rate of return of individual financial accounts is assumed to be 3 per cent. In order to analyse the replacement rates for different levels of income, Flood et al. (2006) classify the mean income for the five years before retirement in three groups: below the first quartile, between the first and third quartiles and above the third quartile. The public pension, the occupational pension and the private pension are calculated.

Replacement rates for different cohorts and income levels are shown in Table 5.2. The transition from the old to the new system occurs gradually. Those who were born in 1937 receive the old pension, while those who were born in 1955 will receive their pensions entirely from the new system. Those born in 1940 receive 70 per cent (14/20) from the old system and 30 per cent (6/20) from the new system. Those born in 1946 receive 60 per cent (12/20) from the new system and 40 per cent (8/20) from the old system. In the table below, average income for the age groups 65–69 and 70–74 is related to the average income for the age group 60–64. The pension age is assumed to be 65. The major component is the public pension. For individuals born in 1955 and with an income in the mid-range, the average public pension is 49 per cent of the average income during the five years before retirement. When we add occupational and private pensions the replacement rate is 74 per cent during the first five years after retirement and 62 per cent after that. The reason for this drop in income for older individuals is that private pension savings and some funded parts of the occupational pensions have a limited payout time. The funded components are more important for younger individuals. For individuals born in 1940 and with an income in the mid-range, the average income during the first five years after retirement is 77 per cent of the average income during the five years before retirement. The public pension is 56 per cent of the income before retirement. The occupational and private pensions have about the same importance, 10 per cent of income before retirement. In the model, private pensions are more important for older cohorts. This might imply an underestimation of private savings for younger individuals.

Table 5.2 Replacement rates for different cohorts and income levels, average income for the age groups 65–69 and 70–74 related to average taxable income for the age group 60–64 (in per cent)

Cohort	Income class	Age 65–69				Age 70–74			
		Taxable income	Public Pen.	Occ. Pen.	Private Pen.	Taxable income	Public Pens.	Occ. Pens	Priv. pen.
1937	< p25	112	88	8	14	105	92	7	3
	p25 – p75	79	60	7	9	74	63	7	2
	> p75	67	43	14	8	64	46	13	3
1940	< p25	97	73	88	13	88	75	7	1
	p25 – p75	77	56	10	10	69	58	8	1
	> p75	67	37	18	10	57	39	15	2
1946	< p25	89	64	13	10	79	66	10	2
	p25 – p75	75	51	14	10	65	52	10	2
	> p75	64	33	21	9	52	34	15	2
1955	< p25	89	62	16	9	77	63	11	1
	p25 – p75	74	49	16	8	62	49	11	0
	> p75	62	31	22	8	46	31	13	1

Notes: The sum of the three components may not add up to the amount shown under taxable income due to rounding up or rounding down.
P = per cent.

Source: Flood et al. (2006), Table 26.

The replacement rates are higher for the lower-income groups. The public pension replacement rate is 13–17 percentage points higher than for the middle-income group (apart from birth cohort 1937). This is due to the guaranteed pension (which gives a higher replacement rate for low-income earners) and to the social insurance ceiling (which gives a lower replacement rate for high-income earners). For high-income earners in younger cohorts the public pension is only about 30 per cent of the income before retirement. This is attributable to the fact that their income exceeds the capped ceiling and the public pension system does not compensate for income losses above the ceiling. However, the occupational pension system does, which is why the occupational pension is more important for high-income earners than for low-income earners.

In Flood et al. (2006) disposable income is also simulated. Benefits other than pensions, such as housing allowances, are added and taxes are withdrawn. Table 5.3 shows replacement rates for different cohorts and income levels regarding disposable income. In general, the replacement rate for disposable income is higher than for taxable income. It is more than 70 per cent for low and middle earners.

To conclude, the oldest cohort has the highest public pension replacement rate. The replacement rate is very similar, however, for the 1946 and 1955 birth cohorts. For the lowest income groups the replacement rate in the public scheme is about 60–65 per cent, around 50 per cent for the mid-range groups and lower for the highest income groups (about 30 per cent). The lower replacement rate for high earners is a result of the capped ceiling in the public pension.

Table 5.3 A pensioner's disposable income as a percentage of his/her average disposable income between 60 and 64

Cohort	Income class	Age 65–69	Age 70–74
1937	< p25	129	143
	P25 – p75	97	97
	> p75	74	71
1940	< p25	110	113
	p25 – p75	89	83
	> p75	78	71
1946	< p25	102	104
	p25 – p75	87	81
	> p75	73	62
1955	< p25	108	102
	p25 – p75	83	73
	> p75	64	54

Note: p = per cent.

Source: Flood et al. (2006), Table 24.

4. THE GENDER IMPACT OF PENSION REFORM

How do the features of a pension system affect women? Women live different lives to men. Typically, they work less in the labour market, have lower earnings, and often have interrupted careers. They also have a longer life expectancy and are more likely to become widows than men are to become widowers.

The Swedish female labour force participation rate is high by international standards and almost as many women as men work. However, women with small children often work part-time. The guiding principle of the Swedish social insurance system is that everyone should support themselves through paid work. In order to facilitate participation in the labour market, Swedish family policy provides subsidised child and elder care. Furthermore, the Swedish labour market is segregated and women's hourly earnings are roughly only 85 per cent of men's.[15]

The effects of the new pension system's design on the outcome for women and men with different labour force participation and earnings have been quantified in a study by Ståhlberg et al. (2005, 2006b). A simple simulation model is used to calculate benefit amounts, replacement rates and rate of return on lifetime contributions for four groups of 'typical' women. The groups include: (a) career woman: same labour force participation and retirement age as men – works full-time for most or all of her career; (b) full-time/part-time woman: works full-time until she has children, alternates between parental leave and part-time as long as the children are young and then goes back to full-time work; (c) 10-year woman: participates in the labour force for ten years early in life, before her marriage and the birth of her children. The 10-year woman is an exception in Sweden. Most Swedish women work far longer than that. The case is chosen to illustrate how those with no pension of their own fare in the new system; and (d) part-time woman: works part-time for most of her career.

For each case, a wage profile is constructed using earnings data from Statistics Sweden for five levels of education. The same calculations are made for a man working full-time and are produced for the five levels of education. The results for the four types of women are then compared to the outcome for the man working full-time, and the ratio between women and career men is calculated. A gender ratio of 1 means that men and women have the same replacement rate, annual annuities, and so on. A gender ratio greater (smaller) than 1 means that women have a higher (lower) replacement rate, higher (lower) annual annuities, and so on, than men. Table 5.4 summarises the women–career men ratio of annual own annuities, replacement rate and rate of return on lifetime contributions for typical earnings profiles. The rate of return is calculated as the ratio of the present value of expected lifetime benefits to lifetime contributions.

The results show that women on average receive lower pension benefits than men. Any pension system having a tight link between benefits and contributions is likely to produce lower benefits for women. Despite this, women have higher replacement rates and higher rates of return on lifetime contributions than men. For example, part-time women's annual pension benefits are 60–70 per cent of those of career men. However, they have replacement rates up to 25 per cent and rates of return which are 20–30 per cent higher than men's. Full-time and part-time women have a rate of return which is about 20 per cent higher than men's. The 10-year woman receives the minimum pension guarantee. Her rate of return on lifetime contributions is 300–400 per cent higher than a man's.

Table 5.4 Crucial features in the Swedish pension with reference to gender aspects

The old pension system	The new pension system
The basic pension and the special pension-tested supplement (paid to those with a low or no ATP) redistributed income in favour of low earners and thereby in favour of women	The (pension-tested) guaranteed pension redistributes income in favour of low earners and thereby in favour of women
The life expectancy of women is higher than that of men. The pension system relied on 'unisex' life tables and redistributed income in favour of women	The pension system relies on 'unisex' life tables and redistributes incom in favour of women
The ceiling on benefits but not on contributions redistributed income in favour of low earners and thereby in favour of women	The ceiling on benefits but not on contributions redistributes income in favour of low earners and thereby in favour of women
Benefits were indexed favouring women because of their longer life expectancy	Benefits are indexed favouring women
Benefits were paid in the form of annuities. This favoured women because of their longer life expectancy	Benefits are paid in the form of annuities. This favours women
The fact that the ATP pension was determined by the 15 best-paid years and that 30 years were enough to qualify for a full pension, while pension contributions were proportional to earnings in all years, may to a certain degree have compensated women for the years they spent at home. But these rules were also to the disadvantage of low income earners (male and female) with long, flat, life income profiles	Pension credits for child rearing favour women The premium pension allows married individuals to transfer pension rights between spouses. This favours women.

The result can be explained by the use of unisex life tables, the minimum pension guarantee, the pension credits for child rearing and the social insurance ceiling. The distributional effects of unisex tables are high, whereas the child credits have less influence on women's pension amounts. The importance of unisex life tables and the provision of pension credits for child-rearing for the redistribution of pension benefits between women and men is shown in Table 5.5. It compares the gender ratio of the replacement rates when unisex life tables are used with the gender ratio of the replacement rates when benefits are calculated using differentiated survival probabilities. At the age of 65, Swedish women, as a group, are expected to live three years longer than Swedish men. The results show that when benefits are calculated using differentiated survival probabilities, women receive a lower replacement rate than men compared to when unisex life tables are used.[16]

Table 5.5 The outcome of typical women as a percentage of career men[a]

	Career woman	Full-time/part time woman	10-year woman	Part-time woman
Annual own annuities	80–100	80*	35–40	60–70
Replacement rate	100–120	100–120	120–145	100–125
Rate of return	115–130	120[b]	310–400	120–130

Notes:
a The first figure in the interval shows those with no upper secondary school education, the last figure is for those with a postgraduate education.
b The outcome is the same for all education groups.

Source: Ståhlberg et al. (2005).

Table 5.6 The gender ratio of the replacement rate when unisex tables are used and when the probability of surviving is diversified according to sex, and with and without child credits

	Women/Career men			
	Unisex tables	Survival probabilities calculated by sex	With child credits	Without child credits
Career woman	1.02–1.21	0.89–1.04	1.02–1.21	1.02–1.21
Full-time/part-time woman	0.98–1.17	0.86–1.00	0.98–1.17	0.94–1.14
Part-time woman	1.04–1.25	0.98–1.03	1.04–1.25	1.00–1.22

Note: The first figure in the interval shows those with no upper secondary school education, the last figure for those with a postgraduate education.

Source: Ståhlberg et al. (2005).

Table 5.6 also shows the effects of the child credits on the gender ratio of the replacement rates. Although the provision of child credits has some positive effects on women's replacement rates, the influence is much smaller than the effect of unisex life tables.

5. INFORMATION NEEDS

The shift in pension design from defined benefit to defined contribution is placing increased demands on the individual to understand how the pension system works, how financial markets operate and how to privately invest in supplementary pension savings. People need to know what pension benefits they can expect and how the amount varies with their choice of retirement age in order to decide how long they need to remain income earners and how much they need to save on their own. This in turn places demands on pension authorities and administrators to inform and raise awareness among prospective pensioners. Recent research also shows that better-informed citizens are more likely to accept reforms.

Insufficient information or knowledge may lead to individuals making decisions that may have negative consequences for their future pension benefits and realising too late that, because they have too little savings, they must delay their retirement or drastically reduce their consumption. One may well ask why people do not themselves acquire the necessary information. There are a number of responses to this question. Pensions are a complex subject and it is both difficult and time-consuming to explore how the system works and what it means in terms of one's own pension. 'Turning a blind eye' can be rational behaviour if the costs of information acquisition appear greater than the rewards. Another explanation, when retirement seems a long way off, is the lack of any feeling of urgency. Gaining information may also incur psychological costs since it may be uncomfortable and disturbing to be reminded that one is getting old. It may also be the case that we retain trust in the state to provide us with adequate pensions and therefore do not think that we need to worry (Sundén 2006).

The difficulty of estimating the size of a future pension varies with the different pension systems. The calculation is often simpler in a defined benefit than in a defined contribution system. In a defined benefit system, the pension is set in advance at a certain level, for example, a certain percentage of final income, and the normal age of retirement is also fixed. Given that one knows how many years of earnings are required for a full pension, it is relatively easy to gauge the level of one's future pension. Even in the less transparent case where the pension benefit is a certain share of lifetime income, it is still possible to estimate pension size reasonably well. Defined benefit systems are often constructed on a pay-as-you-go basis, however, and the uncertainty of this system is that pensions may become smaller if the system is overtaxed. In a defined contribution system with individual accounts, pension size is determined by how much each individual has put into the system along with the interest accrued. In this case, it is much more difficult to express the future pension as a proportion of final income because it will vary with the amount of the dividends and capital gains.

Experience shows that it is difficult to raise the average citizen's awareness of the pension issue. The Swedish pension reform is no exception. It was heralded by a massive information campaign and now each year, every income earner in the country receives the so-called 'orange envelope' which describes how the system works and shows the sum of the person's contributions with accrued interest. It also details the expected annual amount of pension benefits at various retirement ages – 61 (the first year that pensions can be withdrawn), 65 and 70 – in the case where yearly real wages are expected to remain the same as in the present year, and where real wages are expected to increase by 2 per cent per year. The orange envelope is a good initiative and Sweden is one of very few countries that provide citizens with detailed pension information.[17]

To follow up on whether the information offered in the orange envelope has had any appreciable effect since its introduction, a sample of the population has been interviewed each year to discover how the information was received and used. From the answers, we can deduce that knowledge of the pension system is neither particularly great nor has it increased much over time. Central to the new system is the lifetime income principle, but many people are still not aware that this is the major determinant of future pension size. More people know of the premium pension than of the income pension. It is to be expected, however, bearing in mind the considerable attention the premium pension has been given. But it might also indicate that people have not understood that the premium pension is only a small share of the whole public pension. Quite a few never bother to open the envelope, let alone read the contents. Many do not look at their pension projections, and of those who do, most have erroneous expectations. 'Is this all I get?' is the overwhelming reaction. What knowledge there is is unevenly distributed. Older people are more informed than younger ones, which is to be expected. Men know more than women, and those with a higher education more than those with lower levels of education. Blue-collar workers know less than white-collar workers, and those with lower incomes less than those with higher incomes. Sadly, the ones who know least – blue-collar workers, low-income earners, the less-well educated and women – are generally those most dependent on the public system in the sense that they will receive a greater portion of their total income as pensioners from it.

Further, women and the less-well educated tend to overestimate the size of their future pensions more than men and those with a higher education. This means that women and the less-well educated may end up with much lower pensions than they envisaged and find themselves in a very vulnerable position financially, since these groups tend to have fewer alternative pension savings than other groups. It is possible that a longer time perspective is needed in order to draw any far-reaching conclusions from the Swedish information initiative. Nevertheless, in principle, the same results have been produced in several other studies, the majority based on US data. People in general know far too little about their pension systems and their own pensions, and it is most often those who are most dependent on public pensions who know the least.

However, the public pension is not all pension income. Most employees also receive a collective agreement occupational pension emanating from negotiations between parties in the labour market. To make the information about a person's total annual pension more accessible, the National Social Insurance Board and the Premium Pension Agency (PPM), together with private insurance companies, have put together a website on the internet, Minpension.se. The goal is to deliver a picture of each person's total annual pension (public, occupational and private).

Another problem with the individual account system has to do with the extent to which individuals make rational choices. Workers with high risk (variability) in their human capital are at risk of receiving low benefits from the pay-as-you-go part of the public system for two reasons. First, they have lower lifetime earnings that result in lower benefits. Second, pension benefits are automatically adjusted to changes in life expectancy so workers need to extend their work lives in order to receive a given replacement rate. To the extent that workers with high variability in their earnings are less likely to do so, it will negatively impact pension benefits. One way to offset these risks is to take less risk when investing in the premium pension. Palme, Sundén and Söderlind (2007) have examined investment choice in the Swedish individual account system. They find that participants at the bottom of the income distribution take as much risk as those at the top, indicating that they are not diversifying their overall portfolio.

In comparison with defined benefit pensions, defined contribution pensions require more individual responsibility and risk-taking. In the premium pension the individual must decide themselves how pension contributions are to be invested and how they should change over time. Information about the funds is available on the PPM website. The funds are listed by type, and for each fund there is information on the rate of return for the past five years, the risk, and the fee. Setting up and managing a pension savings portfolio is a complex process. Achieving a good mix and nursing this over time calls for individual decision making that places heavy demands on the individual's know-how, dedication and time.

Too many choices can hinder rational decision making. In Sweden, the choice of available funds is far larger than in other countries that have adopted similar systems. Prospective pensioners can choose a maximum of five funds to invest in from a menu of about 800 funds. For those who do not make an active choice there is a default choice administered by the state. The share of non-choosers among newcomers to the system has turned out to be very high. Today, nine out of ten newcomers do not make an active choice. These are, of course, young people enjoying their first incomes and many may make their choices later in life, but the high proportion of non-choosers indicates that the large number of funds is difficult to evaluate and therefore hard to handle. Of those who make an active choice to start with, it would appear that few reconsider their choices in that only a small proportion change their original investment allocations, if we go by those who have changed their original investment allocations. Economic research shows that the more the investment alternatives in a pension system, the fewer the pension savers who make active choices about their savings. A large supply of funds also means higher overall fund management costs.

According to the questionnaire about the orange envelope, more than 80 per cent said that they had too little knowledge to make decisions about pension savings. Clearly, information and education are important components in any pension system and it should be a goal that as many people as possible understand how the system works. However, it is unreasonable to expect everyone to become an investment expert. Instead, it is more important to consider how the pension system might be constructed so that it is easier for savers to choose among alternatives. It seems clear that having so many funds in the Swedish system is actually counter-productive. The Swedish experience may therefore be of interest to countries that are about to introduce individual accounts into their public pension systems; having started with a broad range of funds, it is rather complicated to reduce the number.

What can be done about the problem arising from lack of knowledge? Is it that the information offered is too hard to assimilate? If so, we must consider how information can be imparted in a simpler way. In the USA, financial education in schools has been shown to have some positive and long-term effects. However, experience with financial education indicates that it has limited results. The best thing would be to design a pension system that combines economic stability with ease of decision making on the part of the prospective pensioner.

6. POLITICALLY STABLE?

The new pension system is robust against economic and demographic changes. It is a defined contribution system, which means that more cannot be taken out of the system than has been paid in. The system follows economic developments by means of wage indexation, provides incentives for work in that the pension is calculated on the basis of lifetime income, and takes account into demographic changes by means of the divisor. The premium pension enables wage-earners to share in the return on the capital market. If the liabilities in the pension system exceed the assets, the automatic balancing mechanism (brake) will come into operation to restore financial equilibrium to the system. This will result in a lower annual upwards adjustment to pensions and pension entitlements. These characteristics help to make the system financially stable in the long term.

The system is self-correcting in the case of deficits. But if the citizens in general think that the pension benefits are inadequate or unduly low, the pressure from them on politicians to change the system may become apparent. Difficulties in entering the labour market, a low number of years of paid employment, low wages and a low return on the premium pension may result in certain groups receiving lower pensions than groups that are more favoured in this respect. Low growth leads to a low rate of return on payments to the pay-as-you-go system and, if the brake is applied, pensions and pension entitlements may fall and, when longevity increases, the accumulated pension capital will have to be divided by a higher number, resulting in a lower annual pension. For those born in 1940, for example, the divisor at the age of 65 is 15.7, but 18.1 for those born in 1980. In order to neutralise the effect on pensions of increased longevity, those born in 1980 would need to work until the age of 67 instead of 65 (based on calculations by the Swedish Social Insurance Agency). The automatic balancing mechanism may need to be activated if, for example, the labour supply falls or if the expected longevity becomes higher than the calculated figure, which is based on cross-sectional data and is not a forecast for the respective cohort.[18] It may be possible to compensate for a lower than expected pension by working longer. It is likely that many senior employees will do this, but it may be considerably more difficult for certain other groups, such as workers and lower-level employees, to do so, and it is scarcely possible for the majority of those already in retirement to return to the labour market.

7. CONCLUSION

The reform system in Sweden shows radical change in the philosophy of how to organise support in old age. The defined contribution feature means that each individual bears her or his own costs and that one generation cannot impose a burden on future generations. The design includes strong incentives to work in the labour market, which is one way of lessening the burden of aging. The benefits are determined by accumulated contributions (plus interest) divided by the cohorts' expected lifetime at the time of retirement. In this way the system takes care of increased longevity.

The new system might give lower benefits than the old one, depending among other things, on future growth rates. However, practically all of the employees in Sweden are also covered by collective agreement occupational pension schemes which add a further 10 per cent of final salary. Altogether, the system should give adequate pension benefits for the majority of individuals.[19]

NOTES

1. Financial support from the Swedish Council for Working Life and Social Research is gratefully acknowledged.
2. The ceiling for 2007 is 344 250 SEK, or €36,000.
3. See www.ppm.nu
4. The three options are: (*a*) the income of a parent with young children is topped up to 75 per cent of the average income of all those insured; (*b*) the income determining parental leave pay becomes the covered income and; (*c*) the parent is credited with a minimum pension credit.
5. Benefits are not reduced based on earnings and other pensions and income. This means that voluntary personal savings when young and transfers from members of the extended family when old are not discouraged and that disincentives to work as a pensioner are not introduced.
6. See Granqvist and Ståhlberg (2004).
7. The DC plan for private sector blue-collar workers was introduced in 1996, for local authority and county council employees in 1998, for state employees in 2003, and for private sector white-collar workers in 2007. The transition from the old to the new system occurs gradually. In the public sector the occupational pension is defined contribution on earnings up to the social insurance ceiling, but has remained defined benefit on earnings above the ceiling.
8. Projected state budget outlays for the guarantee pension and contributions for extra credits going into the pension accounts are 1.7 per cent of GDP 2010–2050 (Source: Ministry of Finance, Sweden 2005).
9. See Ståhlberg (2006a) for a description.
10. Registered partners include homosexual couples.
11. To begin with the Social Democratic Party was strongly opposed to introducing financial accounts in the public system. The second largest party, the Moderate Party, argued for a reduction of the scope of the public scheme and the introduction of privatised individual financial accounts. The Liberal Party was also in favour of introducing financial accounts, and generally favoured strengthening the link between benefits and contributions. The Centre Party supported financial individual accounts but had long advocated a flat-rate pension benefit. The latter view was also to some extent shared by the Christian Democratic Party (Könberg et al. 2006).
12. See Borg (2004), pp. 209–210.
13. The Social Democratic Party, the Moderate Party, the Liberal Party, the Centre Party and the Christian Democratic Party reached an agreement. The Left Party and the Green Party opposed the reform. The former wanted only minor revisions to the old ATP system, and still maintains this position; the latter supports a flat-rate system.
14. However, money was transferred from the ATP-fund to the central government to compensate for these 'new' obligations.
15. This is after taking into account of differences in education and training. The length of education is on average the same for Swedish women and men and the difference in training is also very small.
16. A study by Palme et al. (1997) shows significant differences in life expectancy between socio-economic groups. However, the difference between men and women is considerably larger than the difference between socio-economic groups. At the age of 60 the difference in remaining life expectancy between men and women is 4 years while the difference between socio-economic groups is 1.5–2 years.
17. The French pension system has its 'blue envelope'.
18. The Pension System's Annual Report for 2005 sets out the probability and risks of the balancing mechanism being triggered and the results of this (Försäkringskassan 2006).
19. However, it depends on what the pension is supposed to buy. Health care and old age care are highly subsidised in Sweden.

REFERENCES

Boeri, T., A. Börsch-Supan and G. Tabellini (2001), 'Would You Like to Shrink the Welfare State? A Survey of European Citizens', *Economic Policy*, **16** (32), 9–50.

Borg, P. (2004), 'Systemskifte. En studie av tröghet vid fyra brytpunkter inom svensk välfärdspolitik', *Stockholm Studies in Economic History No. 40*, Stockholm: Almqvist and Wiksell International.

Flood, L., A. Klevmarken and A. Mitrut (2006), 'The Income of the Swedish Baby Boomers', Working Paper in Economics No. 209, Department of Economics, School of Business, Economics and Law, Göteborg University.

Försäkringskassan (2006), Pensionssystemets årsredovisning 2005.

Granqvist, L. and A. Ståhlberg (2004), 'Occupational Pensions in Sweden from a Gender Perspective', Hughes G. and Stewart J. (eds), *Reforming Pensions in Europe: Evolution of Pension Financing and Sources of Retirement Income*, Cheltenham UK and Northampton, MA, USA: Edward Elgar, pp. 225–44.

Könberg, B., E. Palmer and A. Sundén (2006), 'The Swedish NDC Reform – The Road to 1994 Legislation, the Long Implementation Phase and Remaining Loose Ends', in Holzmann R. and Palmer P. (eds), *Pension Reform – Issues and Prospects for Non-Financial Defined Contribution (NDC) Schemes*,Washington, D.C.: The World Bank, pp. 449–66.

Kruse, A. and E. Palmer (2006), 'The New Swedish Pension System – Financial Stability and the Central Government Budget', Working Paper, Department of Economics, Lund University.

Palme, J., O. Lundberg, D. Vågerö and Ö. Hemström (1997), 'Klasskillnader i ohälsa och dödlighet kräver robust finansiering av förtidspensionerna', in SOU 1997:166, Stockholm: Fritzes, pp. 603–22.

Palme, M. and A. Sundén (2004), 'Premiepensionen i det reformerade pensionssystemet – är det önskvärt att kunna välja mellan 663 fonder?', *Ekonomisk Debatt*, **32** (3), 6–15.

Palme, M., A. Sundén and P. Söderlind (2007), 'How Do Individual Accounts Work in the Swedish Pension System?' *Journal of the European Economic Association*, **5** (2–3), 636–46, www.ppm.nu.

Selén, J. and A. Ståhlberg (2007), 'Why Sweden's pension reform was able to be successfully implemented', *European Journal of Political Economy*, **23**, 1175–1184.

SOU (1994), *Reformerat pensionssystem, Betänkande av Pensionsarbetsgruppen*, Stockholm: Fritzes.

Ståhlberg, A. (1989), 'Redistribution Effects of Social Policy in a Lifetime Analytical Framework', in Gustafsson B. and Klevmarken A. (eds), *The Political Economy of Social Security*, Amsterdam: North-Holland, pp. 51–65.

Ståhlberg, A. (1995a), 'Women's Pensions in Sweden', *Scandinavian Journal of Social Welfare*, **4**, 19–27.

Ståhlberg, A. (1995b), 'Pension Reform in Sweden', *Scandinavian Journal of Social Welfare*, **4**, 267–273.

Ståhlberg, A., A. Kruse and A. Sundén (2005), 'Pension Design and Gender', *European Journal of Social Security*, **7** (1), 57–79.

Ståhlberg, A. (2006a), 'International study of survivors' pensions: The case of Sweden', Report for Conseil d'orientation des retraites (COR), Paris.

Ståhlberg, A., M. Cohen Birman, A. Kruse and A. Sundén (2006b) 'Pension Reforms and Gender: The Case of Sweden', in Gilbert N. (ed.) *Gender and Social Security Reform: What's Fair for Women?*, New Brunswick and London: Transaction Publisher, pp. 175–205.

Sundén, A. (2006), 'How Much Do People Need to Know About Their Pensions and What Do They Know?', in Holzmann R. and Palmer E. (eds), *Pension Reform – Issues and Prospects for Non-Financial Defined Contribution (NDC) Schemes*, Washington, D.C.: The World Bank, pp. 325–44.

6. A Nation of Risk Lovers: Personal Provision of Retirement Income in Denmark

Finn Ostrup

1. INTRODUCTION

Denmark has a multi-facetted pension system which is characterised by comprehensive coverage. Using the three pillar 'analogy', there is a public old-age pension which provides all citizens with a high income relative to the average wage level. Under the second pillar, practically all groups of wage earners are covered by occupational pension schemes. After improvement through wage agreements at the beginning of the 1990s, the level of funding in occupational pension schemes is increasing. After this build-up has been fully accomplished, the purchasing power for an average pensioner in Denmark will correspond to about 75 per cent of the purchasing power for an average individual in employment. In spite of the coverage provided under these two pillars, recent decades have seen a strong growth in personal pension schemes, causing the third pillar of the pension system to become increasingly important in the Danish pension system.

Personal pensions in Denmark, meaning pension provision based on individual accounts, are characterised by two key features which make them interesting in a broader international context. First, personal pensions benefit from a special tax regime which subsidises personal pension saving. An important question is to what extent these tax subsidies are well-spent and to what extent they are sustainable in a world characterised by personal mobility and by rising international integration of financial markets. A second key feature is that personal pensions are offered not only by life assurance companies but also by banks. The Danish market for personal pensions is marked by strong competition between these two types of financial institutions. In this competition between life assurance companies and banks, banks tend to increase their market share. It may be asked whether this rise in the importance of banks as providers of pensions is a good thing seen from the perspective of protecting pensioners against income short-falls in old age.

This chapter discusses the experience of personal pension provision in Denmark. The chapter is organised as follows. The chapter first gives a broad outline of the rules relating to personal pensions in Denmark. Next follows a discussion of the evolution of personal pensions. The chapter finally discusses some of the main problems facing the Danish system of personal pensions. Several of these issues have been the focus of intense policy debate.

2. THE DANISH PENSION REGIME

The Danish pension system consists of public and private schemes based on three pillars. The first pillar consists of pension schemes that are based on legislation and which cover the population as a whole. Most importantly, the public pension provides all residents in Denmark with a basic pension paid after the age of 65 which is equal to 61,000 DKK or approximately €8,200 (2008 level). This is equivalent to approximately 30 per cent of the average disposable income for Danish wage earners. Those over 65 years with no supplementary incomes receive an additional benefit of up to 61,000 DKK or approximately €8,200, per household (2008 level). This additional benefit is reduced as supplementary income rises. These benefits under the public old-age pension are adjusted with the general increase in prices. On top of these basic benefits, pensioners with low supplementary incomes receive various kinds of means-tested benefits, for example, free dental care, and reduced public transportation charges. The basic public pension is financed as an ordinary expenditure through the government budget. In addition to the basic public old-age pension, Danish residents are entitled to a smaller benefit paid by the Supplementary Pension Fund which is financed through special contributions based on income. Wage earners are furthermore entitled to benefits from a supplementary occupational scheme which by law covers all Danish wage earners and which is financed by contributions based on wage income.[1]

The second pillar in Denmark consists of pension schemes which form part of a wage agreement between, on the one side, an employer or a group of employers and on the other side, a single wage earner or a group of wage earners. At the wage settlements which took place in 1991–93, there was a large expansion of these occupational pension schemes which now cover almost all groups of wage earners. All occupational pensions are fully funded and pensions are determined strictly as a function of the individual person's contributions and returns (net of administration costs) earned on contributions. Contributions are calculated as a certain percentage of the wage income. This percentage is fixed in the wage agreement. The funds are managed by either ordinary life assurance companies, labour-market related life assurance companies or by pension funds. The labour-market life assurance companies and pension funds have been established with the purpose of managing the funds from schemes which cover specific professions (for example, engineers, employees in the financial sector, persons with a higher legal or economic education, and so on). It is a characteristic feature of the Danish occupational pension schemes that funds are fully separated from the firms in which persons have been or are employed.

The third pillar in the Danish pension system consists of personal pension plans that are established by individual persons, that is, they are not based on wage agreements. Personal pension plans have to be established before the age of 60. Pensions can be paid at the earliest from the age of 60. Two features distinguish the system of personal pensions. First, they benefit from a special tax regime and second, personal pension plans can be established both in banks and in life assurance companies. A description is given next.

The problems associated with the rising number of people of old age has been the subject of comprehensive discussion in Denmark. The discussion goes back to the 1980s.[2] The discussion has been characterised by absence of questions concerning the basic design of the Danish pension system with its foundation on the three pillars. Several observers remark that the Danish three-pillar system resembles the system which is recommended by the World Bank in its 1994 report on the design of pension systems.[3] The most comprehensive analysis of the welfare problems raised by the old-age burden in Denmark has been undertaken by the Welfare Commission which was set down by the government in 2003. The final report of the commission submitted in December 2005, gives general support for the basic design of the Danish pension system, recommending only minor changes in the rules applying to the three pillars.[4]

3. RULES APPLYING TO PERSONAL PENSIONS

In Denmark, personal pension saving can be undertaken in either life assurance companies or in banks. If a personal pension plan is established in a life assurance company, a choice exists between three different schemes based on the type of pension benefit: (i) pensions can be paid as a life-long annuity; (ii) pensions can be paid in equal instalments over a period of more than ten years; and (iii) pensions can be paid as a lump sum. In the last two cases, amounts in pension schemes will in the case of death, be paid to surviving beneficiaries. A beneficiary may be any person, independently of the relationship the beneficiary has had with the person who is the holder of the pension. Personal pension plans established in life assurance companies are supplemented by additional insurance policies which provide cover in the case of death before the pension age, sickness, and/or disability. As a new feature, life insurance policies may also cover expenditure for treatment in the case of sickness. Personal pension plans in banks can take two forms: (i) pensions can be paid in equal instalments over a period of more than ten years; and (ii) pensions can be paid as a lump sum.

As noted, a key feature of Danish personal pension plans is that they are subject to a special tax regime. There are three main features of this tax regime.

First, pensions paid out as lump sums are taxed at a flat rate of 40 per cent while pensions paid out as equal-rate instalments or as annuities are taxed as ordinary taxable income, implying that they are subjected to a progressively higher income tax rate. In 2008 the average tax rate on low incomes amounted to 32.8 per cent, and 53.8 per cent on incomes above 335,800 DKK (€45,000). The highest income is taxed at a rate of approximately 53.8 per cent. Second, the return on saving in personal pension plans is subject to a lower tax rate than the tax rate which applies to the return on ordinary saving. Thus, all the return on saving in a personal pension plan is taxed at a flat tax rate of 15 per cent while returns on ordinary savings are taxed at the personal income tax rate, implying that they are taxed at a marginal tax rate which will often be 53.8 percent (see above). Thirdly, in the case of life-annuity plans and personal pension plans involving equal-rate instalments, contributions are deductible in a person's taxable income while benefits in old age are treated as ordinary taxable income under the personal income tax. This tax deductibility represents a tax subsidy to the extent that the tax rate at the time when contributions are paid, is higher than the tax rate at the time when benefits are received. For example, persons who at the time of contributions in 2008 fall into the highest income bracket of 53.8 per cent, obtain allowances on personal pension contributions at a rate of 53.8 per cent. But a saving is made if at the time of retirement the tax rate is lower than 53.8 per cent; for example, if the person falls into a lower tax bracket. It follows that personal pensions are especially favourable for persons who have a high income, implying that they pay the highest marginal income tax rate, and who can count on little or no additional income in old age. With respect to personal pension plans based on lump sums, tax benefits have been largely abolished.

Pension saving undertaken in life assurance companies can take multiple forms. The traditional product is that the company manages the funds. The company issues a guarantee that the annual return or the average annual return on pension saving will not fall below a guaranteed return, for current pension contributions this rate is usually set at 1.5 per cent. For this traditional type of pension product, the legislation requires that at least 30 per cent of the saving is placed in low-risk assets such as bonds and deposits.

There are few constraints on how funds in personal pension plans can be invested. Most importantly, there exists a ceiling of 20 per cent on the share of the pension saving which can be placed in assets issued by a single issuer. There are some further limitations on the amounts which can be placed in non-listed equities.

Since 1999, life assurance companies have offered a range of new products in addition to the traditional pension product. It is a feature of these new products that the investment risk falls largely on the insured, implying that these new products either benefit from no investment guarantee (so-called unit linked schemes) or they benefit from a more limited guarantee than the traditional products, for example, a guarantee for getting contributions back (zero-interest-rate guarantee). In these new products, the insured are offered a range of different investment pools from which to choose. Persons who want to take a larger risk, thus have a possibility of investing in assets with a higher risk while persons with higher risk aversion can choose to invest in assets with a safer return.

Pension saving undertaken in banks can also be managed in different ways. One possibility is that pension saving is placed on a deposit in the bank. In this case, the return consists of the interest income which is received on the deposit. A second possibility is that the saving is placed in a pool of assets which is managed by the bank. Pension savers are offered a choice between different pools with different types of assets, for example, Japanese shares, European bonds and so on. Finally, a third possibility is that the pensioner manages the saving himself, making decisions on the purchase and sale of financial assets over the personal pension account. In contrast to the saving which is made in life assurance companies, no limits are placed on the proportion of funds which can be placed in equities under the personal pension plans which are taken out in banks.

4. THE EVOLUTION OF PERSONAL PENSIONS

Table 6.1 shows the evolution in contributions to personal pension plans in Denmark over the 1990–2005 period. It shows that contributions as a share of personal income has been roughly constant at approximately 2 per cent per annum.

The stability of contributions as a share of personal income to personal pension plans, may seem surprising in the light of a higher proportion of people in the labour market and the widespread discussion concerning the sustainability of the basic public old-age pension. Because of these factors it might have been expected that individuals would have increased contributions to personal pension plans. The fall in the real interest rate, and thus in the real return on saving, throughout the 1990s would seem to have further increased the need for personal pension saving.

A number of factors may explain why personal pension plans have not expanded to a larger extent. First, over the 1990–2005, period, occupational pensions have expanded in coverage, reducing the need for supplementary saving through personal pension schemes. Second, asset prices have shown a large increase over the period. In particular, house prices have increased sharply since 1992. House price increases have increased life-time consumption possibilities, and thus reduced the need for saving, because house-owners can run down house equity through borrowing. Danish commercial banks and mortgage banks have been very keen on lending to house owners.[5] Table 6.1 also shows that there has been a big reduction in household gross saving. A third factor explaining the stable level of personal pension saving, is that during this period there have been some cutbacks in the tax benefits enjoyed under the special tax regime applying to personal pension plans. Thus, with effect from 1994, the personal income tax has been supplemented by a special labour-market tax in which pension contributions are not tax deductible, implying a reduction in the overall tax deductibility of pension contributions. Until 1999, the lump sums paid out under personal pension schemes enjoyed a particularly favourable tax treatment with contributions being fully deductible for personal income tax while lump-sum payments were subject to a tax of only 40 per cent. With effect from 1999, the tax deductions on lump-sum schemes were curtailed, causing a subsequent big fall in contributions for these schemes.

Table 6.1 Contributions to personal pension accounts[a]

	Contributions (billion DKK)	Contributions as a percentage of personal income[b]	Household gross saving as a percentage of personal income[c]
1990	11.1	1.9	8.8
1991	19.0	1.7	8.7
1992	10.8	1.8	7.8
1993	15.1	2.5	6.7
1994	15.2	2.4	3.4
1995	15.2	2.3	5.9
1996	16.0	2.4	4.8
1997	16.7	2.4	3.1
1998	16.5	2.3	3.9
1999	14.7	2.0	1.0
2000	15.0	1.9	4.0
2001	15.7	1.9	7.5
2002	16.1	1.9	7.5
2003	16.8	2.0	8.1
2004	19.4	2.2	4.9
2005	22.3	2.4	2.1

Notes

a The table shows the evolution in contributions to Danish personal pension plans in both life assurance companies and banks.

b Contributions as a share of personable income for households which forms the basis of the personal income tax.

c Gross saving for households and non-profit institutions as a share of personal income.

Source: Danmarks Statistik (Statistical Office of Denmark) (2007). Skatter og afgifter – oversigt 2007 (in English: Taxes and Duties – A Survey 2007). København: Danmarks Statistik.

It may, however, at the same time be seen as a negative development that the increasing role played by banks in the provision of pensions means a reduction in pensions based on life-time annuities. As discussed earlier, pension plans provided by banks are based on savings being paid out either as a one-time lump sum or over a 10-year period in instalments, while only life assurance companies offer life annuities. It is possible that persons at the time of retirement are tempted to spend the full amount of the lump sum or the instalments at the time of receiving them, thus spending pension saving over a limited time period, resulting in periods of relative poverty in old age.

In the current Danish legislation, it is stipulated that pensions plans provided by banks shall be paid out over a period which must be ten years or more. This may seem to be a very short period, especially considering increasing current life expectancy. It might be questioned whether a more appropriate policy would be to increase the minimum period to fifteen years or more.

During the 1980s, it was a main aim of Danish economic policy to increase personal savings with the overall aim of reducing the deficit on the balance-of-payments current account. An expansion of occupational and personal pensions was seen as an important means by which to achieve such a rise in personal savings. Table 6.1 shows that while this aim, behind the expansion of personal and occupational pensions, has not been reached, personal savings have stayed at a low level with no tendency to rise. One explanation is that the positive effect on saving which may arise from the expansion of pension schemes, has been offset by other factors, especially a rise in real house prices and in equity prices, which exert a negative effect on saving. Another explanation is that pension plans have little effect on saving because individuals through financial transactions and especially through easier access to loans from financial institutions, can realise their consumption plans independently of mandatory saving schemes.

5. COMPETITION BETWEEN BANKS AND LIFE ASSURANCE COMPANIES FOR PERSONAL PENSIONS

As discussed in the previous section, personal pension plans can be established both in life assurance companies and in banks. The result has been strong competition in the market for personal pension provision. The competition has especially been characterised by stronger efforts with respect to marketing and by larger product differentiation while price competition has been absent. In this competition between life assurance companies and banks, life assurance companies have lost market shares. This can be seen from Table 6.2 which shows a larger share of contributions being made to schemes which are established in banks.

How can we explain this rise in market shares for banks in the provision of personal pensions? Several factors may be at work. First, banks have closer ties with customers and are therefore in a stronger position with respect to persuading customers to set up pension schemes in banks. Second, life assurance companies offer a bundled product where the management of saving is combined with different types of insurance cover. It may be difficult for customers to look through such bundled products and, in particular, to evaluate the risk cover which is provided through life insurance. Customers may be more attracted to the plans offered by banks because they are simpler. A third reason may be that customers do not sufficiently value the risk cover which is included in the products offered by the life assurance companies, thus preferring the schemes in the banks where they can avoid paying for this risk cover. Finally, life assurance companies may lose out in the competition with banks because life insurance products are less transparent. It has, for example, been difficult to get a break-down of administrative expenses (see below).

Table 6.2 Different types of personal pension plans[a]

	Plans in banks (billion DKK)[b]	Plans in life assurance companies (billion DKK)			
		Total	Schemes with return guarantee[b]	Unit link schemes with return guarantee[c]	Unit linked schemes[d]
1996	6.9	9.1	9.1	-	-
1997	6.8	9.9	9.9	-	-
1998	5.3	11.2	11.2	-	-
1999	6.9	7.8	7.8	-	0.1
2000	6.8	8.2	7.7	-	0.5
2001	6.5	9.2	8.9	1.1	0.3
2002	6.2	9.9	8.2	0.5	0.6
2003	7.1	9.7	8.5	0.2	0.6
2004	10.1	9.3	7.9	0.3	1.0
2005	12.0	10.3	7.9	0.4	1.2
2006	-	9.4	7.2	0.6	1.7

Notes

a. The table shows the evolution in different types of personal pension plans established in banks and in life assurance companies

b. Personal pension plans in life assurance companies with a guaranteed minimum return.

c. Personal pension plans in life assurance companies in which the investment risk falls mainly on the insured.

d. Personal pension plans in life assurance companies in which the investment risk falls exclusively on the insured.

Source: Finanstilsynet (Danish Financial Supervisory Authority) (2007). Statistisk materiale om livsforsikringsselskaber (in English: Statistical Material on Life Assurance Companies). www.finanstilsynet.dk; *Danmarks Statistik* (Statistical Office of Denmark) (2007). *Skatter og afgifter* – oversigt 2007 (in English: Taxes and Duties – A Survey 2007). *København: Danmarks Statistik.*

The very purpose of a pension system is to protect persons against the risk of income shortfalls in old age. It is possible that persons, due to a short time horizon (underestimating longevity) or because they count on the state to step in and care for people in old age, discount the future at a too high a rate, implying that pension saving, if left only to the individual initiative, will be too low. Seen from this perspective, it can be seen as positive that the competition between banks and assurance companies regarding pension saving may increase the total amount of saving, thus causing a rise in total pension saving.

6. THE EXPANSION OF UNIT LINKED SCHEMES IN LIFE ASSURANCE COMPANIES

It follows from Table 6.2 that among the contributions made to plans in life assurance companies, a larger share is being paid to new pension products in which the guarantees offered by the companies concerning a certain minimum return have either been abolished or have been curtailed. This last development means that the schemes offered by the companies have come to resemble the schemes offered by banks, causing a reduction in the overall insurance cover.

A number of reasons may explain this rise in unit linked schemes without guaranteed minimum return. One reason behind the expansion of unit linked schemes can be found in the fall in interest rates since the beginning of the 1980s. This has caused a considerable narrowing of the difference between the market interest rate and companies' guaranteed minimum rate. Companies have reacted to this development by lowering the guaranteed minimum rate, from 4.5 per cent (after deduction of administrative costs) for schemes established in the 1980s to 1.5 per cent in schemes which are established today. This reduction in the minimum guaranteed rate has, however, not matched the fall in market interest rates. This means that there is now a smaller difference between the market rate and the minimum guaranteed rate provided in Danish personal pension plans. The implication is that life assurance companies have to act more prudently in their investment strategies in order not to fall below the minimum guaranteed rate, implying that the minimum guaranteed rate acts as a more important constraint for companies in their investment policies now than previously. In order to fulfil the minimum return guarantee, companies will thus find it increasingly necessary to pursue a cautious investment policy. This tends to cause a lower expected return on company investments. If customers do not sufficiently value the minimum rate guarantee but look to a greater extent at the expected return, this may induce customers to choose unit linked schemes which may offer customers a better prospect of higher returns.

Furthermore, in order to avoid a situation where the minimum return guarantee becomes effective, companies actively pursue a policy where they try to persuade customers with a minimum return guarantee to shift to personal pension plans offering no such guarantees. In order to persuade customers to shift to unit linked schemes with no guaranteed return, companies hold out to customers the prospect of a higher return on the non-guaranteed plans.

A further reason behind the expansion of unit linked schemes in life assurance companies can probably be found in the stronger preference for risk which has been characteristic of investors in world financial markets at least since 2003. This is a trend which has been characteristic not least of Danish investors who over recent years have demonstrated their risk appetite by expanding investments to a number of risky projects such as real estate in foreign countries and mutual funds based on equities issued in emerging economies.

Seen from a pension perspective, the main purpose of pensions being to reduce risks related to the standard of living in old age, it can be seen as negative that the trend towards a reduction of the minimum guaranteed rate reduces the insurance element in personal pensions. Pensioners will come to rely more on the return which can be reached in the market and less on guarantees which are supplied by the life assurance companies. It may further be seen as negative that companies, through the removal of the minimum return guarantee, have the possibility of pursuing a more risky investment policy. Minimum return guarantees can be defended on the ground of the discipline which they impose on pension scheme managers who become unable to pursue risky policies which may be to the benefit of managers but not to the benefit of investors. As an example, managers in pension schemes may have an incentive to invest in large corporations in order to play a role in major corporate decisions.

In the debate in Denmark, these objections to the expansion of unit linked schemes seem, however, to carry little weight. The trend towards an expansion of unit linked schemes has, on the contrary, met with wide approval by the competent authorities. For example, the 'Bremer Committee' (see Section 7) notes with satisfaction that the expansion of unit link schemes will offer customers the prospect of a higher average return and also make it possible to offer customers a wider range of investment possibilities. The Bremer Committee also argues that minimum return guarantees may give customers a false impression of future pensions insofar as it will be impossible, in the case of a further fall in the interest rate, to meet the guarantees.[6]

7. TRANSPARENCY AND FREEDOM OF CHOICE IN PERSONAL PENSION SCHEMES

For many years, life assurance companies in Denmark have been criticised because of the lack of transparency in their products. First, life assurance companies sell a bundled product, comprising of a savings product and different types of insurance cover. It has been difficult for customers to get an overview of the amounts which are paid to each for each of these different products. Second, many of the costs in the insurance companies have not been visible to customers because they have been paid from investment income, implying that insurance companies have used part of the investment income to cover costs which are not directly applicable to individual customers, for example, costs related to the acquisition of new customers, costs related to investment management and so on.

In 2002, the Danish liberal-conservative government established a committee (the so-called 'Bremer Committee') whose brief was to analyse the system of private pensions with the purpose of making recommendations as to how customers could be offered a wider freedom of choice regarding their investments and with respect to shifting individual pension schemes between different providers.[7]

In its report, the 'Bremer Committee' argues that freedom of choice with respect to investments makes it possible for customers to choose an investment profile which will meet their individual preferences with respect to risk and expected return. The committee also notes that the minimum return guarantees offered in the traditional life insurance products make it impossible for customers to freely choose their own investments. From an analysis of the costs associated with moving personal pension plans between life assurance companies, the committee concluded that these costs were very high. Thus, in the case of one insurance company, it cost no less than 14–15,000 DKK (€1,040– €1,120) to move a pension plan with a value of 98,000 DKK (€13,130) to another company. The committee finally recommends that greater efforts should be made to increase transparency concerning pension plans in life assurance companies and concerning the total income which is received by an individual person as a result of pensions received under various schemes from all the three pillars in the Danish pension system.

As a result of political pressure originating from the work of the Bremer Committee, insurance companies and banks providing personal pensions, have now reduced costs related to moving personal pension plans between providers. In order to increase transparency regarding pension plans, a special internet platform (PensionsInfo.dk) has been established which makes it possible for individuals to get a full overview of the pensions which they are to receive from public pension schemes, from occupational schemes, and from personal pension schemes. Finally, companies have agreed to provide a breakdown of administrative costs so that customers can see the amounts which are being used for investment management, marketing, and so on. Companies have promised that this last breakdown of administrative expenses will take effect from 2009.

8. IMPLICATION OF THE TAX REGIME FOR PERSONAL PENSIONS

As discussed in the previous section, personal pensions are subject to a special tax regime which implies the deductibility of contributions from personal income tax, while benefits in old age are treated as part of personal income, thus being taxed at the going tax rate at the time of retirement. This tax regime implies a subsidy for pensions insofar as the tax rate in old age is lower than that at the time when contributions are made. In addition, the return on pension fund assets is subjected to lower taxation than ordinary saving.

Little or no discussion has taken place in Denmark concerning the basic design of the tax regime for personal pensions. It may, however, be questioned as to what extent the design of the tax regime is appropriate from the perspective of providing persons with an adequate income in old age and from the perspective of contributing to other social and economic goals. The main opposition party, the Social Democratic Party (the Danish equivalent of the Labour Party in the UK) has as part of their political platform that a ceiling should be placed on the amounts which can benefit from tax deductibility for personal pension contributions.

The possibility of deducting contributions from taxable income constitutes an incentive to increase pension saving for persons with a short time horizon, as these persons place too large a weight on the immediate prospect of receiving a tax relief while not properly taking into account the subsequent taxes which are to be paid in old age. This may be seen as positive to the extent that the main problem facing the pension system is too little saving being made for old age. It may, however, at the same time be seen as negative if persons, due to the possibility of immediate tax relief, are tempted into saving too much.

The special tax regime has clear distributional implications, because tax relief is given for those persons who are taxed at a high marginal tax rate during employment and who have a fall in taxable income and hence tax rates at the time of retirement. No statistics exist concerning the income distribution of those who have established personal plans but there is little doubt that these schemes have been used extensively by persons in high-income tax brackets. The tax relief will in particular, be important for persons who have a relatively high income in employment but who have little supplementary pension cover in old age. It is, however, difficult to estimate the size of this tax subsidy. Thus, most high-income groups are covered by pension schemes with a high replacement rate and it is therefore doubtful to what extent the possibility of shifting taxable income to the retirement period constitutes a general tax subsidy for high-income groups. The expansion of occupational schemes, both with respect to the size of contributions and with respect to the groups covered, further tends to reduce the size of tax subsidies which result from personal pension plans. Tax subsidies may, however, be increased by postponing pension payments made from occupational schemes. In most occupational schemes, it is possible to postpone pension benefits to the age of 70.

The special tax regime for personal pensions in Denmark may also have some effects on labour supply. For persons in employment, it is possible to lower tax payments by contributing to personal pension plans. Insofar as persons, due to lower income in retirement, are taxed at a lower rate when pensions are paid out, one may expect the tax deductibility of contributions to personal pension plans to raise the labour supply for persons in the work-active period. Personal pensions may, however, at the same time weaken the incentive to work for persons older than 60 years. This is because, in order to benefit from a lower tax rate on pensions from personal plans, persons above 60 years have an incentive to reduce supplementary income by retiring earlier. The tax regime for personal pension plans may therefore have two contrary effects on the labour supply. For persons younger than 60, the tax deductibility gives an incentive to work more due to a lower tax rate on labour income. Persons older than 60 years with pension plans may, however, reduce their labour income, in particular by retiring earlier, in order to avoid pension income being taxed at a higher marginal income tax rate.

The special tax regime also makes the pension system less transparent. Individuals may overestimate the value of their total pension saving because they may overlook the fact that pension savings are taxed at the time of retirement.

The deductibility of pension contributions in taxable income corresponds to persons receiving a loan from the government which is re-paid at the time of retirement. The proceeds from this loan are invested, either by individuals or by the financial institutions, in financial assets. This has implications for the functioning of financial markets, implying a rise in the supply of government bonds to finance a higher budgetary deficit at the time of the tax deductibility and an increase in the demand for those financial assets which are required for the funding of personal pension plans. As personal pension funds are to a large extent invested in equities and other risky financial assets, the overall result is a rise in the total risk incurred by Danish society as a whole. This can be seen as positive. It may, however, also be seen as undesirable insofar as tax deductibility provides individuals with financial means that can be used for speculative purposes.

The tax deductibility of pension contributions increases the size of funds which are managed by financial institutions. The result is the generation of revenue for financial institutions. These tax reductions thus constitute a government subsidy for the financial sector which raises earnings for mutual funds and for funds management in banks and life assurance companies.

Finally the special tax regime for Danish pensions raises problems in regard to cross-border migration. The system will be unsustainable if persons exploit it to deduct pension contributions at the high marginal Danish tax rate in their work income while they move to countries with low taxation of pension benefits in old age. In order to prevent such a situation from arising, the Danish government has concluded double-taxation agreements with a number of countries which give Denmark the right to tax pensions. Until now, however, it has been impossible to obtain such double-taxation agreements with France and Spain and persons who move to France or Spain in old age, have therefore been able to escape taxation. The government now intends to use unilateral Danish legislation to prevent the pension system from being exploited by such tax reliefs. It may, however, be asked whether it will be possible in the long run to maintain the right to tax pensions in a world where cross-border migration becomes more common and considering that the free mobility of persons is one of the fundamental objectives pursued by the European Union.

9. CONCLUSION

This chapter has analysed some features of the system of personal pension provision in Denmark. A key feature of the Danish pension system is that personal pensions are subject to a special tax regime which means that contributions are deductible against personal income tax while pension benefits are included as part of taxable income at the time of retirement. It is a further feature of the Danish system that personal pension plans can be established not only in life assurance companies but also in banks. This chapter has discussed a number of implications which result from these features of personal pensions. In the Danish debate on pension provision, it has especially been seen as a problem that personal plans established in life assurance companies are characterised by low transparency and high costs related to moving accounts between different providers. The special tax regime may create a possibility of increasing the tax subsidy by increasing income during working life while retiring earlier, and thus reducing supplementary income at the time of retirement when one is eligible for pensions through the personal pension plans. The tax regime may thus have the overall effect of reducing labour supply. The tax deductibility of pension plans contributions also constitutes a subsidy for financial institutions, because it corresponds to a loan granted by the government to individuals that can be used for investments, for example, in equities and other risky assets.

NOTES

1. This scheme is known as Arbejdsmarkedets Tillægspension (ATP) (in English: The Labour Market Supplementary Pension Scheme).
2. See Ostrup (1996) for a survey of the Danish literature until 1995.
3. World Bank (1994).
4. See Velfærdskommissionen (2006)
5. A fall in property prices in 2007 – 08 has thus led to losses and the collapse of some Danish financial institutions. Source: *Financial Times*, August 26, 2008 p. 7.
6. There is a comprehensive literature in Danish on the implications of minimum return guarantees in pension schemes. A contribution in English is Jensen and Sørensen (2001).
7. The report is published as Danish Ministry of Economic and Commercial Affairs (2003). The work in the Bremer Committee has subsequently been discussed in a number of contributions in Danish, see for example, Andersen and Søgaard (2006).

REFERENCES

Andersen, Lennart L. and Flemming B. Søgaard (eds) (2006), *12 perspektiver på pension*, [in English: 12 Perspectives on Pensions] (text in Danish), Copenhagen: Thomson

Danish Ministry of Economic and Commercial Affairs (2003), *Større valgfrihed i pensionsopsparingen*. [in English: Larger Flexibility in Pension Saving] (text in Danish). København: Økonomi-og Erhvervsministeriet.

Jensen, Bjarne A. and Carsten Sørensen (2001), 'Paying for Minimum Interest Rate Guarantees: Who Should Compensate Who?', *European Financial Management*, **7**, 183–211.

Ostrup, Finn (1996), 'The Outlook on Supplementary Pensions in the Context of Demographic, Economic and Social Change: The Development in Denmark', *Social Europe*, Supplement 7/96, 57–75.

Velfærdskommissionen (2006), *Fremtidens velfærd – vore valg*. [In English: The Future Welfare – Our Choices] (text in Danish), www.velfaerd.dk.

World Bank (1994), *Averting the Old Age Crisis*, Oxford: Oxford University Press.

7. Personal Provision of Retirement Income in the UK[1]

Barbara Waine

1. THE UK PENSIONS REGIME

The UK pensions system operates with a basic state pension and an additional pension (for a description of the former, see Appendix F Pensions Commission 2004b). Originally the latter existed in the form of employer sponsored occupational schemes, although only for a privileged minority of the workforce (Hannah 1986, p. 40). A major theme of the political debates over pensions from the mid-1950s to the mid-1970s was how to extend additional pensions to those without occupational cover. The Labour Party both in and out of office proposed the introduction of a state earnings-related scheme while Conservatives supported the expansion of occupational schemes. The 1975 Social Security and Pensions Act, introduced by the Labour government, was seen as a long term framework within which additional pensions could develop.

The Act was a compromise. Labour, whose earlier policy stance had been to design a scheme in which occupational provision would effectively be replaced by state provision, accepted the existence of an occupational pensions sphere which, by this time, covered around half of all employees, while the Conservatives accepted a State Earnings-Related Pension Scheme (SERPS) for those not covered by occupational schemes. However, this harmony between the parties was to be short-lived. The Conservatives returned to office in 1979 and during the 1980s introduced a number of important changes to the pensions regime which they inherited. Firstly the indexing of the basic pension to earnings or prices was discontinued. Pensions were to be linked only to prices and, as earnings generally rise faster than prices, this meant that over time the basic pension would become of marginal importance.

Secondly the 1986 Social Security Act introduced a number of changes in the sphere of additional pensions: SERPS was to be retained (the original plan had been to abolish it) but in a modified form; occupational pensions schemes were retained but membership could no longer be a condition of employment and encouragement was given to employers to operate such schemes on a defined contribution basis in addition to a defined benefit basis. While benefit levels in the former depend upon the level of contributions and investment returns, with the latter benefits at the point of retirement are guaranteed with the pension calculated either as a proportion of final salary or a revalued career average. The Act also offered an additional choice for employees, an Approved Personal Pension (APP), an individual money purchase scheme as an alternative to occupational pensions and a modified SERPS. (Weaver 2006, pp. 15–18 provides a lucid account of this major policy change). The APP was not a new vehicle for saving; individual personal pensions had been used by the self employed for many years. (In line with the accepted nomenclature the APP, will hereafter, be referred to as the Personal Pension (PP)).

While the Labour Party had mounted a vigorous opposition to the 1986 pension reforms by the time that they were returned to office in 1997 their policies on pensions had undergone considerable change (Waine 1998, pp. 159–61). Their commitment to their predecessor's policy of restraining public expenditure (Burchardt and Hills 1999, Chapter 2) together with a commitment to reconstructing the Welfare State in terms of an emphasis on opportunity and individual responsibility required a pensions policy related to these objectives. This was developed in A New Contract for Welfare: Partnership in Pensions (Department of Social Security, DSS 1998). The basic state non-means-tested pension would remain but, following the changes introduced by the Conservatives, would continue to be raised in line with prices (DSS 1998, p. 3). (The Pensions Act 2007 has restored the link with earnings but not until 2012). SERPS was to be replaced with a State Second Pension for low earners (that is, those earning less than £9,000 per annum) for whom a private second pension was not an option. Both occupational and personal pensions would continue. The centrepiece of New Labour's proposals was the Stakeholder Pension (SHP) aimed at middle-income earners (those earning between £9,000 and £20,000). Like the PP, the SHP was an individual money purchase scheme. It was argued that 'this new type of pension combines the low overheads and the high security of occupational pension schemes with the flexibility of the best personal pensions' (DSS 1998, p. 5).

The changes to additional pension provision in the 1986 Act were justified in three ways. Firstly concerns about the increasing cost of SERPS, which was a pay-as-you-go (PAYG) unfunded scheme. The Conservatives claimed that in the context of an ageing population such a scheme would require unacceptably high levels of personal taxation for future generations. Secondly Britain was becoming an 'enterprise economy' characterised by frequent job changes which could not be reconciled with occupational pensions based upon employment involving long tenure.

The final justification for the 1986 changes lay in the distinctive political philosophy embraced by the Conservatives from the 1970s, neo-liberalism (Waine 1995, pp. 318–20). A key component of this philosophy was possessive individualism and the consequent limitation of state power (Beland 2005, pp. 13–19). Personal property ownership was a crucial aspect of this approach and the Conservatives sought to promote it via the privatisation of social housing, nationalised industries (with the object of spreading share ownership) and the extension to employees of the ability to opt in to private pensions. The political rationale for personal ownership was that it brought increased self-respect and independence.

These justifications for individualised provision were broadly shared by the post-1997 Labour governments. Firstly there was a recognition of the impact of an ageing population, accompanied by a decline in those of working age (DSS 1998, p.13). Secondly, a view that the pension system required modernisation to meet the needs of a modern competitive economy (DSS 1998, p. 25). Thirdly there was the accommodation to the central tenets of neo liberalism which had transformed the party post 1985 (Hefferman 2003, pp. 49–58). Thus there was a continuity in the commitment to personal ownership and independent provision.

2. INDIVIDUALISING PENSION PROVISION: THE PERSONAL PENSION AND THE STAKEHOLDER PENSION

While the PP and SHP had ideological objectives at the same time they were presented as arrangements to help people save for their retirement. This section will consider the experience of both in this respect.

The PP and the SHP share a number of features. The final pension is linked to contributions paid by individual members. Employers must make a minimum contribution equivalent to what they would have paid in national insurance contributions on behalf of the employee; this is known as the contracted out rebate. They are not obliged to make any additional contributions and a significant number do not. Administrative costs are set against contributions and the accumulated fund is used to purchase an annuity, (Inland Revenue 2000, pp. 76–76). Problems can emerge at each stage. The purpose of the contracted out rebate is to provide a pension broadly equivalent to the foregone state additional pension. However, as Jarvis (2001, p. 17) states, there is 'no guarantee that the rebates invested in a private pension will produce a final pension of an amount equivalent to the state benefits foregone' (see also the discussion in Blake and Turner 2007, pp. 57–58). Age-related rebates (increasing with age) were introduced in 1993. However, they were capped in order to retain control of public expenditure on pensions and this particularly penalised older workers. The effect of the cap together with concerns about whether the generally low level of contributions into a PP could lead to a reasonable pension has led many pension providers to advise those with a PP to opt back into the state scheme. The Department for Work and Pensions (DWP) estimated that, in 2004, 500,000 people abandoned their personal pension and moved back into the state system and that a further 250,000 would do so in 2005 (Cohen 2005).

Secondly an individual's 'pension pot' depends upon returns from investment of the premiums. Watson Wyatt, the pension specialists, noted that in 2006 falling interest rates and lower investment returns meant that after twenty years of saving, the pension pot would be less than half what it would have been ten years previously (Timmins 2006).

Thirdly not only are benefits in personal pensions restricted by minimum contributions and falling returns but also by the administrative costs of providing individual contracts which do not have the economies of scale of large company or state schemes. It has been estimated that the costs for administration and fund management of an individual account reduces its value by an average of 25 per cent over an individual's working life (Orszag 1999, pp. 6–7). As a result the fund available for investment is severely reduced (see the discussion in Gillion et al. 2000, pp. 323–4). There is a significant difference here with the SHP, where the limit on the permitted level of administrative costs was initially set at 1 per cent and for those joining after April 2005 at 1.5 per cent for the first ten years (House of Commons Treasury Committee 2006, p. 10).

Finally, a personal pension fund must be used to buy an annuity: initially this was at the age of 60, increased to 75 in 1995. The intention here was to allow individuals to defer purchase of their annuity to a more opportune time if annuity rates were falling. However as Blake and Turner (2007, p. 56) point out few workers make use of this opportunity, annuitising at the time of retirement. Neither do they shop around for the best deal on annuities; rather they purchase with the insurance company managing their account (HM Treasury 2006, p. 24).

The Conservative government launched an extensive media campaign highlighting the merits of the PP in contrast to both state and employer provision (Cohen 2005). In addition it offered a series of financial inducements. In order to get around the problem that the PP was inherently less attractive for older workers, as later contributions are likely to mean a smaller accumulated fund, the percentage of income which attracted tax relief varied with age. These tax reliefs were accompanied by a number of financial incentives or subsidies financed from the National Insurance Fund. The estimated gross cost of these subsidies to the Fund was in the region of £9.3 billion (National Audit Office 1990, para. 3.18). While the subsidy from the National Insurance Fund attracted considerable controversy, this was not replicated in respect of the tax expenditures attached to the new PP. Hughes and Sinfield (2004, p. 178) argue that these expenditures would of course grow as the PP became more established and yet they were not mentioned in debates or discussions.The current estimate for the annual cost of this relief is £3.4 billion (HM Revenue and Customs (HMRC 2007, Table 7.9).

The PP was initially very successful with a take-up of 5 million by the end of 1992–93 (DSS 1994, p. 9). However, as early as 1990 complaints began to surface about the possibility of 'mis-selling' (in the sense that having purchased a PP, people would in retirement be worse off than if they had remained in their original schemes). Accusations of 'mis-selling' focused attention on the sales practices of insurance agents for whom commission payments made up a large proportion of their salary (Waine 1995, pp. 325–326; Gillion et al 2000, p. 321). 'Sales' took priority over 'advice giving' (House of Commons Treasury Committee 2006, p. 11). In 1993 the Securities and Investment Board (now the Financial Services Authority) commissioned a report on the selling of the PP over the previous two and a half years. It was estimated that 50 per cent of those who had taken out a PP as an alternative to remaining in an occupational scheme had been 'missold' this product. It was recommended that those who were the victims of 'mis-selling' should either be reinstated in their original scheme or, if this were not possible, offered financial compensation. The process of rectifying the effects of 'mis-selling' began under the last Conservative government; redress though was slow and one of the first actions of the Labour government elected in May 1997 was to put additional pressure on the major insurance companies to speed up this process (Eaglesham 1997). However, it was not until mid-2002 that the review finally drew to a close, with compensation having been offered to over 1.6 million people at an estimated cost of nearly £12 billion pounds to the pension providers (Mackintosh 2002).

While the SHP has not been mired in controversy and scandal it has had a 'limited effect' (Pensions Commission 2004a, p. 92). At the end of the financial year 2004–5 while there were 6.9 million contributors to a personal pension there were only 1.6 million to a SHP (HMRC 2007, Tables 7.4 and 7.5). The vast majority of the schemes identified by employers were 'empty shells' with no contributory members (Pensions Commission 2004a, p. 92; McKay 2006, p. 76). The limited impact of the SHP might be a reflection of the lack of trust by consumers in financial services, in turn, a response to the 'mis-selling' of the PP in the 1980s and 1990s (Ring 2005, p. 355).

The United Kingdom has now had individualised pension provision for two decades; the current government has announced its intention to continue and extend this form of provision even though there is no substantial evidence that such individualised provision has improved or will improve the pension entitlements of a substantial proportion of scheme participants. Indeed evidence suggests the contrary. A significant proportion of the PPs are minimum contributions only (HMRC 2007, Table 7.3), the fund values remain low (HMRC 2007, Table 7.13). Very few PPs are now sold to employees on average or below average earnings (Pensions Commission 2004a, p. 90) and this also applies to SHPs (Weaver 2006, p. 24). Lapsed policies are also an issue. Blake and Turner (2007, p. 59) drawing on research by the Pensions Investment Authority note that 'very few personal plan members are likely to maintain plan membership for long enough to build up an adequate pension'. The Department for Work and Pensions (DWP 2006e, p. 517) found that 31 per cent of those participating in a SHP terminated their contracts in the same year in which they took them out. Referring to the role of individualised pension provision in the 1980s and 1990s, the Pensions Commission (2005a, p. 28) spoke of the 'misguided attempts to extend personal pensions to segments of the market where the economics only appeared to work in periods of exceptional return'. Such segments are likely to include the low paid, those who take time out of the labour market to care for children and elderly relatives and those with irregular patterns of employment. (These groups are likely to be disproportionately made up of women both now and in future, see the discussion in Price 2007a, pp. 49–50).

3. EXTENDING INDIVIDUALISED PENSION PROVISION

The final section of this chapter focuses on the most recent proposal for the reform of pensions, namely the introduction of Personal Accounts (PA) in 2012. The key question is whether PAs will remedy the problems identified with the PP and SHP and secure the objective of tackling inadequate saving for retirement.

The Green Paper 'Simplicity, Security and Choice: Working and Saving for Retirement', stated that current 'estimates show that up to 3 million people are seriously undersaving for retirement…[and] a further group of 5 and 10 million people may want to consider saving more' (see Department for Work and Pensions (DWP 2002, pp. 4–5). The focus was on how to increase levels of saving. The government's response was two-fold. Firstly it sought to remove obstacles to saving by simplifying the tax regime for pensions (DWP 2002, p. 5). Secondly it established the Pensions Commission to review private pensions and to consider whether there was a case for moving beyond the existing voluntarist approach (Pensions Commission 2004a, p. ix). A central proposal of the Commission to encourage additional saving for retirement was the creation of a new second-tier pension scheme, the National Pensions Savings Scheme (NPSS). The key features would be automatic enrolment for all employees not covered by other adequate pension arrangements but with a right to opt out. Compulsion was rejected as it failed to take account of individual preferences and circumstances. There would be a minimum contribution of 8 per cent of earnings between the primary threshold (the level of income at which national insurance contributions become payable by employer and employee) and the upper earnings limit (the level of income beyond which the employee ceases to pay national insurance contributions) with 4 per cent contributed by the employee, 3 per cent by the employer and 1 per cent from tax relief. An independent centralised authority would be responsible for investing contributions and in order to ensure that the maximum funds were available for investment the scheme should aim for the Annual Management Charge (AMC) of no more than 0.3 per cent which was comparable to that found in schemes run by large employers (Pensions Commission 2005a, p. 133). There was a general acceptance of the Pensions Commission recommendation that a new approach to pension saving which went beyond the voluntary approach was required (Pensions Commission 2006, p.16).

The Pensions White Paper published in May 2006 announced the government's intention of introducing a new pensions vehicle which would provide 'a simple way for people to take responsibility for the income they want in retirement' (DWP 2006a, p. 16). Personal Accounts were closely modelled on the NPSS (DWP 2006a, p. 31). A more detailed exposition of the government's proposals followed in December (DWP 2006c). The response to the consultation exercises initiated by both White Papers indicated widespread support for the principle of PAs (DWP 2006b, p. 32; DWP 2007, p. 7–8) even if there was disagreement on particular features. The Personal Accounts Delivery Authority was created by the Pensions Act 2007 with the remit of designing and building an infrastructure to implement Personal Accounts and further legislation in 2008 will deal with the details of the PA itself.

Having described Personal Accounts the chapter will now assess how far, if at all, they are likely to represent an advance on earlier forms of individualised pension provision in leading to higher levels of saving for retirement. Three features of PAs have the potential for contributing to this objective. Firstly automatic enrolment for those aged 22 and over earning above the primary threshold; secondly a minimum contribution level; thirdly a proposed cap on Annual Management Charges of 0.3 per cent. The case for auto-enrolment uses evidence from both the UK and USA, which points to the association between it and increased participation rates (DWP 2006a, p. 63) and by definition a decline in lapsed policies, identified as a key problem with the PP (Pensions Commission 2005a, p. 111; DWP 2006a, p. 43). The employer contribution is seen as having two main advantages: an increase in employee participation and an increase in incentives to save (DWP 2006a, p. 69). An important difference between the PP/SHP and Personal Accounts is the intended low AMC charges (DWP 2006a, p. 59). As the White Paper points out, a high AMC reduces an individual's accumulated fund. For example, with an AMC of 1.5 per cent, an individual saving for 40 years will lose 20 per cent of their pension (DWP 2006a, p. 60). Low charges are regarded as a 'key feature for the success of Personal Accounts' (DWP 2007, p. 48).

Certain other features though which PAs share with PPs and SHPs could act in a contrary direction. The PA like its predecessors, is a defined contribution scheme: contributions are invested in funds and the accumulated fund is converted into an annuity. As the White Paper states as with 'all defined contribution products, the value of an individual's fund can fluctuate over time due to changing investment performance' (DWP 2006a, p. 57). While the risk can be mitigated by developing an investment strategy that progressively moves funds into less volatile investments as an individual approaches retirement, 'there is no absolute guarantee that the value of the fund would be more than the value of contributions invested' (DWP 2006a, p. 57). The White Paper also states that the value of the investment will not 'be underwritten by government' (DWP 2006a, p. 57), a position reiterated by John Hutton (then Secretary of State for Work and Pensions) in his evidence to the House of Commons Work and Pensions Committee (2006a, p. 39). While poor returns could perhaps be mitigated if an individual chose to save the maximum allowed in a PA (£3,600 based on 2005 earnings (DWP 2007, p. 93), experience of the PP and SHP suggests that few contributors will save up to the limit (HMRC 2007, Table 7.3). As noted a low AMC (0.3 per cent in the long term, 0.5 per cent in the short term (DWP 2006c, p.94) is crucial to a successful delivery of the PA. However, whether this level of charges is achievable is a matter of controversy and many in the pensions industry have argued that they are unrealistically low (DWP 2007, p. 51; House of Commons Work and Pensions Committee 2007a, p. 42)

As with the PP and SHP the accumulated fund from investments will be used to purchase an annuity. Referring to DWP commissioned research by Canon and Tonks (2006), the White Paper argues that annuities offer good value for money (DWP 2006a, p. 58). However, the authors themselves note that there are variations in annuity rates which are caused by variations in interest rates (Canon and Tonks 2006, p. 48). A perhaps unintentional by-product of this report is that it highlights the difficulties from the point of view of the consumer in engaging with the annuities market. There is a high administrative cost in providing individual annuities (Blake and Turner 2007, p. 59) but the bulk purchase of annuities (favoured by the Pensions Commission 2005a, p. 384) which would mirror the bulk purchase of the original investment funds is rejected as too costly due to the need to negotiate regularly to find suitable deals (DWP 2006c, p. 109).

With the PA, a lifetime median earner who started saving at around the age of 30 could expect to achieve a replacement rate of around 45 per cent with 30 per cent coming from the state pension system and 15 per cent from the 8 per cent contribution to the NPSS/PA (Pensions Commission 2005a, p. 274; DWP 2006a, p. 67). The preceding paragraphs have indicated certain features of the PA which might militate against this (see also House of Commons Work and Pensions 2006b, pp. 349–350). Three additional points are relevant here; firstly the extent to which individuals are aware of the risk involved in enrolling into a defined contribution scheme. (For a comprehensive discussion of the different types of risk involved in pensions saving in particular how defined contribution schemes expose individuals to uncertainty with respect to their future income see the Pensions Commission 2004a, pp. 104–113). Although people might not be compelled to take such risks a heavy financial penalty will be incurred in opting out because of the loss of the employer's contribution and that from tax (House of Commons Work and Pensions Committee 2006b, Ev. 351). If the returns are not in line with expectations this could lead to accusations of 'mis-selling' (House of Commons Work and Pensions Committee 2006a, pp. 38–39).

Secondly there is also a question of the impact on poverty levels. Notwithstanding various redistributive policies pursued by Labour governments since 1997, there has been a clear trend to increasing pay inequalities (See Dickens, Gregg and Wadsworth 2000 on both wage inequality and the relative immobility within the earnings distribution). In such a context a significant 'low pay' problem could mean that even relatively high replacement rates (that is well above the 45 per cent 'target' for median earners) will still leave a significant group of retired people in poverty (see the discussion on this point in Bridgen and Meyer 2005, p. 7–9). Thirdly both the Pensions Commission (2005a, p. 278) and the White Paper (DWP 2006a, p. 196) calculated savings and returns using the model of the median earner with a continuous working history who started saving aged 30. While both recognise that individuals experience patterns of employment and earnings which do not conform to this model (Pensions Commission 2005b, pp. 199–216.; DWP 2006a, p. 196) neither seem to explore the impact of these experiences on the required level of savings to reach the replacement rate of 45 per cent of median earnings. The Pensions Commission (2004a, pp. 150–157) does, however, acknowledge that the rate of pension contributions to secure an 'adequate' pension will vary with planned retirement age, number of years of saving, return on investment and so on). Bridgen and Meyer (2005, pp. 11–15) using the assumptions of the Pensions Commission have demonstrated in their discussion of savings and 'risk biographies' that individuals who have breaks in employment, combine different types of employment and thus have variations in income would require unrealistic levels of saving to achieve the desired replacement rate. In addition, Steventon (2006, pp. 3–4) has identified the self-employed and individuals combining low earnings and interrupted contributions as more likely to have reduced returns from PAs than those in continuous full-time employment.

The obstacles that women experience in the area of pensions, for example, low incomes, periods out of the labour market, have been extensively documented (Ginn 2003; Pensions Commission 2004a, chapter 8; DWP 2006d). Several of the reforms introduced in the Pensions Act 2007 such as the restoration of the link between earnings and the basic state pension and the qualification for that pension after thirty rather than thirty-nine years of contributions or caring credits, are likely to benefit future generations of women (Price 2007a, pp. 50–52). It is the view of the Equal Opportunities Commission (House of Commons Work and Pensions Committee 2007b, Evidence 53–56) and the DWP (2006d, p. 25) that the PA could provide the potential for significant improvements to women's pension outcomes. The right to claim an employer's contribution distinguishes the PA from its predecessors. However the final pension for a woman in a PA as with a man is still determined by the vagaries of the market in respect of the accumulation of the investment fund and the purchase of annuities. Indeed, with the latter, women will continue to experience an existing discrimination, as insurers are not required to provide unisex annuities (Price 2007a, pp. 53–54). The White Paper (DWP 2006a, p.

64) initially proposed that those earning less than £5,000 p.a. (predominantly women) were to be excluded from a PA; this has now been amended and such low earners will now be able to participate but with no requirement for an employers contribution (DWP 2006c, p. 53). This contradicts the arguments in the White Paper noted here, that such a contribution encourages participation; this group of employees will have little incentive to contribute and at such a low level of earning might well be advised not to do so (Price 2007a, pp. 52–53). Using previously unpublished data on stylised individuals provided by the Pensions Commission, Price (2007b, p. 580) concludes that it is unlikely that the proposed reforms will provide an income equivalent to 45 per cent of median earnings in retirement for the majority of women, as paid work histories will continue to play a significant part in the accumulation of income in later life.

4. CONCLUSION

The aim of this chapter has been to present a critical analysis of various phases of individualised pension provision in the UK over the past 20 years. While these phases have their own distinct character they also have certain common themes. In particular individualised provision has operated with two overarching objectives. The first was to create a form of provision which emphasised the importance of promoting individual choice in pension provision and independence from the state. There were differences of emphasis between the Conservatives and Labour but both, – Labour following its conversion to at least certain precepts of neo-liberalism – have supported individualised provision as a central plank of pensions policy. However, as Rose (1996) has pointed out, such policies have not involved the withdrawal of the state. Rather state intervention has been central to the policy of individualised provision by providing a variety of incentives and inducements to the creation of a 'prudential' subject providing for his/her retirement (Rose 1996, p. 340) via the private market (Rose 1996, p. 342). The second central objective was that individualised provision would give a basis for adequate incomes in retirement without substantial support from the state.

However, both aspects have proved problematic. In the period when the Personal Pension was the centrepiece of policy far from 'prudential' subjects making sensible decisions over their pension provision, the dominant motif was one of individuals inexperienced in making such decisions falling prey to mercenary selling tactics. Ironically the state was brought back in, via the regulatory framework, to enforce redress. Stakeholders pensions escaped the opprobrium associated with Personal Pensions but encountered a severe shortage of savers. The problems of the latter policy have now engendered a third phase of individualised provision, that is, Personal Accounts. Yet here the tensions between the two objectives have resurfaced. The policy on Personal Accounts has sought to respond to the very real problems of transaction costs eating into often modest contributions. However auto-enrolment, while it has an obvious appeal in terms of avoiding the very low take up problems associated with Stakeholder Pensions, sits uneasily with conceptions of the 'independent' saver. Furthermore doubts regarding how far Personal Accounts will meet the test of adequacy remain. The optimistic account of very low transaction costs remains untested; the suitability of such accounts for those with interrupted work histories are still in question; and even if replacement targets are attained the question remains will they give adequate retirement incomes if contemporary trends to greater labour market inequality continue? After two apparent failures it is by no means clear that individual accounts will provide a case of 'third time lucky'.

NOTE

1. My thanks to Adrian Sinfield for comments on an earlier draft of this article. The author is responsible for the final version.

REFERENCES

Beland, Daniel (2005), 'Framing the Ownership Society: Ideas, Institutions and Neo-Liberal Social Policy', paper presented at the Annual Meeting of the Research Committee (Poverty, Social Welfare and Social Policy) of the International Sociological Association, Chicago.

Blake, D. and John Turner (2007), 'Individual Accounts for Social Security Reform: Lessons from the United Kingdom', *Discussion Paper PI-0707*, London: The Pensions Institute, pp. 55–60.

Bridgen, P. and Traute Meyer (2005), 'Towards a 'Balanced' Approach to Pensions Reform? Individuals, the State and Employers in the Restructuring of Post-Retirement Income in the UK', *Discussion Paper PI-0509*, London, UK: The Pensions Institute.

Burchardt, Tania and John Hills (1999), 'Public expenditure and the public/private mix', in Martin Powell (ed.) *New Labour, New Welfare State? The 'Third Way' in British Social Policy*, Bristol, UK: Policy Press, pp. 29–49.

Canon, Edward and Ian Tonks (2006), Survey of Annuity Pricing, DWP Research Report 318., Leeds, UK: Corporate Document Services.

Cohen, Norma. (2005), *A Bloody Mess*, The American Prospect, available on the Web only at www.prospect.org.

Department for Work and Pensions (DWP) (2002), *Simplicity, Security and Choice: Working and Saving for Retirement*, Cm. 5677, London: The Stationery Office.

Department for Work and Pensions (DWP) (2006a), *Security in Retirement: Towards A New Pensions System*, Cm. 6841, London: The Stationery Office.

Department for Work and Pensions (DWP) (2006b), *Security in Retirement: A New Way to Save*, Summary of Responses to the Consultation, Cm. 6960, London: The Stationery Office.

Department for Work and Pensions (DWP) (2006c), *Personal Accounts: A New Way to Save*, Cm. 6975, London: The Stationery Office.

Department for Work and Pensions (DWP) (2006d), *Gender Impact of Pension Reform*, available at www.gov.uk/pensionsreform/pdfs/GenderimpactAssessment.

Department for Work and Pensions (DWP) (2006e), *Second Tier Pension Provision 1978/9 to 2003/04*, at www.dwp.gov,uk/asd/asd1/dsu/second_tier/second_tier.asp.

Department for Work and Pensions (DWP) (2007), *Personal Accounts: A New Way to Save*, Summary of Responses to the Consultation, Cm. 7121, London: The Stationery Office.

Department of Social Security (DSS) (1994), *Personal Pensions Statistics 1992/93*, Revised Edition, London: Government Statistical Service.

Department of Social Security (DSS) (1998), *A New Contract for Welfare Partnership in Pensions*, Cm. 4179, London, UK: The Stationery Office.

Dickens, R., P. Gregg, and J. Wadsworth (2000), 'New Labour and the Labour Market', *Oxford Review of Economic Policy*, **16** (1), 95–111.

Eaglesham, J. (1997), '"Shame" Campaign Threat', *Financial Times*, 17/18 May 1997.

Gillion, Colin, John Turner, Clive Bailey and Denis Latulippe (eds) (2000), *Social Security Pensions: Development and Reform*, Geneva, Switzerland: International Labour Office.

Ginn, Jay (2003) *Gender, Pensions and the Life Course: How Pensions Need to Adapt to Changing Family Forms*, Bristol, UK: The Policy Press.

Hannah, Leslie (1986), *Inventing Retirement: the Development of Occupational Pensions in Britain*, Cambridge, UK: Cambridge University Press.

Hefferman, Richard. (2003), 'New Labour and Thatcherism', in Andrew Chadwick and Richard Hefferman (eds) *The New Labour Reader*, Cambridge, UK: Polity Press, pp. 49–58.

HM Revenue and Customs (2007), *Pensions*, at www.hmrc.gov.uk/Stats/pensions/.

HM Treasury (2006), *The Annuities Market*, London: HM Treasury.

House of Commons Treasury Committee (2006), *The Design of the National Pensions Savings Scheme and the Role of Financial Services Regulation*, Fifth Special Report of Session 2005–06, HC 1074-I, London: The Stationery Office.

House of Commons Work and Pensions Committee (2006a), *Pension Reform*, Fourth Report of Session 2005–06, HC 1068-I, London: The Stationery Office.

House of Commons Work and Pensions Committee (2006b), *Pension Reform*, Fourth Report of Session 2005–06, HC 1068-II, Memoranda submitted by Tony Lynes, Ev 344-353, London, UK: The Stationery Office.

House of Commons Work and Pensions Committee (2007a), *Personal Accounts*, Fifth Report of Session 2006–07, HC 220-I, London: The Stationery Office.

House of Commons Work and Pensions Committee (2007b), *Personal Accounts*, Fifth Report of Session 2006–07, HC 220-II, Memorandum submitted by the Equal Opportunities Commission, Ev 53-56, London: The Stationery Office.

Hughes, Gerard and Adrian Sinfield (2004), 'Financing pensions by stealth: The Anglo-American model and the cost and distribution of tax benefits for private pensions' in Gerard Hughes and Jim Stewart (eds) *Reforming Pensions in Europe: Evolution of Pension Financing and Sources of Retirement Income*, Cheltenham, UK and Lyme, US: Edward Elgar, pp. 165–193.

Inland Revenue (2000), Inland Revenue Statistics, London: HMSO.

Jarvis, Tim (2001), *Stakeholder Pensions*, Research Paper 01/69, London: House of Commons Library.

Mackintosh, J. (2002) 'Deadline nears for mis-sold pension payouts', *Financial Times*, 28 June.

McKay, Stephen (2006), *Employers' Pension Provision Survey 2005*, DWP Research Report No. 329, Leeds, UK: Corporate Document Services.

National Audit Office (1990), *The Elderly: Information Requirements for Supporting the Implications of Personal Pensions for the National Insurance Fund*, HC 55, London: HMSO.

Orszag, Peter (1999), *Administrative Costs in Individual Accounts in the UK: Executive Summary*, Washington, D.C.: Center on Budget and Policy Priorities.

Pensions Commission (2004a), *Pensions: Challenges and Choices, the First Report of the Pensions Commission*, London: The Stationery Office.

Pensions Commission (2004b), *Pensions: Challenges and Choice the First Report of the Pensions Commission*, Appendices, London: The Stationery Office.

Pensions Commission (2005a), *A New Pension Settlement for the Twenty-First Century: Second Report of the Pensions Commission*, London: The Stationery Office.

Pensions Commission (2005b), *A New Pension Settlement for the Twenty-First Century: Second Report of the Pensions Commission*: Appendices, London: The Stationery Office.

Pensions Commission (2006), *Implementing an Integrated Package of Pension Reforms: Final Report of the Pensions Commission*, London: The Stationery Office.

Price, D. (2007a), 'The pensions white paper: taking account of gender', *Benefits: the Journal of Poverty and Social Justice*, **15** (1), 45–58.

Price, D. (2007b) 'Closing the gender gap in retirement income: what difference will recent UK pension reforms make?' *Journal of Social Policy*, **36** (4), 561–84.

Ring, P. J. (2005), 'Security in pension provision: a critical analysis of UK government policy', *Journal of Social Policy*, **34** (3), 343–64.

Rose, N. (1996), 'The death of the social? refiguring the territory of government' *Economy and Society*, **25** (3), 327–356.

Steventon, Adam (2006), *Are Personal Accounts Suitable for All?*, London: Pensions Policy Institute.

Timmins, N. (2006), 'Income from pensions down by 80% in ten years, warns specialist', *Financial Times*, 28 February.

Waine, B. (1995), 'A disaster foretold: the case of the personal pension', *Social Policy and Administration*, **29** (4), 317–334.

Waine, Barbara. (1998), 'Paying for pensions', in Helen Jones and Susanne MacGregor (eds) *Social Issues and Party Politics*, London: Routledge, pp. 155—167.

Weaver, Kent (2006), *The Politics of Parallel Pensions: Lessons from the United Kingdom for the United States*, Boston, USA: Center for Retirement Research, Boston College.

8. Personal Provision of Retirement Income in Poland

Marek Szczepański

1. INTRODUCTION

This chapter describes and analyses trends in Individual Pension Schemes (IKE) and the barriers and prospects for the development of personal pension provision in Poland.

The chapter is organised as follows: Section 2 describes the main features of the old and the new old-age pension system in Poland. Section 3 describes the Individual Pension Scheme (IKE) in Poland. This is a supplementary pension system which was introduced in 2004. Section 4 examines the macro costs, that is the cost of tax relief and the micro costs in terms of fees and charges. Costs and returns are then considered jointly. Finally section 5 gives some conclusions in terms of evaluation of the current development of IKE and necessary steps which would be required if individual pension provision in Poland were to become more widespread.

2. THE OLD AND THE NEW OLD-AGE PENSION SYSTEM IN POLAND

Supplementary pension systems, including personal pensions, should be analysed in context of the pension system as a whole. Hence this chapter begins with a description of the mandatory public pension system. In Poland almost 100 per cent of the population are covered by some pension provision. The pensions system includes old-age pensions, disability pensions and survivor pensions. According to different eligibility rules, different benefit formula and different ways of contributing money for different groups, the pension system can be usefully divided into three subsystems: the employee pension scheme, the farmers pension scheme and the pension schem for military and police (see Table 8.1). The most important (in terms of number of participants and expenditure) is the employee pension scheme. The farmers scheme is financed by farmers' contributions and a state subsidy (about 90 per cent of the income of the farmers pensions scheme consists of a state subsidy). The benefits for farmers are relatively low. The pension scheme for the military and police has a relatively generous formula. This scheme is a pay-as-you-go scheme. The benefits are paid directly from the state and the participants do not have to make any contributions. The main focus of this chapter is the employee pension scheme.

Table 8.1 The number of pensioners[a] and average monthly gross pensions

average benefit level (in PLN)[b]	2004	2005	2006
Total	9213	9169	9151
Persons covered by non-agricultural social security system	7504	7524	7565
payment	1141	1171	1261
old-age pensioners	4012	4168	4625
payment	1289	1306	1361
disability pensioners	2158	2014	1594
payment	898	926	1019
survivor pensioners	1334	1342	1346
payment	1090	1119	1205
Individual farmers	1709	1645	1586
payment	747	758	803
old-age pensioners	963	1272	1247
payment	785	794	841
disability pensioners	702	328	295
payment	696	619	639
survivor pensioners	44	44	44
payment	737	711	813

Notes
a annual average in thousands.
b monthly average.

Source: Concise Statistical Yearbook of Poland CSO, 2007, p. 177.

In Poland the mandatory part of the pension system covering most employees is complicated. From 1999, two mandatory old-age pension systems have been operating in parallel to each other: the old pension scheme – for persons receiving old-age pensions and for persons above 50 years of age at the point of the introduction of the pensions reforms and the new pension scheme which applies to those who have not reached the age of 50 years at the point at which reforms were introduced, that is persons born after 31 December 1948. In the transition period both old and new pension systems are operational and will co-exist until at least

2034 (the retirement date of men who have chosen the new system in 1999, at the age of 30 and who will reach retirement age at the age of 65). After 2034 all retirement pensions in Poland will only be paid out from the new pension system.

Table 8.2 Introduction of the new pension system by age group

New system (people born after 31 Dec. 1948)		Old system
People born after 31 December 1968	People born before 1 January 1969	People born before 1 January 1949
Automatically covered by the new system; OA[a] contribution automatically split between two accounts [NDC[b]+FDC[c]]	Automatically covered by the new system; OA[a] contribution either split between two accounts or paid into one account [(NDC[b]+FDC[c]) or NDC]	Stay in the old system (no possibility of switching to the new system) no accounts

Notes:
a OA – old age
b NDC (notional defined contribution) – individual accounts not traded in financial markets, bringing rate of return equal wage sum growth (GDP growth in long run).
c FDC (financial defined contribution – individual accounts based on traded instruments.

Source: Góra, M. (2003a).

The Old Pension System

The old pension system was based on a PAYG financing method and defined benefit rules. The new multipillar pension system consists of a notional defined contribution pay-as-you-go first pillar, a mandatory defined contribution, privately-managed, funded second pillar and a voluntary funded defined contribution third pillar. The third pillar consists of Employee Pension Plans (PPE) and Individual Pension Schemes (IKE). There are also other long-term saving plans provided by financial institutions (banks, investment funds, life insurance companies and so on). Some of these are called 'pension plans'. But unlike PPE and IKE, the commercial pension plans are not covered by institutional regulations and state incentives for the third pillar. That is why they are not treated as a part of the Polish pension system in this chapter but rather as one of a wide range of financial products.

The right to the old-age social insurance-based pension is acquired by women aged 60 years with at least a 20-year contributory and non-contributory period and men aged 65 years with at least a 25-year contributory and non-contributory period. Contributory periods are periods in which pension insurance contributions were paid, as well as periods of military service, or service in the police force, employment in border and prison services, and periods in which maternity benefits are claimed. Non-contributory periods include, among others, periods of claiming sickness allowance, bringing up children (three years per child, but not more than six years in total), taking care of persons requiring permanent care and periods of university study. Non-contribution periods are reckoned at the rate not exceeding one-third of contributory periods.[1]

There are many exemptions to statutory pension eligibility criteria. For example, the old-age pension may be acquired by a woman who has reached the age of 60 years and has completed at least a 15-year contributory and non-contributory period and a man aged 65 years with a 20-year contributory and non-contributory period.

The formula used to calculate a pension in the old system included a strong social or redistributive component via an adjustment called a 'base amount'. The base amount consists of average earnings reduced by social insurance contributions deducted from the insured persons in the preceding calendar year. The old-age pension in the old system is then calculated in the following way: OLD AGE PENSION = 24 per cent of the base amount + 1.3 per cent of the basis of assessment for each contributory year + 0.7 per cent of the basis of assessment for each non-contributory year. The base amount adjustment thus served to compensate for shortfalls in contribution years. The pension from the old system may not be higher than 100 per cent of the basis of assessment, and the basis of assessment may not be higher than 250 per cent of the base amount. The replacement rate of higher-income earners was proportionally lower than that of lower-income earners, resulting in a redistribution of old-age income between these two groups. Moreover, the social component (the base amount) can be easily changed by political decisions.

The old pension system is managed by ZUS (Social Insurance Institution). The same public institution manages the first pillar of the new system.[2]

Basics of the New Pension System

The new pension system in Poland was first introduced in 1999. This was a radical reform, changing the logic and foundations of the system. The changes involved a switch from a pay-as-you go system with extensive redistribution effects to a system which was less redistributive and with a greater reliance on funding. This has been combined with parallel shift from defined benefit scheme to defined contribution schemes.[3]

Góra (2003), one of the reform team-leaders, summarises the main principles of the new system principles as follows.

1. An emphasis on a mandatory part of the pension system.
2. Separation of the old-age part of social security (OA) from the non-old-age part of social security (NOA).
3. Termination of the OA part of the previous system (for those not already retired).

4. Creation of a new OA pension system, based entirely on individual accounts.
5. Splitting each person's OA contributions between two accounts, one account is a notional defined contribution (NDC) account and the second account is a financial defined contribution account (FDC).
6. Annuitisation of account values (NDC and FDC) at the moment of retirement.
7. Minimum pension supplement on top of both annuities if their sum is below a certain level (this supplement is paid out of the state budget).
8. Both accounts are annuitised at the same time and play exactly the same role within the social security system.[4]

Table 8.3 Classification of the new old-age pension scheme

Classification	1st pillar	2nd pillar	3rd pillar
System management	public	private	private
Participation in the system	compulsory	compulsory	voluntary
Financing	pay-as-you-go principle	funded	funded
Calculation of benefit amount	a defined contribution system	a defined contribution system	a defined contribution system
Social objective	determined basic level of benefits	determined basic level of benefits	higher standard of benefits

Source: Social Insurance in Poland – Information Facts (2006), p. 39.

In the new old-age pension system the social insurance pension will be granted from ZUS (the institution in charge of social insurance-based payments) and from a notional capital fund. The amount of the new old-age pension received from ZUS is calculated according to the amount of pension contributions after indexation collected after 31 December 1998 and the amount of the so-called initial capital[5] after indexation divided by average life expectancy, expressed in months, for persons of retirement age.

The formula used in calculating the old-age pension in the new system is as follows: Old age pension = sum of collected and indexed pension contributions and the indexed capital, divided by average life expectancy expressed in months for persons in the retirement age group.

The new partially privatised pension system in Poland should ensure risk diversification because the accumulation of pension capital is partially based on the rule of traditional inter-generational agreement (pay-as-you-go financed) and partially on capitalisation (privately managed mandatory open pension funds).[6]

The system is thus dependent on the labour market through PAYG contributions, as well as on the capital market. Those in favour of these reforms argued that this would ensure the pension system was more viable in the context of an aging society, than traditional pay-as-you-go systems. However, whether a partially privatised pension system partly dependent on funding will be more viable than a PAYG system in the future depends on many variables, for example, rates of return on investment funds and costs (administration, regulation, investment and marketing). It is not obvious, as many have argued, that in the long run, funded systems are less risky than PAYG pension systems. Pension funds are exposed to many risks, for example investment risk. Marketing costs of funded systems are much higher than the costs of a PAYG system. Inflation poses another risk to retirement pensions paid out of a funded pension system.[7] Polish pension reform leaders were aware of problems with both PAYG and funded systems. But it was argued that reforms would diversify risk rather than eliminate all risks connected with pension schemes. It was argued that: 'Since each of the pillars has different types of risks, especially after retirement, the system's overall risk will be more diversified. Of course, pay-as-you-go and funding both offer individuals a measure of certainty about their future, but neither method can insure against common aggregate shocks'.[9] However a comparison of the relative risk of a PAYG system compared with a funded system, or an assessment of the risks from a pension system which relies on both PAYG and funding, requires several assumptions. For example if a funded system is always more risky that a PAYG system, any increase in funding necessarily increases the overall risk of the pension system. Risks from both systems may also not be independent, for example, stock market falls could be associated with rising unemployment and reduced PAYG payments.

The changes in the old-age pension system in Poland also included changes in the way pensions are financed. Contributions for old-age insurance are shared equally between employers and employees (each side pays 9.76 per cent contribution). From a total old-age pension contribution of 19.52 per cent, 7.30 per cent is transferred to a fund. That means that ZUS (Social Insurance Institution), which is responsible for paying out pensions, collects nearly one-third less income from old-age insurance contributions. This deficit in the pension system during the transition period must be covered by a subsidy from the state budget – as long as the old pension exists (that is, 2034). The cost of transition from a PAYG to partially funded old-age system is high, approximately 1 per cent of GDP each year.

One significant aspect of the reforms which has been subject to criticism within Poland is that the replacement rate will fall. Various calculations have shown that the replacement rate under the reforms would fall to a level of 50–60 per cent for men, whose retirement age is 65 years, and 40 per cent or less for women who retire five years earlier. Some projections show that the reform will also cause wage replacement rates to fall to levels below the minimum stipulated in international standards (for example, in ILO conventions) in future years.[9] Such long-term projections are not precise. But there is no doubt that the new system provides only basic security for old-age protection from poverty.

Table 8.4 Comparision of replacement rates in 'the old' and 'the new' pension system[a]

Features of the person obtaining the old-age pension[b]				
Sex	age	% of average earnings	'old system'(%)	'new system'(%)
Woman	60	50	91	–
Woman	60	100	67	43
Woman	60	250	52	43
Woman	65[c]	50	96	63
Woman	65[c]	100	73	63
Woman	65[c]	250	58	63
Man	65	50	96	63
Man	65	100	73	63
Man	65	250	58	63

Notes:
a Using optimistic assumptions.
b Each of these persons must have worked 30 or 35 years (when they are then eligible to receive the old-age pension at age of 65).
c The retirement age of women in Poland is 60. This simulation shows that a shift of retirement age to 65 would increase the old-age pension benefit of women to the level of pensions of men.

Source: Szumlicz, T. (2005).

In order to maintain living standards in old-age future pensioners will be obliged to participate in additional supplementary pension systems, such as the Employee Pension Programs (PPE) existing from 1999 and/or Individual Pension Schemes (IKE) launched in 2004, or accumulate capital in other ways, such as life insurance, investment funds, property, and so on.

The reform package was called 'Security through Diversity'. From a socio-technical point of view this description was very attractive and effective. The new system was promoted in the mass-media as a three pillar system. In reality, the reformers concentrated their attention on the mandatory public pension scheme. Although the law on voluntary Employee Pension Programs (a part of the third tier) had been passed in August 1997 (and amended many times since then), collective savings for supplementary pensions are very poorly developed in Poland. In 2007 only 1,101 such occupational pension systems were active in less than 1 per cent of registered enterprises (data form the end of June 2007). Total assets of occupational pension schemes in 2007 amounted to PLN 3.5 billion (€0.9 billion). Only about 290,000 employees were members of occupational pension schemes (less than 2 per cent of the working population).[11] The reasons for the collapse of the PPE system are not explored in this chapter but warrant further research.

Individual pension schemes in Poland could not compensate for the poor development of collective pension agreements. Until the introduction of Personal Pension Schemes (IKE) in 2004 there was no support by the state institutional framework for individual pension provisions. It was argued that employees, especially those with average or lower salaries, who were not members of any supplementary pension schemes (collective or individual) will be confronted with a significant decrease in income and living standard after retirement unless further supplementary pension provision were introduced.

3. FEATURES AND DEVELOPMENT OF INDIVIDUAL PENSION SCHEMES (IKE)

Individual Pension Schemes (IKE) were introduced in September 2004. It was the intention of the Ministry of Labour and Social Policy to create personal pension provisions as an additional source of pension income funded via capital accumulation and also to introduce a range of insurance products for future pensioners. The IKE pension arrangements in the form of individual savings accounts managed through financial institutions, were supposed to be widespread. They were designed to be attractive to not only better-off employees but also for people with average or lower income such as women, people with atypical working careers, for example, part-time workers. The former minister of Labour and Social Policy responsible for introducing IKE pensions and other reforms, Krzysztof Pater, had forecast that 1.5 to 3.5 million citizens would participate in the system of additional pension provision in the first year. However, at the end of 2006 the number of IKE pension accounts was only about 840,000 and the total value of assets amounted only PLN 1.3 billion (about €360.1 million). In June 2007 the number of IKE accounts reached 886,509 with total assets of PLN1.8 billion (approximately €0.5 bn). The number of those participating amounts to about 6 per cent of the working population in Poland (about 15.2 million people). In comparison the number of members of the mandatory open pension funds (II pillar) in Poland amounts over 13.1 million persons and their total assets amounted to PLN 142.8 billion (€39.7 billion).[12]

The law regulating IKE pensions[13] has been coordinated with other regulations of the new Polish pension system, especially with the law on occupational pension schemes (for example – the possibility of transferring between IKE and occupational pension schemes without losing tax incentives – see Table 8.5). The IKE system is regulated by the Polish Financial Supervising Authority (a state regulator of all financial institutions in Poland, including the pensions industry).

The following are the main characteristics of Individual Pension Schemes.

1. Only one IKE account per person is exempt from capital gains tax (CGT).
2. Those with Individual Pension Schemes (IKE) may transfer to an Employee Pension Programmme, that is from an individual into a group form of pension provision, and from one financial institution providing IKE accounts to another.

Table 8.5 Tax reliefs for occupation pension schemes (PPE) and individual pension schemes (IKE)

	Employee Pension Programs (PPE)	Individ. Pension Schemes (IKE)
Tax incentives	Tax reliefs for employer: The contribution to PPE by an employer (up to 7% of employee's gross earnings) is treated as a cost for the company. That means that corporate income tax (CIT) is reduced by this amount. Tax reliefs for employee: Tax exemption from capital gains tax (CGT) for PPE funds. Possibility of transferring funds from PPE to IKE without paying CGT. Benefits paid from occupational pension schemes are exempt from personal income tax (PIT).	Tax exemption from capital Gains tax (CGT) up to a yearly limit of payments on IKE (1.5 average forecasted earnings for each year). Possibility of transfer Funds from IKE to PPE Without paying CGT.
Other supports	The contribution to PPE is free from additional costs (such as contributions to social insurance) for an employer. Control of Financial Supervising Authority over PPE in companies – when PPE is managed by internal Employees' Pension Fund and in external financial institutions which manage PPE, such as investment funds and life insurance companies.	Control of the Polish Financial Supervision Authority over financial institutions managing IKE accounts (life insurance companies, investment funds, banks and stock brokers companies).

3. There is also a possibility of leaving the IKE system before reaching retirement age. The financial institution responsible for the IKE (bank, life insurance company, investment funds company, stock broker office) might allow some payments before the due retirement age or a transfer of capital assets, but only for a period of one year after signing a contract. The IKE participant can withdraw funds (before reaching retirement age) only by taking a lump sum. Such a withdrawal is then subject to tax and the IKE account must be closed.

4. The law guarantees the possibility of cashing in an account aged 60 (or in the case of particular professional groups) without losing any tax incentives. However, it is also possible to have an IKE account for a longer period (until the age of 70) and accumulate more capital in the pension account.
5. Assets accumulated in IKE accounts may be inherited. A future pensioner may specify in a contract one person or more, who would inherit the accumulated lump sum in the event of death. Such a decision can be taken or changed during any point in the contract.

As already discussed, the state has introduced tax incentives for those entering IKE contracts. The IKE savings accounts is exempt from capital gains tax (CGT), but only up to a certain amount. This tax relief is limited to 1.5 times of the forecast of the average gross salary (this was equal to PLN3,521 in 2006 and PLN3,697 in 2007). The financial institutions which provide IKE pension accounts have spent relatively less money on promoting these products than the mandatory open pension funds (OFE) introduced in 1999. IKE savings accounts are promoted mostly only via the internet (on home web sides of the investment funds, life insurance companies, banks and brokerage offices which manage IKE accounts) and through personal selling as well as cross-selling with insurance or banking financial products.

In December 2006, most of the 840,200 IKE accounts were managed by insurance enterprises (634,600) of which the majority were managed by the biggest Polish insurance company – PZU Życie. However the average payment into an IKE contract managed by Polish insurance companies is the lowest for any management group. They amounted to PLN1226 (€331) in 2006. This is partly due to the way IKE accounts are structured by life insurance companies: only part of the payments are invested in capital funds, the other part is used to pay for life assurance. The average payment into an IKE of all types (four categories) in 2006 was PLN2199. At the same time over 144,000 thousands accounts were managed by investment fund companies, and about 53,200 by banks. The smallest number of accounts are operated by stock brokers 8,200, although payments into these accounts are the highest at PLN3211, €868).

The latest available data from 30 June 2007 (Figure 8.1) shows systematic but relatively slow growth in the number of IKE accounts and total assets. The relative share of different forms of Individual Pension Schemes is shown in Table 8.6. There is relatively little change over the period June 2006 to June 2007. The most popular are IKE schemes managed through life insurance companies and the least popular through banks. The most recent data shows that the number of IKE accounts in banks has decreased compared with the same period in 2006. This form of IKE has not been popular, because most of those with IKE accounts prefer accounts whose funds are invested directly on the Polish capital market, for example, those accounts provided by investment funds and life insurance companies.

Table 8.7 shows that at the end of June 2007, investment funds managed the largest proportion of assets in IKE accounts (46.6 per cent), even though their market share of individual IKE accounts was only 19.3 per cent. Insurance companies managed the second largest proportion of funds (37.7 per cent).

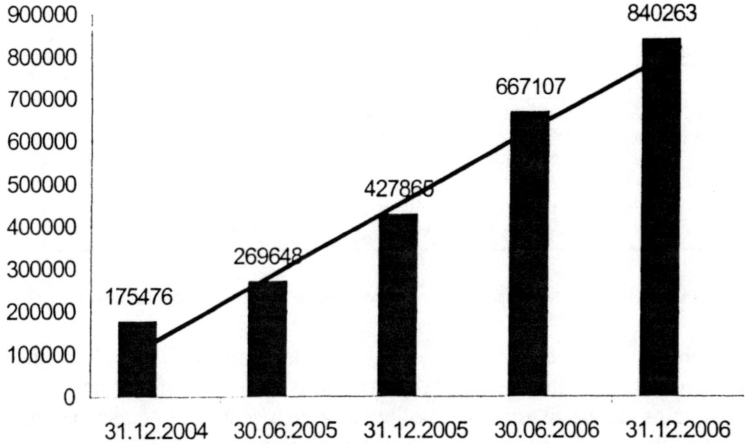

Source: Polish Financial Supervising Authority, Ministry of Labour and Social Policy.

Figure 8.1 Development of individual pension schemes, 2004 – 2006

Table 8.6 Number of IKE accounts 30 June 2006 –30 June 2007

Institution providing IKE accounts	Number of IKE Accounts ('000.)		Market share (%)		Change (%)
	June 2006	June 2007	June 2006	June 2007	2007/06
Insurance comp.s	484,912	659,232	72.7	74.4	135.9
Investment funds	121,179	171,208	18.2	19.3	141.3
Stock brokers	7,509	8,254	1.1	0.9	109.9
Banks	53,507	47,815	8.0	5.4	89.4
Total	667,107	886,509	100.0	100.0	132.9

Source: Polish Financial Supervising Authority, www.knf.gov.pl (accessed 15 December 2007).

Table 8.7 also shows that the total value of assets in IKE accounts in 2007 was PLN1.8 billion (€0.5 bn). This is not a large amount compared with the total value of assets of occupational pension funds of PLN 142.8 billion (€40 bn). IKE accounts own a very small proportion of the total value of shares quoted on the Polish stock exchange. This is in contrast with assets of mandatory pension funds which have a significant influence on the Warsaw Stock Exchange and on total investment in the Polish economy.

Table 8.7 Assets in IKE accounts June 2006–June 2007

Financial institution	Assets value ('000 PLN)		Share in total assets value (%)		Change (%)
	June 2006	June 2007	June 2006	June 2007	2007–2006
Insurance comps.	346,684	668,164	35.7	37.7	192.7
Investment funds	421,283	824,494	43.4	46.6	195.7
Stock broker comps.	57,435	90,844	5.9	5.1	158.2
Banks	144,822	186,784	14.9	10.6	129.0
Total	970,223	1,770,2860	100.0	100.0	182.5

Source: Polish Financial Supervising Authority, www.knf.gov.pl (accessed 15 December 2007)

The majority of those who save in IKE accounts are those with high income and/or wealth. For this group, tax allowances in terms of exemptions from capital gains tax are likely to be too low to give incentives to contribute to IKE accounts. However the majority of Polish employees have relatively low incomes, particularly in comparison with average salaries in the European Union. Over 95 per cent of incomes are taxed at the lowest tax rate. For this group the requirement to save large amounts which cannot be withdrawn before reaching retirement age is a disincentive.

There are different ways of accumulating funds within IKE accounts as shown in Table 8.8. The main differences are:

1. the scope of potential investment strategies;
2. level of investment risk;
3. the level of contributions;
4. the method of securing savings in case of potential bankruptcy of the company managing the account.

4. ANALYSIS

Public interest in IKE schemes has been much lower than government projections. Many experts have openly criticised the policy of pension provision via IKE schemes. For example Szumlicz has argued that the wrong pension 'philosophy' has been chosen and that the possibility of creating an additional source of old-pension income has not been realised. The new pension system for old-age pensions should be attractive for most future pensioners, and not just for those with the highest income.[15]

Table 8.8 Differences in individual forms of saving within individual pension schemes (IKE)

Institution	Risk	Expected return on capital	Level of contribution
Insurance companies	Depends on investment: from low to high	from low to high	Up to 150% of average earnings
Investment Funds	from low to high	from low to high	Up to 150% of average earnings
Banks	low	low	Up to 150% of average earnings
Stockbroker	high	high	Up to 150% of average earnings

Source: Based on Brzozowska and Dawidowicz (2007).

The reason for the poor development of IKE personal pensions requires deeper analysis. It is not just a problem with tax incentives and fiscal policy, but also with the overall costs of tax relief and costs to individuals (in terms of fees, charges, and so on) and returns to IKE accounts. Other determinants influencing the development of IKE pensions are the general awareness of Polish citizens of pension issues and the marketing and selling strategies of financial institutions which provide products for IKE system.

An assessment of the effectiveness of tax reliefs for pension provision through IKE accounts would require sophisticated financial projections and calculations. A very simple example proves that tax relief connected with IKE pension provision is relatively small. For instance, in 2007 the limit of IKE saving exempted from CGT amounted PLN3,670 per annum (about €966). The capital gains tax in Poland is at a rate of 19 per cent and applies not just to capital gains but to interest on deposits, as well as gains from Stock Exchange investments. Hence this relief amounts to an interest income exemption or an exemption from capital gains up to a specified amount. So, for a person who uses the full amount of tax reliefs (PLN3,670) and receives a 10 per cent gain after 12 months, the yearly relief from capital gains tax would amount to 19 per cent of PLN 36. This amounts to PLN69.73 (about €18.35). Only returns over a long time period (20 to 30 years) makes the exemption from capital gains tax relevant, because over a long period payments reinvested many times might generate interest payments significantly surpassing the capital paid up on the IKE account (see Table 8.9).

If an IKE account owner withdraws the lump sum even after 30 years of contributions (PLN62,679.48 from example given in Table 8.9), he or she would lose the tax relief (that is, PLN5,491.07 in the example given in Table 8.9). The risk of loss of tax relief (exemption from the capital gains tax) is large and clear to those who contribute to an IKE scheme, even though they may not understand other forms of risk connected with long-term savings and investments.

In reality, returns and the effect of tax relief will be lower. The IKE system participant must pay fees and charges to the financial institution managing an IKE account. For example, a 1 per cent handling charge (a distribution fee collected from each payment) means that contributions will be reduced by 1 per cent and the accumulated sum will be lower. The fee for asset management reduces the rate of return and any capital gain. For example, if the rate of return on IKE accounts is 5 per cent, then with an asset management fee of 1 per cent the rate of return will reduce to 4 per cent.

Table 8.9 A simulation of the effects of 30-year contributions to an IKE account (including tax relief)

Monthly payment (in PLN)	75.0
Rate of return	5.00%
Savings period (years)	30.0
Handling charge (from each payment)	0.0%
Fee for the assets management	0.0%
Final sum in PLN (accumulated capital plus interest), including:	62,679.48
Net payments in PLN (capital)	27,000.0
Gain in PLN	28,900.38
Effects of tax relief (19% capital gains tax rate) in PLN	5,491.07
Amount of extra pension paid from the third pillar (IKE) during 15 years (180 months) in PLN	348.22

Source: own calculation.

It is obvious that the microeconomic costs of IKE accounts – charges and fees payed by the participants – have a considerable impact on the development of individual pension accounts. The law establishing IKE accounts required the disclosure of all fees and charges. However the structure of fees and charges of different types of IKE accounts is not transparent. A comprehensive statement of fees and charges of all financial institutions managing IKE accounts is not available.[16]

In 2007 Individual Pension Schemes were managed by 13 out of a total 31 life insurance companies operating in Poland, by 14 out of 29 investment funds, by 4 out of 48 stock broking companies (including 10 banks providing stock broking services) and by 8 out of 68 commercial banks including 3 co-operative banks. It can be assumed that the fees and charges are more or less similar in the same type of financial institution managing IKE accounts. Competition in this segment of the financial market in Poland is not intense and financial institutions providing IKE pension accounts are not under competitive pressure to reduce fees and charges.

The calculations shown in Table 8.10 show that the return on IKE accounts in 2007 (including the capital gains tax exemption) was generally lower than the return on investments in government bonds (which do not have an associated tax incentive). The only exception in the Personal Pension Schemes examined was an IKE managed by Skarbiec Akcja investment fund. In addition an IKE account in PKO BP brokerage office was more profitable than an investment in government bonds for some investors.

In short the tax relief for IKE pension accounts is not sufficient to increase returns net of costs compared with returns on government bonds. A simple and easy investment in government bonds (with greater liquidity and lower risk) had higher returns. The real winners from the introduction of IKE accounts were not future pensioners but the financial institutions because of their profits from fees and charges.

The results of this analysis lead to the conclusion that tax relief from CGT is relevant only over a long period for an IKE account. Thus the incentive to contribute to IKE accounts for future retirement income is relatively weak.

People who contribute to Individual Pension Schemes do not obtain tax relief from personal income tax (PIT) on their payments to IKE accounts. Many experts in Poland consider that giving a tax exemption on contributions to IKE accounts would create greater incentives and thus increase both flows of funds into IKE accounts and coverage, although at a greater cost in terms of tax expenditures. Traditionally, Polish citizens have been very responsive to opportunities to reduce personal income tax. The experience with tax relief for investments in treasury bonds (a tax relief that does not exist any more) shows that such tax incentive could be very attractive and efficient. A key issue is the cost in terms of tax foregone in changing from tax incentives based on capital gains tax relief to personal income tax (PIT) relief. The cost in terms of the decrease of state tax revenues is dependent on the number of IKE participants, the amounts contributed and the rate of return on IKE accounts. It will also depend on how much of the IKE contributions are shifted from other forms of savings and investments. The simulation prepared in the Ministry of Labur and Social Policy in 2002, before the IKE system was put into operation, assumed that 90 per cent of persons with the highest income (the third tax group) would use the tax relief and transfer part of their contributions from other forms of personal savings into IKE accounts, thus reducing tother forms of personal saving. The simulation assumed that 70 per cent of those on average and higher income (the second tax group) would join IKE schemes, but that this would result in only 50 per cent of 'new money', the other 50 per cent consisting of a transfer from existing savings schemes. Those with lower income (the first tax group in Poland) were assumed to contribute just 20 per cent of 'new money' to IKE system (the rest shifted from other forms of savings). With these

Table 8.10 Returns on IKE savings accounts managed through chosen financial institutions in Poland over the period January 2001–December 2007

Financial Institution	Yearly max. payment into IKE savings account in 2007	Fees and charges of financial institution providing IKE	Return on IKE savings account (with the exemption from capital gains tax) Final value of IKE savings after a year	Benchmark - return on Gov.bonds (subject to capital gains tax)
1	2	3	4	5
IKE from Skarbiec Kasa – Investment Fund of Monetary Market	PLN 3697	0.9% charge for managing assets (calculated on the value of units of the investment fund) no handling charge	3.63 % – 0.9% = 2.73% PLN 3697+ PLN3697 x 2% = 3697(1+ 0.0273) PLN = PLN 3797.93	4.2% – 0.19(4.2) ≅ 3.40% (interest on Gov. bonds minus 19% capital gains tax) PLN 3,697 + 3,697 x 3.4% = PLN 3,697 (1 + 0.034) =PLN 3,823
IKE based On Skarbiec Akcja – Investment Fund of Stocks (Shares)	PLN 3,697	4.0% charge for managing assets (calculated on the value of units of the investment fund) no handling charge	10.39% – 4.0% = 6.39% (return on investment in stocks minus asset management fee) PLN3697 + (3697 x 6.3%) = PLN 3697(1 + 0.0639) = PLN 3953.20	3.40% PLN 3,823
PZU IKE (IKE managed through PZU life insurance company) PZU FIO POLONEZ (PZU investment fund of bonds)	PLN 3,697	1.5% charge for managing assets (calculated on the value of units of the investment fund) 3.4% handling charge (collected from every payment)* PLN50 – yearly contribution for life insurance	1.7% – 1.5% = 0.2% (return on investment in stocks minus asset management fee) PLN 3,697 – PLN 3 697 x 3.4% – 50 PLN = PLN 3521 (yearly payment on IKE minus fees and charges) PLN 3,521 + PLN 3,521x 0.2 = PLN 3,521 x (1 + 0.002) = PLN 3,528 (yearly payment on IKE minus fees and charges multiplied by annual rate ofreturn of the Polonez open investment fund)	3.40% PLN 3,823

Table 8.10 (continued)

PZU IKE (managed by PZU life insurance) PZU FIO KRAKOWIAK (PZU investment fund of shares)	PLN 3,697 4.0% asset management fee 3.4% handling charge PLN 50 – yearly contribution for life insurance		.25% – 4.0%= 4.25% PLN 3,697 – PLN3 697 x 3.4% – PLN50 = PLN3521.31 PLN 3,521.31 (1+ 0.0425) = PLN 3,670.96	3.40% PLN 3,823
PKO BP SUPER IKE (managed by PKO BP Bank)	PLN 3,697	no handling charge	3.3% PLN 3,697+ (3,697 x 3.3%)= PLN 3,697(1 + 0.033) = PLN 3,709.20	3.40% PLN3,823
IKE DM PKO BP (savings account in PKO Brokerage Office)	PLN 3,697	0.25% of assets value yearly – fee for providing IKE brokerage account	Rate of return dependent on yearly change of value of the chosen securities listed on the Warsaw Stock Exchange. In 2007 the index of the Warsaw Stock Exchange (WIG) increased 5.2%, but some shares by more than 50%. There were also many shares which lost value. Hence precise calculation of returns on IKE held in brokerage offices is not possible. Some investors may have had returns of more than 20% in 2007.	3.40% PLN3,823

Note:
a The calculation assumes that the yearly limit of payments into an IKE account (3697 PLN in 2007) is paid in one lump sum (one payment at the beginning of January).

Source: Data from individual financial institutions, own calculations.

assumptions, and assuming 1.7 million participants, pay 1.5 per cent of average earnings annually into an IKE account, the cost of the capital gains tax relief would reach PLN16 million, and assuming 3.5 million participants, PLN26 million. The expected cost of tax relief for the first year was PLN 8.3 million – a relatively modest amount.[17] The simulation took into consideration the alternative costs of another possible tax incentive: the tax relief from personal income tax (PIT) paid every year. The authors of the exercise assumed that this alternative cost of tax relief would be much higher (more than PLN400 million in three years) and would be too expensive for the state budget. The expert opinion did not consider the cost of IKE accounts to individuals (for example, charges and fees paid to financial institutions). The simulation exercise assumed the existing institutional structure and law relating to IKE accounts. In reality, the costs of tax relief were much lower, because the number of IKE accounts is less then 1 million, and not the assumed 3.5 million.

The Ministry of Finance has rejected the possibility of introducing tax relief from personal income tax in 2006 and in 2007. Instead, the Ministry of Labour and Policy has prepared a new concept of tax relief for IKE savings. This new concept includes the old concept of tax incentives but with new conditions. These include higher annual payment limits exempted from capital gains tax and a new possibility of partial withdrawal of assets from IKE accounts without losing the tax incentive for the remainder of the capital left in an IKE pension account.

5. DETERMINANTS OF THE DEVELOPMENT OF INDIVIDUAL PENSION SCHEMES

The development of Individual Pension Schemes in Poland has been influenced by various factors at the level of the State and the individual. There are also institutional, legal, and demographic factors as well as more subjective and more difficult to measure, psychological factors.

The decision to open an IKE account and on the choices available with IKE accounts depend on the following key variables.

1. Insurance awareness.
2. Material status.
3. Age of the potential pensioner.
4. Level of knowledge of the reformed pension system in Poland and Polish financial markets.
5. Knowledge of state incentives to participate in the Individual Pension Account System.

The choice of particular Individual Pension Schemes is also determined by the level of costs faced by individuals associated with each scheme, for example, financial institutions' commissions, trading costs and costs of maintaining the account.

Awareness of the necessity to participate in additional voluntary pension systems has become more common in Poland, if adequate retirement incomes are to be achieved. However pension awareness in itself may not be sufficient to encourage less wealthy persons to save money in a systematic, long-term way in order to increase their retirement income.

Those who advocated the introduction of personal pensions in Poland IKE argued that they would have mass appeal. However only those whose incomes are above the average national average have opened IKE accounts. Wealthy persons in Poland (as in other countries) have numerous opportunities to use various forms of saving and investment, which are much more flexible than Individual Pension Schemes and do not need special tax incentives for personal pension provisions.

The level of knowledge about capital markets and IKE products linked to capital markets has been relatively low. A poor government information campaign when the new supplementary pension system (IKE) was introduced in 2004 and relatively low interest by financial institutions in promote the new product resulted in only persons especially well-informed persons, have decided to open an Individual Pension Scheme.

6. CONCLUSION

Most factors determining development of personal pension provisions in Poland might be called barriers rather than development opportunities.

The main barriers to the development of Individual Pension Schemes development are:

1. lack of sufficient economic and financial incentives to save within Individual Pension Schemes. A limited exemption from the 19 per cent capital gains tax is not a sufficient incentive, furthermore, costs connected with such accounts in financial institutions reduce the significance of this tax incentive;
2. IKE savings accounts are not well targeted; they are not attractive enough for low earners;
3. the IKE account viewed as a long-time savings product is not sufficiently flexible;
4. the hidden costs of managing IKE accounts through financial institutions which decrease returns on this savings account;
5. the overall level of average earnings and savings in Poland, which is much lower than in most EU countries,
6. the costs of early withdrawal of part of all the accumulated lump sum before the age of 60;
7. the regulations on institutions offering Individual Pension Schemes which are overly burdensome;
8. a poor level of support and information provided by financial institutions to those with IKE accounts;
9. the failure by public institutions to provide detailed and accurate information about IKE accounts.

On the other hand, with reform Individual Pension Schemes could be become more widespread in Poland and could be a means for certain individuals to provide retirement income.

1. IKE accounts provide flexibility in relation to the sort of assets that may be held.
2. There is an option to change from one kind IKE account to another.
3.. The fact that in the event of an account holders death, IKE assets may be inherited by a spouse, and so on.
4. The possibility of paying varying amounts into an IKE account.

From our analysis a general conclusion can be made that IKE accounts are not attractive to an average member of an existing pension scheme. The current structure and incentives available to participate in an UKE scheme in particular can be criticised.

In order to improve take-up the following changes should be made.

1. In order to make IKE accounts more attractive consideration should be given to switching to a tax incentive based on income tax rather than on capital gains tax.
2. Allow the withdrawal of a lump sum which would not affect the value of existing capital gains tax allowances.
3. Simplify the procedures and requirements for financial institutions which manage IKE accounts.

It would also be necessary to devote considerable resources to to inform individuals on IKE pension plans. Hence, participation in IKE schemes needs to be extensively supported by the State. This is particularly important for persons with average and lower earnings. The development of occupational pension schemes (so-called Employee Pension Plans) cannot be treated as an alternative to individual pension provisions. Poland is different from many other EU countries in that there is no pressure from employees or representative organisations (especially trade unions) to create occupational pension schemes. Employees are more likely to seek demand more earnings in the short-term than additional pension provision in the future.

In conclusion it is not only the IKE system, but the whole concept of the third pillar pension system in Poland that needs to be deeply reconsidered and modified.

NOTES

1. *Social Insurance in Poland. Information, facts (*2006), ZUS, Warsaw, pp. 34–38. accident insurance.
2. ZUS (Social Insurance Institution) plays a crucial role not only in the pension system (old and new) but also in the whole social insurance system in Poland. The Social Insurance Institution,

among others, establishes the entitlement to and pays on a monthly basis pensions to approximately 7.2 million people, it establishes the entitlement to and pays sickness allowances, maternity allowances, care allowances, compensatory allowances, rehabilitation benefts, death grants. It also conducts medical examinations and takes decisions on entitlement to social insurance benefts.

3. Wiktorow, A. (2007), p. 485.
4. Góra, M. (2003a), p. 8.
5. The initial capital is a new element of the Polish old-age pension scheme. This capital means accounting for the period of paying contributions 1 January 1999, for persons aged not more than 50 years. It is assessed for each insured person born after 31 December 1948 who has been paying before 1999 a contribution to the social insurance or for whom such contribution was paid by the contribution payer. For each of these persons a theoretical old-age pension will be calculated, that the insured person would have received on 1 January 1999. The amount of the initial capital is recorded on the account of the insured person, and together with pension contributions is a subject to indexation starting from 1 June 2000 up to the moment of retirement of the insured person. Explanation based on: *Social Insurance in Poland. Information, facts (*2006), op. cit., p. 38.
6. According to the Law on Organisation and Operation of Pension Funds from 18 August 1997 (Journal of Laws No. 139/97, position 934) 'a fund is a legal person'. The scope of activities of a Fund is the collection and investment of finacial resources intended for payment of cash benefits to members who have attained pension age. A Funds governing body is a Pension Fund Society, established in accordance with the provisions of the Law.' http://www.knf.gov.pl/en/ /Images /ustawa_OFE_eng_tcm21-5092.pdf (accessed: 10 December 2007).
7. Barr, M., Ekonomia polityki społecznej (The Economics of the Welfare State), translatiopn by M.Żukowski, Akademia Ekonomiczna w Poznaniu (Poznań Univeristy of Economics), Poznań 1993, pp. 231–2.
8. Chlon, A., Góra, M., Rutkowski, M. (1999).
9. Fultz, E. (2004), p. 57. See also Stopy zastąpienia. Projekcje stóp zastąpienia w nowym systemie emerytalnym (Replacement rates. Projections of the replacement rates in new pension system, Urząd Nadzoru na Funduszami Emerytalnymi (State Supervising Authority of Penson Funds, which has been later on integrated with other supervising institutions of Polish financial market in Polish Financial Supervising Authority), Warsaw 2002, pp. 60–70.
10. Rynek pracowniczych programów emerytalnych w 2006 roku (Market of occupational pension funds in Poland in 2006), www. knf.gov.pl, Warsaw, September 2006 (accessed 10 December 2007).
11. IKE na koniec roku 2006 (IKE at the end of 2006*)*, www.mps.gov.pl (accessed 10 January 2007).
12. Ustawa o pracowniczych programach emerytalnych (Law on Occupational Pension Schemes), Journal of Laws, 2004, No. 116, item 1207, http://ks.sejm.gov.pl/proc4/ustawy/855_u.htm (accessed: 15.12.2007). Ustawa o indywidualnych kontach emerytalnych (Law on Individual Pension Schems), Journal of Laws, 2004, No. 116, item 1205, http://www.mps.gov.pl/pliki _do_pobrania/240831 (accessed: 15.12.2007).
13. Data from Ministry of Labour and Social Politics, www. http://www.mps.gov.pl (accessed: 10 December 2007).
14. Szumlicz, T. (2006), pp. 265–6.
15. Financial institutions enclose only general information about fees and charges to the IKE arrangements and send back to other documents for details (for example fees and charges defined in statutes on investment fund company). Polish Financial Supervising Authority does not gather data about fees and charges collected through financial institutions form IKE savings accounts.
16. Szumlicz T. (2006), pp. 264–5.

REFERENCES

Barr, M.(1993), Ekonomia polityki społecznej (The Economics of the Welfare State), translated by M. Żukowski, Akademia Ekonomiczna w Poznaniu (Poznań Univeristy of Economics), Poznań 1993.

Brzozowska, K., and Dawidowicz, D. (2007), *III filar systemu emerytalnego w Polsce – próba oceny, maszynopis niepublikowany* (Third pillar of pension system in Poland – estimation trial, unpublished manuscript), Gdańsk.

Chlon, A., Góra, M., and Rutkowski, M. (1999) , *Shaping Pension Reform in Poland: Security through Diversity*, Social Protection Discussion Paper, No. 9923.

Fultz, E. (2004), 'Pension Privatisation in Hungary and Poland: A Comparative Overview', in Hughes, G. and Stewart, J., (eds), *Reforming Pensions in Europe. Evolution of Pension Financing and Sources of Retirement Income*, Cheltenham U.K., Northhampton, MA, USA.: Edward Elgar Publishing.

Góra, M. (2003a), 'The New Polish Pension System: An Example of a Non-Orthodox Approach to Pension Reform', PIE Discussion Paper Series No. 168, Tokyo: The Institute of Economic Research, Hitotsubashi University.

Góra, M. (2003b), *System emerytalny (Pension System)*, Warsaw: Polskie Wydawnictwo Ekonomiczne (Polish Economics Publishing Company).

Hanau, P., Steinmeyer, H.-D., Wank, R. (2002) Handbuch des europäischen Arbeits –und Sozialrechts (HEAS), München: Beck Verlag.

Kalabarczyk P., 'Indywidualne Konta emerytalne – analiza przypadku. Reforma systemu emerytalnego – ucieczka do przodu' (Individual Pension Schemes – case analysis. Pension system reorganisation as a runaway forward), forum: *Polski rynek kapitałowy w Europie XXI wieku* (Polish Capital market in Europe of the XXI century), Warsaw, 18 January 2005.

Kowalski J. (2004), 'IKE – stracona szansa na lepsze emerytury?' (Individual Pension Schemes: Lost Chance for Better Pensions?), 'Gazeta Ubezpieczeniowa' (Insurance Newspaper), 17 November.

Ministry of Labour and Social Policy (2005), Projects of Changes in Acts: on Individual Pension Schemes and on Occupational Pension Schemes, available at http://www.mps.gov.pl.

National Bank of Poland (2006), Rozwój rynku finansowego w Polsce w 2005 roku (Development of Polish Financial Market in 2005), Warsaw, available at http://www.nbp.gov.pl.

Ostrowska, K. (2005), 'Indywidualne konto emerytalne. Skazani na porażkę' (Individual Pension Schemes. Fated to Loose), *Rzeczpospolita* (Republic), 5 September.

Schmähl, W., Horstmann S. (2002), *Transformation of Pension Systems in Central and Eastern Europe*, Cheltenham U.K., Northhampton, MA, USA.: Edward Elgar Publishing.

Stopy zastąpienia (2002), *Projekcje stóp zastąpienia w nowym systemie emerytalnym* (Projections of Replacement Ratios in the New Pension System in Poland), Warsaw: Urząd Nadzoru nad Funduszami Emerytalnymi (Supervising Authority on Pension Funds).

Szczepański, M. (2006), Dylematy reformy polskiego systemu emerytalnego (Dilemmas of Polish Pension System transition), Poznań: Wydawnictwo Politechniki Poznańskiej (Poznań University of Technology Publishers).

Szczepański, M. (2007), 'Rentenreformen in Polen und Deutschland. Gemeinsame Herausforderungen, verschiedene Strategien', *Osteuropa Wirtschaft*, 3/2007, pp. 223–48.

Szumlicz, T (2006), *Ubezpieczenia społeczne. Teoria dla praktyki (Social Insurances. Theory for Practice)*, Bydgoszcz-Warsaw : Oficyna Wydawnicza Branta,.

Walczykiewicz, B. (2004), 'Indywidualne konta emerytalne' (Individual Pension Schemes), *Służba Pracownicza* (Workers' Service), number 10.

Wiktorow, A. (2007), 'Pension Reform in Poland', *The Geneva Papers*, No. 32.

Żukowski, M. (2006), Reformy emerytalne w Europie (Reforms of Retirement Pensions in Europe), Wydawnictwo Akademii Ekonomicznej w Poznaniu (Poznań University of Economics Publishers), Poznań. ZUS, Warsaw: Social Insurance in Poland.

Information, ZUS.
Żytniewski, M (2006). Statement during a conference 'Capital Pension Insurances in Poland: Prospects for a Citizen, Entrepreneur and System Operator', 28 November, Warsaw.

PART II

Public Policy and Private Provision

9. The Matthew Effect: Why Current Pension Policy Helps the Rich Get Richer

Kim De Witte, Paul Roels and Yves Stevens

1. INTRODUCTION

This chapter examines individual voluntary pension provision (IVPP) in Belgium. Various forms of individual pension provision are compared with one another. IVPP is popular in Belgium because of tax incentives. Due to the Belgian tax regime, the exact size of the tax incentive is not transparent for most people. Only tax specialists are in a position to estimate the size of the incentives available. The chapter tries to clarify the issue of the size and hence the cost of tax incentives for personal pension provision.

The effect of tax incentives for pension provision in Belgium is to contribute in an important way to what is referred to as the 'Matthew effect'. Middle or higher income classes tend to be the main beneficiaries of social benefits and services, even if these are primarily targeted at the poor. This chapter argues the same is true of tax incentives, in particular those associated with personal pension provision. The main beneficiaries are higher income groups. This raises issues of the effectiveness of tax policy in relation to personal pensions as a tool of social policy. Tax incentives for pension provision should be justified in the overall context of the welfare state and social justice. This chapter will analyse some data on the profiles of the beneficiaries of the tax incentives for IVPP. This analysis will also clarify the position of IVPP in the overall old age income distribution of retired persons in Belgium.

2. THE MATTHEW EFFECT

The Matthew effect refers to a sentence in a parable in the Gospel of Matthew:

'For unto every one that hath shall be given, and he shall have abundance: but From him that hath not shall be taken away even that which he hath.[1] The parable deals with a sower of seed. His seeds fall on all kinds of soil: roads, rocks and thorns as well as on good soil. For Christians the seeds symbolise the word of God that, although it is spread to everyone, is only received by those whose heart and mind is open. In social policy it means that the effect of the seeds – the policy measures targeted at particular groups – will only benefit those that are aware of the measures and live in conditions that allow them to benefit from them.

In social policy the Matthew effect is seen as creating inequality. Legal systems regard all people as equal, but this equality rule leads in practise to another inequality. Due to socio-cultural and socio-political factors, those with higher incomes will benefit relatively more from social policy measures than those with lower incomes. In general, persons with higher incomes have greater opportunities to claim legal rights. This is because they have more personal resources and greater access to resources. Through social contact and position they also have greater opportunity to claim legal rights. Legally these rights are the same for lower incomes, but they lack the possibility or experience to claim them. For example, legally everybody has the same possibility of participating in pension savings and of benefiting from associated tax allowances. However in order to be able to contribute to a pension, income is first needed. Obviously, not everybody has the same opportunities for earning income and benefiting from the associated tax allowances.[2]

Public, Private and Social Goods

In economics a public good is defined as a good that is non-rival in consumption and non-excludable. This means that consumption of the good by one individual does not reduce the amount of the good available for consumption by others and no one can be effectively excluded from using that good (for example clean air, national defense, public fireworks and so on). A private good is the opposite of a public good: it is excludable (for example to those who have not paid for it) and rival in consumption (consumption by one consumer prevents simultaneous consumption by other consumers).

A social or merit good is a private good for which consumption is stimulated by the government for various reasons, including social policy. A society decides that individuals should have a particular social good on the basis of a norm other than responding just to consumer preferences. This norm could be the public interest, common well-being or general welfare. A social good would be under-consumed in a free market economy. Because of its positive externalities, consumption is stimulated by the government through social policy measures.[3]

Is Voluntary Pension Provision in Belgium a Social Good?

Belgian individual voluntary pension provision is not a public good (IVPP). A participant in IVPP is only entitled to returns and contributions on their own pension scheme and the consumption from this pension scheme excludes consumption by others. In other words, IVPP schemes in Belgium are excludable and rival in consumption and can therefore be considered as a private good. A question arises can IVPP schemes be considered a social good? Various reasons can be found to promote and stimulate pension savings. For instance, governments could assume citizens to be myopic. Or governments could anticipate that state pensions will not be maintained in real terms in the future, due to demographic and socio-political changes. To evaluate a good as a social good, the scope and the budgetary cost of the policy measures are also relevant. Therefore the question arises, whether and to what extent Belgian IVPP can be considered as a social good. This is the first issue to be considered in this chapter.

A Matthew Effect Within Belgian IVPP?

If Belgian IVPP can be considered as a social good, the question that arises is what means are used to stimulate demand for IVPP schemes in Belgium? The answer is tax policy. The incentive to participate to Belgian IVPP is given via tax allowances, resulting in a reduction in income tax. The choice of this instrument for social policy, means that higher income categories will benefit more than lower ones. This is for a number of reasons. First, the legislation concerning tax allowances for Belgian IVPP is very complicated, thus excluding those without detailed knowledge of the tax system or the resources to pay for tax advice. Second, in order to obtain a tax reduction, one must pay taxes first, and the higher an individual's income the greater the tax saving.

The Matthew effect is related to the distribution of social goods. The presence of the Matthew effect does not mean that social goods are distributed in the same way as private goods in a free market economy. The distribution of social goods would be much more unequal if there were no social policy. The Matthew effect means social inequalities that are at the basis of unequal distribution in the free market economy continue to work in the distribution of social goods. In other words, the Matthew effect means that the actual distribution of social goods differs from the normative distribution, that is the distribution originally planned by social policy. This inequality in practice can only be overcome by introducing a more selective social policy so that the differences in opportunities to benefit from a particular policy are legally translated into rules requiring unequal distribution and applied to different income categories. Whether and to what extent the Matthew effect is present within Belgian IVPP is the second main question to be answered in this chapter.

3. THE MAIN FORMS OF INDIVIDUAL VOLUNTARY PENSION PROVISION IN BELGIUM

Different forms of individual voluntary pension provision exist in Belgium. The main forms are via life insurance, pension savings and voluntary pensions for the self-employed. The common features of these different forms are: the voluntary character of participation; the contributory character of funding; and the management of the assets by private operators, such as insurance companies or financial institutions.

Tax Allowances

If certain conditions are fulfilled, specific tax allowances apply. These incentives distinguish IVPP from ordinary long-term saving. Within each form of IVPP, retirement and survivors' benefits can be agreed upon, either separately or combined. This chapter only focuses on the retirement benefits.

One feature of the tax allowances for personal pension provision is that they can be cumulated. In other words, a household can benefit at the same time from tax allowances for a life insurance or mortgage, from the tax allowances for pension savings and in the case of a self-employed worker, from tax allowances for voluntary pension for self-employed.

Individual Life Insurance

The main characteristics of individual life insurance agreement is that an annuity or lump sum is provided at the moment the insured person dies or reaches a certain age. Individual life insurance is accessible for everybody, irrespective of professional status. An individual life insurance agreement is financed by premiums paid by the subscriber. The size of the premiums is agreed and stated in the insurance contract.[4] The premiums are invested in so-called 'with profit insurance contracts' that guarantee a capital value, based on a fixed interest rate.[5] The subscriber can within the same basket of tax incentives also choose investment in real estate through a tax incentive based on a mortgage loan and debt insurance that is linked to the mortgage loan.

The tax allowances for individual life insurance only apply if the following conditions are met.[6]

1. The taxpayer must be the insured person and the beneficiary of the retirement benefit.[7]
2. The contract must be contracted by the taxpayer before the age of 65.
3. The contract must have a minimum duration of 10 years.
4. The contract has to expire at the earliest by the age of 65.[8]
5. Only products with a guaranteed investment return are eligible for tax allowances.

Mortgage repayments for one dwelling are also eligible for tax allowances. More or less the same tax allowances apply as for personal pensions. The maximum amount on which tax allowances can be obtained (subject to certain limits mentioned below) is determined jointly by life insurance and mortgage payments. In other words, if a household already has a high mortgage, it may be impossible to obtain a further tax allowance for life insurance products.[9]

The calculation of tax allowances on life insurance premia is complex. The holder of an individual life insurance policy is entitled to a tax allowance on her premiums, in the form of a tax reduction, deducted from taxes due on earned income after calculation of the final income tax due by the policy holder.[10]

The amount of the tax reduction is calculated as a percentage of the premiums paid in a particular tax year. This percentage is based on a special tax rate, the so-called ameliorated average tax rate. The ameliorated average tax rate is based on the average tax rate applicable to the taxpayer's income, without taking into account the tax relief in relation to family members for the taxpayer.[11] If the ameliorated average tax rate is lower than 30 per cent, a minimum percentage of 30 per cent will be allowed as a tax deduction. If the ameliorated average tax rate is higher than 40 per cent, a maximum percentage of 40 per cent will be allowed as a tax deduction.

Life insurance premiums that are allowed as a tax deduction are limited to 15 per cent of the first income tax bracket of €1,660 plus 6 per cent of the remaining net taxable earned income. An absolute maximum of €,1990 per year may be deducted against tax. Net taxable earned income is defined as earned income after deduction of associated costs and other amounts determined in the Income Tax Act.[12] The allowance of €1,660 is a non-indexed amount stated in tax law. The maximum amount of €1,990 is an indexed amount (income year 2008, tax year 2009).[13]

Given the above mentioned restrictions, the maximum tax reduction a contributor to life insurance with a taxable income of more than €30,676.50 is entitled to is equal to €796 per year (for the income year 2008 and tax year 2009).[14]

If life insurance premiums or even a part of these premiums lead to a tax reduction, the benefits of the insurance contract will be taxed.[15] The applicable tax treatment is that of the so-called special tax regime for long-term savings.

Different tax rates also apply depending on the age of the taxpayer at the moment of payment of the benefits. If the benefits are paid five years prior to the expiration of the contract, which currently occurs in almost all cases, once the contributor reaches the age of 60, a tax is levied on the surrender value of the contract at that moment. The tax rate in this case is 10 per cent.[16] This tax is paid by the insurer. Once this tax is paid, the benefits are free of income tax for the individual. This means that premiums paid between the age of 60 and 65, will trigger a tax reduction without further taxation of the benefits.[17]

Returns that derive from participation in the profits of the insurance company (profit sharing) are not taxed as part of the personal income tax of the beneficiary, if they are paid at the same time as other benefits.[18]

Example

In the case of a person with a net earned income of €25,000, the maximum amount of life insurance premiums that will be taken into consideration for tax allowances is 15 per cent × €1,660 + 6 per cent × (€25,000 − €1,660) = €1,649.40. Suppose that the special average tax rate for this person is equal to 35 per cent. A tax reduction of €1,649.40 × 35 per cent = €577.29, will apply. The taxpayer will be able to deduct an amount of €577.29 from her taxes to be paid in the appropriate tax year.

In the case of an insured amount or a surrender value of the life insurance contract of €100,000 at the age of 65, the surrender value will be taxed at 10 per cent on a once off basis (if the above mentioned conditions are fulfilled). The total taxation of the benefits from the life insurance contract will be €10,000.

Pension Savings

Pension savings is the generic term for three forms of long-term saving that benefit from a same special tax regime: (1) pension savings insurance; (2) collective pension savings; and (3) individual pension savings.[19] Pension savings are accessible for everybody. Pension savings insurance is very similar to individual life insurance. The main differences relates to tax allowances. Only the products with a guaranteed investment return are eligible for tax allowances.[20] Pension savings accounts and individual pension savings are offered by financial institutions (mainly banks). Contributions for pension savings accounts are used to buy units in investment funds. These funds are popular because they allow a wide choice of assets and risks. Contributions for individual pension savings are invested in shares chosen by the individual.

Tax allowances for pension savings may be claimed only if the following conditions are fulfilled.[21]

1. The insurance contract must be concluded or the account must be opened by a resident of the EEA between the age of 18 and 65.
2. The contributor must be the beneficiary of the life cover.
3. The contract has to be concluded or the account has to be opened for a minimum duration of 10 years.
4. Payments during a taxable period may only be made for one account or insurance contract.

The pension saver is entitled to a tax allowance on contributions in the form of a tax reduction, which is from taxes due on earned income.[22] The reduction is applied after calculation of the final income tax due by the pension saver.

The amount of the tax reduction is calculated in the same way as a tax reduction for life insurance premiums, that is as a percentage of the contributions paid for pension savings in a particular tax year. This percentage is based on a special tax rate, the so-called ameliorated average tax rate. The ameliorated average tax rate is based on the average tax rate applicable to the taxpayer's income, without taking into account the tax relief for the family situation of the taxpayer.[23] If the ameliorated average tax rate is lower than 30 per cent, a minimum of 30 per cent will be allowed as a tax reduction. If the ameliorated average tax rate is higher than 40 per cent, a maximum of 40 per cent will be allowed.[24]

The contributions taken into account are capped at a maximum of €830 per year.[25] Therefore, the maximum tax allowance a contributor can obtain is €324 per year (indexed amount for the tax year 2007).[26]

Benefits are taxed at a rate of 10 per cent if the payment takes place at the normal retirement age (65 years for men and until 1 January 2009, 64 years for women).[27] Payments that result from profit sharing are not taxed if paid at the same time as the other benefits.[28]

Example

The maximum amount of pension savings a person can contribute is €830, which is independent of income. Suppose that the special average tax rate for this person is equal to 35 per cent. A tax reduction of €830 × 35 per cent = €290.50 will apply. The taxpayer will be able to deduct an amount of €290.50 from taxes to be paid in the tax year involved. Suppose that the accumulated sum of pension savings is €50,000 at the age of 65, this amount will then be taxed at 10 per cent on a once-off basis (if the above mentioned conditions are fulfilled). The total taxation on the accumulated sum of pension savings benefits is €5,000.

Voluntary Pensions for the Self-employed

A specific individual voluntary pension provision (IVPP) for the self-employed was introduced in Belgium because state pensions for self-employed workers in Belgium were low.[29] [30] This pension provision is available for self-employed workers and their helpers (including a helping spouse), who pay the necessary social security contribution to the social security scheme for the self-employed.[31]

Self-employed workers who wish to participate in a voluntary pension have two options: either they pay extra contributions to their social insurance fund, which will use these contributions for an individual life insurance;[32] or they pay the contributions directly to an insurance company.[33]

Pension agreements for voluntary pensions for the self-employed are no more than individual life insurance schemes designed to a specific model set up by Belgian law. The self-employed workers pay contributions. These contributions are considered as individual accrued reserves. A guaranteed return is provided with respect to the net contributions.[34]

Tax allowances for voluntary pensions for self-employed persons apply only if the following conditions are fulfilled.

1. No surrender of the accrued reserves before the age of 60.
2. Payment of a yearly minimum contribution of €100.
3. Payment of the social security contributions in accordance with social regulations for the self-employed.

Tax allowances for voluntary saving only apply when the accumulated sum of contributions cannot be surrendered before the age of 60.[35] Earlier surrender is not allowed.[36] The contributions paid are considered as contributions based on social law.[37] As a consequence, these contributions are entirely deductible as costs against income. They thus reduce taxable income. There is no contribution tax applicable.

The contributions a self-employed worker is allowed to pay are capped at 8.17 per cent of earned income. This is subject to an absolute maximum of €2,686.05 (indexed amount for the tax year 2008).[38] The contribution rate of 8.17 per cent is increased to 9.40 per cent and a maximum absolute amount of €3,090.44 for so-called 'social pension agreements'.[39]

A distinction must be made between payment as a lump sum and payment as an annuity with respect to the taxation of pension benefits. Payment as a lump sum is converted for tax reasons in a fictive annuity, calculated as a percentage of the lump sum. This percentage will depend on the starting age of retirement, 3.5 per cent at the age of 60 and 5 per cent at the age of 65. If the person remains in active work until the age of 65, the fictive annuity will be calculated on only 80 per cent of the lump sum instead of 100 per cent. In other words, the fictive annuity will as a consequence become 4 per cent of the lump sum.

The amount of the yearly (fictive) annuity is added to other income and taxed at the normal rates which are progressive with income. The fictive annuity must only be declared during a given number of years:[40] That is 13 years if the lump sum is paid before the age of 65 and 10 years if the lump sum is paid at the age of 65.

If the pension is not paid as a lump sum, but as an annuity, the amount of the annuity is added to the rest of the income and taxed at the progressive tax rates on income. Discussion exists over whether the payments of pension benefits are subject to a special social security tax of 3.55 per cent.[41] In addition, a municipal tax is applicable. In Belgium each municipal authority has the right to charge tax. This tax is expressed as a per cent of the income tax. The per cent is determined by each municipality and varies between 0 and 12 per cent with an average around 7 per cent.

Example

For a self-employed person with a gross earned income of €30,000, the maximum amount of contributions that can be paid is equal to €30,000 × 8.17 per cent = €2,451.[42] These contributions are considered as costs in earning income. They may be deducted from gross earned income. Net taxable income will thus decrease by €2,541.

If it is assumed that the accumulated sum of contributions at the age of 65 is equal to €50,000, the self-employed worker is active until the age of 65 and obtains payment as a lump sum, for ten years, 5 per cent of 80 per cent of €50,000, that is €2,000 will be added to the rest of the income of the taxpayer and taxed progressively. In addition a municipal tax will be applied. The percentage will depend on the municipality where the taxpayer lives.

The different forms of individual pension provision can be cumulated. A self-employed person can benefit tax allowance for voluntary pension for the self-employed, tax allowance for life insurance and tax allowance for pension savings. An employee can benefit from the tax allowance for life insurance and the tax allowance for pension savings.[43]

Table 9.1 gives a summary of the complex nature of tax exemptions that apply to personal pension provision in Belgium.

4. THE COST OF TAX ALLOWANCES FOR INDIVIDUAL PENSION PROVISION

In order to estimate the cost of tax allowances for IVPP, we compare contributions to IVPP with an investment in what we refer to as ordinary long-term saving, that is investment in financial products which do not benefit from tax allowances. In order to make this comparison, certain assumptions are made based on average values. For the purpose of this chapter, we wish to examine whether and to what extent the tax allowances in general benefit those with higher incomes than those with lower incomes. The following are some of the key assumptions made:

1. average return on investment for both ordinary long-term saving and IVPP of 4 per cent[44];
2. guaranteed interest rate on the contributions paid of 2.5 per cent;

Table 9.1 Summary of individual voluntary pension provision in Belgium

Life insurance	Pension savings	Voluntary pension for self-employ.
Accessible for everybody.	Accessible for everybody.	Accessible only for self-employed
Conditions for tax allowances: taxpayer is beneficiary of contract signed before age 65 contract with a minimum duration of 10 years contract expires at the earliest age of 65 only products with a guaranteed investment return	Conditions for tax allowances: resident of the EEA aged between 18 – 65 the taxpayer is the beneficiary of the contract minimum duration of 10 years one account or insurance contract per person and period savings can only be withdrawn at the normal retirement age	Conditions for tax allowances: no surrender of the accrued reserves before age 60; minimum payment of €100; per year; payment of the social security contributions in accordance with social regulations
Tax reduction equal to: 30- 30 – 40% of the premium: paid maximum premium per year equal to 15% of the first income bracket of €1,660 plus 6% of the remaining net taxable professional income with an absolute maximum of €1,990	Tax reduction equal to: 30–40% of contributions paid maximum contributions of € 830 per year Each spouse is entitled to the tax reduction.	Contributions are deductible asprofessional costs, capped at 8.17 % of earned income, with a maximum of € 2,686.05 (9.40% and absolute maximum of € 3,090.44 for social pension agreements). No contribution tax, because the contributions are considered as social security contributions.
No premium tax applicable. The benefit of the contract is taxed if (a part of) the premiums lead to a tax reduction.	Savings are taxed if (a part of) the contributions lead to a tax reduction.	The pension benefits are taxed. The payment is a lump sum converted to a fictive annuity, calculated as a percentage of the lump sum equal to: 3.5% at the age of 60 5% at the age of 65 (on 80% of the lump sum if active until the age of 65)
Payment between age 60 –65: Taxation at: 10% for the part of the benefits that correspond with premiums paid since 1993; Taxation at 16.5% for the part of the benefits that correspond with premiums paid before 1993	Taxation at: 10% for the Part of the savings that correspond with contributions paid since 1993 Taxation at 16.5% for part of the savings that correspond with the contributions paid before 1993	The fictive annuity is taxed with other income at progressive rates for: 13 years if the lump sum is paid before the age of 65, 10 years if the lump sum is paid at the age of 65
Payment before age 60: surrender values paid as a lump sum: taxed at a special tax rate of 33% annuities taxed with the other professional income at progressive rates		If pension is paid as an annuity, the annuity is added to rest of income and taxed progressively. Municipal tax around 8% of the Income tax paid by the taxpayer

3. participation rate in the profit of the insurer or financial institution of 1.5 per cent;
4. insurance costs as a percentage of the contributions paid (front loading) of 5 per cent;
5. municipal tax of 6 per cent.[45]

The applicable average tax rate and marginal tax rate will depend on the income (adjusted for tax allowances) of the person involved. The comparison is made between lower and higher income categories. In the example, lower income categories are subjected to a marginal tax rate of 40 per cent and to an average tax rate of 30 per cent.[46] Higher incomes are taxed at a marginal tax rate of 50 per cent and an average tax rate of 40 per cent.[47]

Given the similar tax treatment of life insurance and pension savings, these forms of pension provision can be treated together. However employees compared with self-employed workers are treated separately because of very different tax treatment.

Cost of Tax Reliefs for Employees

In order to make comparisons between different tax brackets, we assume that €100 is received as an increase of gross salary per annum. The entire amount is saved or invested over a 30-year period (between the age of 35 and 65). The employee can either invest all the net income derived from this €100 gross salary in ordinary long-term saving products. Alternatively the net of tax salary increase can be paid in to an IVPP. Table 9.2 shows the net results of these different choices, after 30 years and after final taxation of the benefit.

Table 9.2 Comparative returns on savings and pension products for different tax categories for employees

Tax Bracket	Ordinary long-term saving (1)	Life insurance and pension savings (2)	Difference between (1) and (2)
Lower incomes	€2,920.60	€3,674.20	26 %
Higher incomes	€2,383.13	€3,497.72	47 %

Table 9.2 shows that assuming the same return on capital for pension products and long-term saving, the after-tax returns to a pension product over 30 years are 26 per cent greater than a savings product for lower incomes and 47 per cent greater for higher incomes. This is solely due to tax allowances. Three conclusions can be drawn from Table 9.2.

1. The tax allowances for IVPP has a real impact for all taxpayers.

2. The net result after taxation of an investment in IVPP is higher for lower income categories than for higher income categories. In other words, the tax system is redistributive (the strongest shoulders carry the heaviest load).
3. The incentive to participate in IVPP is relatively higher for higher incomes than for lower incomes (47 per cent increase in returns compared with 26 per cent). In other words, the higher the marginal tax rate a person is subjected to, the greater the incentive to participate in IVPP.

Self-Employed

For the self-employed we also assume a yearly investment of €100 received as income, over a period of 30 years (between the age of 35 and 65). The self-employed worker can decide to invest this €100 in an ordinary long-term saving product, or in pension products or in voluntary pension for self-employed. In the latter case the €100 will not be considered as part of his gross income but as a cost in earning income. Table 9.3 gives the net results of the various options, after 30 years and after final taxation.

Table 9.3 shows a comparison of the capital that can be obtained in ordinary long-term saving with life insurance, pension savings and voluntary pension for a self-employed person with a gross income of €100, given the assumptions already stated.

Table 9.3 Comparative returns on savings and pension products for different tax categories for self-employed

	ordinary long-term saving (1)	Life insurance and pension savings (2)	voluntary pension self-employed (3)	difference between (1) and (2)	difference between (1) and (3)
Lower incomes	€2,724.14	€3,591.05	€4,452.28	32 %	163 %
Higher incomes	€2,105.86	€3,388.04	€4,276.66	63.5 %	203 %

If the same return on capital is assumed for returns on ordinary savings and life insurance and pension savings, the extra return over a 30 year period is equal to 32 per cent for those with lower incomes and 63.5 per cent for those with higher incomes. The same comparison for those with voluntary pensions for the self-employed results in an extra return of 163 per cent for those with lower incomes and 203 per cent for those with higher incomes.

These extra returns are due to tax allowances. Similar conclusions can be drawn from Table 9.3 as for Table 9.2:

1. the tax allowances for IVPP have a real impact for all taxpayers;
2. the net return after taxation of an investment in IVPP is higher for higher income categories than for lower income categories;

3. the incentive to participate in IVPP is relatively higher for higher incomes than for lower incomes: 63.5 per cent extra return compared with 32 per cent for life insurance and pension savings and 203 per cent compared with 163 per cent for voluntary pensions for the self-employed;
4. the voluntary pension for the self-employed gives rise to greater tax savings than for individual life insurance. This is caused by three elements (a) a tax deduction at marginal tax rates results in higher tax allowances compared to the tax credit on individual life insurance, (b) the amount invested in a voluntary pension for self-employed influences the level of income on which social contributions for the first pillar are levied, and (c) the tax paid on distributions is lower. The amounts contributed by a self-employed person within a voluntary pension scheme are treated for tax purposes as if they were social security contributions.

5. WHO CAN CONTRIBUTE TO AN IVPP?

The participation rate in, and amounts of contributions to an IVPP are not systematically centralised in Belgium. Relevant data must be gathered from different sources and different studies.[48]

Participation in IVPP

According to Gieselink et al. (2003), the participation rate of the income tax-paying population in life insurance and pension contracts for the year 1999 was 29 per cent for single persons and 59 per cent for married persons.[49] According to Wuyts et al. (2007) the participation rate for life insurance and pension savings rose by 38 per cent between 1993 and 2003. This author found that the most important factors for participation in life insurance and pension savings are: high income, age, marital status, being self-employed and owning a home.

According to the Belgian Banking, Finance and Insurance Commission in 2005 only 19.54 per cent of all self-employed workers in Belgium participated in the voluntary pension for self-employed. The participation rate of the so-called 'free professions' was 28.08 per cent[50] Only 11.6 per cent of the self-employed workers who retired in 2005 were entitled to payments from voluntary pensions for the self-employed.[51] The most important factors for participation in a voluntary pension for the self-employed are high income and practicing a so-called 'free profession'.[52]

Table 9.4 shows the participation rate for life insurance and/or pension contracts by income bracket. Income is a very important factor for participation in IVPP. Of the single persons with a monthly income less than €750, only 9.1 per cent participate in IVPP. For those with a monthly income above €2,000 almost 50 per cent participate in IVPP.

Table 9.4 Participation in IVPP and income [a]

Participation in life insurance and/or pension savings per income bracket					
Single Person[b]			Married persons[c]		
Less than	€750	9.1 %	Less than	€1,500	31.3 %
Between	€750 −1,350	23.3 %	Between	€1,500–2700	50.5 %
Between	€1,350 −2,000	34.0 %	Between	€2,700–4000	63.7 %
More than	€2,000	48.7 %	More than	€4,000	74.8 %

Notes:
a Gieselink et al. (2003) p. 206 and 219.
b X^2, p-value (DF = 3) is respectively 445.833 and $p<0.0001$.
c X^2, p-value (DF = 3) is respectively 258.221 and $p<0.0001$.

According to Gieselink et al. (2003), opposite trends can be observed with regard to the effects of income on participation for life insurance and pension savings. For life insurance the effect of income has increased participation between 1992 and 1999. For pension savings the effect of income has decreased participation between 1992 and 1999 (on the other hand the effect of owning a home has increased for married persons).[53]

Wuyts et al. show a decline in the average income of contributors between 1993 and 2003, of 11 per cent in real terms. This decrease in real incomes (incomes adjusted for inflation) is highest for age categories that showed the sharpest increases in participation rates (aged 45–64). For the younger age categories (aged 25–35) no decrease in average income of contributors can be seen. For the youngest age category (age 20–25) there has been an increase in average income of contributors.[54]

Table 9.5 shows that home owners participate more in Life Insurance/Pension Savings compared to non-home owners: about 50 per cent of single persons who own a home, participate in life insurance and/or pension savings against only 20 per cent of single persons who rent their home.[55] A possible explanation for the relationship between home ownership and participation in life insurance and/or pension savings, is that home ownership is regarded as a form of income. Persons who participate in occupational pensions participate significantly more in life insurance and pension savings. Self-employed participate more in, and contribute more to IVPP than employees, which is in line with the fact that they receive a lower state pension.

Table 9.5 Participation in life insurance/pension savings and home ownership, occupational pension and employment status

		Single %	Married persons %
Home ownership[a]	Rented accommodation	21.0	39.7
	Ownership with mortgage	53.0	62.5
	Ownership without mortgage	44.8	64.7
Occupational pensions[b]	Yes	41.0	53.5
	No	20.3	45.6
Employment status[c]	Employee	28.0	57.8
	Self-employed	41.7	64.1

Notes:

a. For singles X^2, p-value (DF = 2) is respectively 405.326 and $p<0.0001$. For married persons X^2, p-value (DF = 2) is respectively 120.211 and $p<0.0001$.

b. For singles $X^2 = 32.031$, $p < 0.0001$, DF = 1. For married persons $X^2 = 6.065$, $p = 0.0145$, DF = 1.

c. For singles X^2, p-value (DF = 1) for pension savings, life insurance and one of both are respectively 22.647 ($p<0.0001$), 90.350 ($p<0.0001$) and 179.251 ($p<0.0001$). For married persons the variable gives the professional status of the husband. X^2, p-value (DF = 1) for pension savings, life insurance and one of both are respectively 4.516 ($p<0.0001$), 16.037 ($p<0.0001$) and 7.634 ($p<0.0001$).

Contributions to IVPP

Households with a higher total income contribute more to life insurance and pension savings. Besides income, age, marital status, being self-employed, and home ownership also lead to higher contributions for life insurance and pension savings.

According to Gieselink et al. 80 per cent of those who participated in pension savings in 1999 paid the maximum contributions and benefited from the maximum tax reduction. For life insurance only those with low incomes paid the maximum premiums. This could partly be explained by the fact that tax allowances for mortgages are part of the global maximum amount for life insurance. Gieselink et al. (2003) did not take incentives for mortgages into account.[56]

Table 9.6 shows that in relation to voluntary pensions for the self-employed 40 per cent of the active affiliates pay a contribution of €2,000 or more per year. For persons that practice a so-called 'free profession', this percentage is higher at 60 per cent.

According to the Banking, Finance and Insurance Commission the figures shown in Table 9.6 indicate that higher income is an important factor for participation and contribution to the voluntary pension by self-employed.

Table 9.6 Contributions to voluntary pensions for self-employed in 2005

Contributions	Self-employed %	'Free professions'
Between €100–500	8.87	3.63
Between €500–1,000	21.48	16.74
Between €1,000–1,500	15.66	6.84
Between €1,500–2,000	13.92	13.56
More than €2,000	40.07	59.23

Note: Report of the Banking, Finance and Insurance Commission, Tweejaarlijks verslag betreffende het vrij aanvullend pensioen voor zelfstandigen (Bi-annual report regarding the Voluntary pension for self employed), July 2007,available at www.cbfa.be.

6. IVPP WITHIN THE OVERALL OLD AGE INCOME OF ELDERLY IN BELGIUM

An evaluation of Belgian IVPP needs to be made within a much larger framework. This framework should include the overall old age income of the elderly in Belgium and the budgetary cost of tax allowances for IVPP.

State Pensions and Occupational Pensions

State pensions in Belgium are low (except for civil servants). The average state pension for employees in 2005 was equal to €1,019.14 for men and €742.30 for women. The average state pension for self-employed workers in 2005 was equal to €682.62 for men and €472.03 for women. For civil servants the average state pensions in 2005 were equal to €1,980.09 for men and €1,488.55 for women. Different system apply to calculate state pension for employees, for self-employed and for civil servants.[57]

Occupational pensions are in general not mandatory. Few sectors have a mandatory occupational pension scheme. Most employees have no occupational pension. For the lucky ones with an occupational pension, contributions often remain rather low.[58]

In order to evaluate the importance of IVPP in total old age income in Belgium, Gieselink et al. (2003) compared total contributions to IVPP, with the total contributions to occupational pensions and with the total payments of state pension benefits in the same year. This comparison can be questioned. Two main problems arise: (1) State pensions in Belgium are organized on a PAYG system, whereas IVPP and occupational pensions are contributory systems based on funding;[59] and (2) The comparison compares contributions to IVPP and to occupational pensions with benefits from the state pension.

The comparison is nevertheless interesting, not with regard to the exact amounts, but with regard to the evolution of IVPP within the overall old age as Gieselink et al. (2003). Gieselink et al. made calculations for the year 2000. In order to evaluate the evolution, we made calculations for the years 1989 and 2006. By calculating the contributions to life insurance, we also took the contributions linked to a mortgage into account.[60]

According to Gieselink et al. (2003), total contributions for life insurance and pension savings in 2000 amounted to €10 billion or 4.2 per cent of GDP. This amount was three times higher than the total contributions for work-related pensions in 2000. Based on the data from the Banking, Finance and Insurance Commission, we calculated that total contributions for life insurance and pension savings amounted to €16 billion in 2006 (5.4 per cent of GDP).[61] The total contributions for life insurance and pension savings in 2000 represented 50 per cent of the total payments for state pensions in 1999.[62] This proportion has increased since then. Therefore we can conclude in general that IVPP is of growing importance in the overall old age income of elderly in Belgium.

Costs and Benefits of the Tax Allowances for IVPP

There are different sources showing the costs of tax allowances for IVPP. The Belgian Minister of Finance presented the estimated net budgetary costs of the tax allowances for IVPP in the Belgian Senate. In addition two studies calculated these costs and their main beneficiaries. The three different sources reach more or less the same conclusion. We did not find any relevant data with regard to the voluntary pension for the self-employed.

According to the Minister of Finance, the net cost of the tax allowances for life insurance (without taking into account the tax allowances for the reimbursement of mortgages) and pension savings is €339 million in 1996 and €532 million in 2005. This is around 0.36 per cent of the state budget. Table 9.7 shows the figures for the period 1996–2005.[63]

The figures in Table 9.7 are similar to those in studies of Algoed et al. (2000) and Wuyts et al. (2007).[64]

Table 9.7 Estimated net cost of the fiscal allowances for life insurance (without mortgage) and pension savings € millions (2005 prices)

Tax year	1996	1997	1998	1999	2000	2001	2002	2003	2004	2005
Cost of life insurance	173	182	185	196	202	196	205	213	216	217
Cost of pension savings	166	176	185	212	230	243	268	289	300	315
Total cost	339	358	370	408	432	439	473	502	516	532

According to Wuyts et al (2007) total contributions to life insurance and pension savings eligible for tax allowances amounted in 2003 to €1,786 billion. Given the fact that the contributors are entitled to a tax reduction of 30 to 40 per cent, the budgetary cost of the tax allowances for life insurance and pension savings in 2003 was between €568 and €757 million.[65] In this study they also did not include the cost of tax reliefs on contributions for life insurance linked to a mortgage.

Algoed et al. (2000) show that the tax allowances for life insurance (without allowances for mortgage reimbursements) and pension savings represented in 1996 (tax year 1997) a cost in terms of tax foregone of €372 million. Algoed et al. also calculated the tax allowances for life insurance linked to mortgage reimbursements. These tax allowances were €628 million in 1996. In total, the tax allowances for life insurances and pension savings in 1996 (taking mortgage reimbursements into account) were €1 billion or 1.12 per cent of the state budget for that year.

Algoed et al. (2000) also studied the distribution of the allowances for life insurance and pension savings. According to their study, more than 70 per cent of these incentives went to less than 30 per cent of the tax payers (with a taxable income above €25,000 in 1996). More than 40 per cent of the incentives went to 12 per cent of the tax payers (with a taxable income above €37,500 in 1996).

Social Policy and Pension Provisions in Belgium

The benefits of social security schemes – including pension benefits – are of greatest value for those who are not the most needy within society. Social policy redistributes income proportionally more to socially higher income classes than lower classes. Some might say that this effect of social policy is an inherent element of the design of current social policy. Hence it should not be considered a negative aspect. In this view, pension systems and social security are not meant to be redistributive in the first place.[66] The systems are set up to maintain the existing income flow. In this vision the Matthew effect is not 'wrong' but is inherent to an imperfect system.

Others have argued that the efficiency of the social security system is determined by the level of the benefits for those who rely exclusively on the public system. The preservation of living standards (based on insurance principles) fails if the system cannot provide at the same time a decent minimum income standard for everybody.[67] This minimum income standard is a human right, and does not mean that social security should be limited to this minimum standard.[68]

Tax and social policy should take account of all components of a pension system. Tax and social policy should be especially concerned with those who currently have low pension incomes and with those who are likely to have low state and occupational pension income in the future. This latter group are the intended targets to participate and contribute more to IVPP. However we saw in this chapter that the tax system in Belgium gives far greater incentives to those with higher incomes to participate and contribute to IVPP. The philosophy behind Belgian IVPP is therefore more closely related to income replacement and not to a guarantee of a decent minimum income standard for everybody. This is an ideological choice, made by society.

The inequality resulting from tax and social policy can be overcome by introducing more selective social policy measures. For example, for Belgian state and occupational pensions, certain caps apply. Once these caps are exceeded, no more tax incentives are allowed.[69] The same system could be applied to IVPP. Once a certain accumulated sum of global pension provisions is reached (that is an accumulated sum of state pension, occupational pension and IVPP), no more tax incentives for IVPP could be allowed. The savings that this would entail for the state budget could be used to increase minimum state pensions. A more selective policy, directed towards a decent minimum standard for everybody, is possible if society makes the choice to do so. However, such choice must be made within overall pension policy. This means that the total cost of tax concessions must be taken into account for all different income groups and their relative pension wealth. from all different pension forms of pension income.

7. CONCLUSION

The two main questions asked in this chapter were: (1) whether and to what extent Belgian IVPP can be considered as a social good and (2) whether and to what extent the Matthew effect is present within the tax allowances for Belgian IVPP.

We defined a social good as a good that is under-consumed in a market economy, but because of positive externalities, its consumption is stimulated by the government. We saw that tax allowances for those with individual pension policies have a real impact for all taxpayers who participate, regardless of their income level. Under an assumption of the same return on capital for IVPP and long-term saving, the surplus over an ordinary savings account of a yearly investment of €100 over 30 years in IVPP is between 26 per cent and 203 per cent. This is entirely due to tax incentives. Furthermore we saw that the budgetary cost for IVPP is not negligible. This cost amounts to more than 1 per cent of the state budget if we take account of allowances for reimbursement of mortgages. However, the tax incentives are capped. Above certain amounts, contributions to IVPP do not entail any additional tax allowances. Therefore, we can conclude that Belgian IVPP can be considered as a social good up to the level tax allowances are granted.

The Matthew effect means that social inequalities that generate unequal distribution in the free market economy continue to work in the distribution of social goods. With regard to social policy, it means that the actual distribution of social goods differs from the normative distribution, that is the distribution originally planned for.

Sociological and econometric studies show that high income is a determining factor for participation and contributions to Belgian IVPP. This finding could be sufficient to conclude that the Matthew effect is present. However, a detailed analysis of the tax incentives for IVPP raises the question if these incentives are designed for the lowest income categories. It appears that the target group for the tax incentives are those categories with higher incomes. Tax incentives are such that the lowest income categories cannot benefit at all. This finding can be deduced from (1) the instrument of social policy that is used to stimulate IVPP and (2) the way the social policy measures are set out. The instrument of social policy is a tax reduction. In order to qualify for a tax reduction, one must pay taxes first. Given the fact that lowest income categories (unemployed, those caring for children, disabled, and so on) do not pay any taxes, a tax reduction cannot be an incentive for these categories to participate in IVPP. Second, the way the tax reduction is given is more valuable to higher incomes categories than lower incomes categories (the surplus of investment in IVPP over ordinary saving, for lower income categories varies between 26 and 163 per cent and for higher income categories between 47 and 203 per cent). The way the tax reduction is implemented effectively compensates higher income categories for the higher progressive income taxes they pay.

Some argue that this effect is inherent in social policy. Hence it should not be considered in a negative way. From this viewpoint, pension systems and social security are not meant to be redistributive in the first place. The systems are set up to maintain the existing income flow, based on an insurance idea, and not designed to ensure a decent minimum income standard for people with insufficient state and occupational pension provision. In this vision the Matthew effect is not 'wrong' but is inherent in an imperfect system. Others argue that this is not necessarily so in social policy, nor in social policy for IVPP. It is an ideological choice, made by society. Another choice is possible through more selective social policy measures. These choices should always be considered within overall old age policy. The IVPP is but one element in this policy. Elements such as the overall cost of tax incentives, the minimum wage, the minimum pension and guaranteed incomes for the elderly are other elements to be taken into account when evaluating pension policies.

NOTES

1. Matthew XXV:29, King James Version (Anglo-Saxon version) or Mattheus 13:12, Roman Catholic. The 'Matthew effect is directly at variance with a concept of justice which can be equated to equality. See Aristoteles, Ethique à Nicomanque, E6, 1113, a 14 who states 'Justice is equality'.
2. Deleeck (1983), 33; H. Deleeck (1991).

3. Musgrave (1957) introduced the concept of a merit good. We prefer the notion social good, which we will use here. According to Musgrave, different rationales can be found for the existence of merit goods. There may be more acceptance for income redistribution in the form of goods, rather than *purchasing power*. Consumption of merit goods needs to be stimulated because (1) when consumed, a merit good creates positive *externalities* (there is a divergence between private benefit and public benefit and most consumers only take into account private benefit) and (2) most individuals are short-term utility maximisers and so do not take into account the long term benefits of consuming a merit good. Examples of merit goods include education, subsidized housing, health care. See Musgrave (1957).
4. The subscriber can choose between classical and universal life insurances. In classical life insurance the contributions are calculated in accordance with a previously defined benefit. The periodicity, the size of the contributions and the tariffs that are applied are fixed in advance. In universal life insurance the benefit equals the capitalised value of the contributions and there is only a tariff guarantee on paid premiums.
5. Only contracts with a guaranteed technical interest rate are taken into account for tax allowances. The maximum interest rate that can be guaranteed is fixed by the Commission for Banking, Finance and Assurance, the Belgian control authority. At present it amounts to 3.75 per cent, but most insurers apply lower rates. In some older contracts higher guaranteed rates, up to 4.75 per cent still exist.
6. Art. 145/1(2), 145/4 and 145/6 Income Tax Act.
7. In the event of death, the benefits must be stipulated in favour of the spouse or relatives up to the second degree of the taxpayer. When the life insurance contract is assigned in order to amortization or as security for a mortgage loan, the benefits must be stipulated, in the event of death in favor of the person who acquires the full property or usufruct of the dwelling.
8. The maturity date is stipulated in the insurance contract and can be freely agreed upon together with several other aspects. In order to benefit from tax relief, this age condition is required.
9. Tax allowances for pension savings and, in the case of a self-employed worker, for voluntary pension for self-employed, remain accessible.
10. This tax reduction is actually a tax credit converted into a tax reduction.
11. Tax rates in personal income tax in Belgium are progressive. For each of the following brackets of taxable income, the rates are (income year 2008):
    € 0 – €7,560 → 25 per cent
    €7,420 – €10,760 → 30 per cent
    €10,570 – €17,920 → 40 per cent
    €1,7610 – €32,860 → 45 per cent
    €3,2270 – and over → 50 per cent
12. Article 145/2 Income Tax Act.
13. Article 145/6 Income Tax Act. Within a household, these limits apply to each individual separately. The maximum amount of €1,990 is reached at a net taxable income of €30,676.5. Depending on income, a lower maximum amount will be taken in consideration. For example, the maximum amount for someone whose net taxable income is €2,0000 will be €1,349.40 (15 per cent × €1,660 + 6 per cent × (€2,0000 – €1,660)).
14. Maximum contribution of €1,990 multiplied with the maximum tax rate of 40 per cent gives a maximum tax relief of €796.
15. Article 39, (2), a Income Tax Act. As a consequence, benefits from unit-linked insurance contracts are never taxed in Belgium, given the fact that only life insurance products with a guaranteed investment lead to tax reduction.
16. For the part of the surrender value which corresponds with premiums paid before 1 January 1993, the tax rate is 16.5 per cent.
17. Articles 184–187/6 Code of Taxes. If the benefits are paid before the age of 60, they will be subjected to personal income tax at the moment of payment. In this situation, a different regime applies to surrender values paid as a lump sum and payments as an annuity: (1) surrender values paid as a lump sum more than 5 years before expiration of the contract, are taxed to a special rate of 33 per cent (the part of the surrender value that corresponds with the contributions paid before 1 January 1993, is taxed progressively (article 171, 1°, f and article 515bis Income Tax Act), (2) annuities will be joined with the other income from professional activities and taxed progressively.
18. Article 40 Income Tax Act.

19. See articles 145/8 to 145/16 of the Income Tax Act for the main principles concerning pension savings.
20. The subscriber can choose between classical and universal life insurance products. Universal life products can be chosen with or without guaranteed investment return.
21. Articles 145/8 and 145/9 Income Tax Act
22. As for individual life insurances, it is actually a tax credit converted afterwards in a tax reduction.
23. See footnote 11 for the progressive tax rates in personal income tax in Belgium.
24. Article 145/2 Income Tax Act.
25. Article 145/8 Income Tax Act.
26. Maximum contribution of € 810 multiplied with the maximum tax rate of 40 per cent = €324.
27. Article 171, (2) Income Tax Act. For the part of the payment that corresponds with contributions paid before January 1993, the tax rate is 16.5 per cent. In relation to payment of individual life insurance benefits, the payment of pension savings benefits is only taxed if the contributions led to a tax reduction (article 39, 3° Income Tax Act).
28. Article 40 Income Tax Act.
29. The average state pension for self-employed workers on 1 January 2005 was €682.62 a month for men and €4,72.03 a month for women. The average state pension for employees (white and blue collar) on 1 January 2005 was €1,019.14 a month for men and €742.30 a month for women.
30. For medical and paramedical professions, this specific IVPP is slightly different. These professions are entitled to some extra payments (for example a financial contribution to IVPP is paid by the statutory social security institutions).
31. Article 52bis (1) Royal Decree no 72 of 10 November 1967 and article 44 (1) Act of 24 December 2002.
32. Article 52bis 2 Royal Decree no 72.
33. Article 44 §1 Act of 24 December 2002.
34. This means that the pension institution will have to guarantee at least the sum of the net contributions at the retirement age (article 47 Act of 24 December 2002).
35. Article 49 Act of 24 December 2002.
36. Two exceptions: transfer to another operator and mortgage.
37. Article 52bis 3 Royal Decree no 72 and article 45 Act of 24 December 2002.
38. Article 44 2-4 Act of 24 December 2002.
39. For social pension agreements, 10 per cent of the contributions are attributed to the solidarity scheme. The solidarity scheme that is offered depends from the pension institution. Mostly it covers against disability and death risks. Also bankruptcy risk can be covered (article 46 and 54-57 Act of 24 December 2002).
40. Article 169 Income Tax Act.
41. The so-called INAMI tax (tax for the National Institute of Sickness and Disability), article 191, 1, 7, Act of 14 July 1994 and article 3 Royal Decree 15 September 1980.
42. For social pension agreements, the maximum amount of yearly contributions is €32,876.96 × 9.40 per cent = €3,090.44.
43. A self employed director of a company can also benefit from a 2nd pillar workplace pension. Contributions to the 2nd pillar are tax deductible if the total benefit from state pension and 2nd pillar pension does not exceed 80 per cent of the normal salary. The voluntary pension of self-employed will be included in order to assess if the tax limit on these contributions for the 2nd pillar is reached. Individual life insurance and pension savings are not taken into account.
44. This assumption is made for the sake of the example. It could be argued that the return on capital of IVPP products with a guaranteed minimum investment return, would on the long term be a little lower than the return on capital of ordinary long-term saving products without a guarantee.
45. In Belgium each municipality has the right to charge a municipal tax. This tax is calculated as a per cent of income tax. For example a municipal tax of 6 per cent on income tax, will give result in the following tax paid: if the income tax paid by a person is equal to €5,000, the municipal tax will be €5,000 × 6 per cent = €300.
46. These tax rates are applicable for persons with a gross annual income around €20,000 (see above for the marginal tax rates in Belgium).
47. These tax rates are applicable for persons with a gross annual income exceeding around €35,000.

48. The main sources are tax declarations. Other sources are the Panel Study of Belgian Households, the reports of the National Bank of Belgium and the Banking Finance and Insurance Commission, data from the National Institute for Statistics, reports of the Ageing Commission. The main studies that analyzed participation in and contribution to life insurance and pension savings are: Algoed et al (2000); Gieselink et al (2003); Wuyts (2007). With regard to the voluntary pension for self-employed, the Banking, Finance and Insurance Commission of Belgium published a detailed report in July 2007.
49. This is the participation rate for the working population that submits an income tax declaration. The population that submits no income tax declaration (estimated at 14 per cent) is not taken into account (Gieselink et al 2003 p. 166).
50. Members of a 'free profession' are doctors, pharmacists, dentists, physiotherapists, lawyers, bailiffs and notaries.
51. Banking, Finance and Insurance Commission Report, July 2007, 37, available at www.cbfa.be..
52. Banking, Finance and Insurance Commission Report, July 2007, 13. Those who pay a contribution of less than €100 per year are not taken in consideration.
53. Gieselink et al. (2003), p. 212.
54. Wuyts et al. (2007), p. 57.
55. Gieselink et al., 204–219. The link between home ownership and participation to IVPP is no coincidence. As explained above the reimbursement of mortgages for the one and only dwelling also leads to tax allowances. More or less the same tax allowances as those for individual life insurance apply. The maximum amount on which a tax allowance can be obtained is determined jointly for life insurance and mortgage reimbursements.
56. Gieselink et al. (2003) p. 220.
57. For employees, the state pension is equal to 60 per cent (single person) or 75 per cent (couple) of yearly income assuming 45 years contributions (pension formula = yearly wage/45 × 60 per cent (or 75 per cent for a couple)). However, the wage that is taken in consideration is capped (for example the wage taken in consideration for 1981 is capped on €20,697.62 and for 2007 on €44,994.88).
58. Report of the Banking, Finance and Insurance Commission, *Tweejaarlijks verslag betreffende de sectorale pensioenstelsel* (Bi-annual report regarding the sector pension schemes), July 2007, www.cbfa.be.
59. See Kune (2007), in O.W. Steenbeeck, and S.G. Van Der Lecq, (ed.), (2007), 247.
60. As explained above the reimbursement of mortgages for a dwelling also leads to tax allowances. These tax allowances are or less the same as tax allowances for individual life insurance. The maximum amount on which a tax allowance can be obtained is determined jointly for life insurance and mortgage repayments.
61. The accumulated reserves for voluntary pension for self-employed is very limited. In 1996 amounted to €28 million and amounted to €72 million in 2000 (Gieselink et al. p. 59).
62. Gieselink et al. (2003), p. 71
63. Source: Questions and answers in the Belgian Senate 2006–2007, nr. 3-90, p. 10461–10463 (Question nr. 3-6352 of Ms Van de Casteele dd. 07.12.2006).
64. Algoed, et al (2000) and Wuyts et al (2007).
65. There is a debate amongst economists as to whether pension provisions represent new saving or are substitute for other forms of saving that is simply a rebalancing of the savings portfolio
66. Van Langendonck (1994), p. 84
67. Deleeck, et al. (1983), p. 33; Deleeck (1991).
68. Kapuy et al. (2008) pp. 53–72
69. The tax deductible contribution for occupational pensions may not constitute a pension that exceeds 80 per cent of the sum of the 1st and 2nd pillar pensions.

REFERENCES

Algoed, K., Callatay D.E. , and Roels P., (2000), 'Iedereen gelijk voor de fiscale wet – Tous égaux devant la legislation sociale' (Everybody equal for the tax law), *Life & Benefits*, 7–16 May, (published in French and Dutch).

Attanasio, O., Banks J., and Wakefield M., (2004), *Effectiveness of Tax Allowances to Boost (Retirement) Saving: Theoretical Motivation and Empirical Evidence*, IFS Working Paper, 04/33.

Banking, Finance and Insurance Commission (2007), *Tweejaarlijks verslag betreffende het vrij aanvullend pensioen voor zelfstandigen (Bi-annual report regarding the voluntary pension for self employed)*, July 2007, available at www.cbfa.be (only available in Dutch).

Belgian Ageing Commission, Reports 2001, 2002, 2003, 2004, 2005 and 2006, available at www.docufin.fgov.be (only available in Dutch).

Deleeck, H., Huybrechts, J. and Cantillon, B. (1983), *Het Mattheüseffect. De ongelijke verdeling van de sociale overheidsuitgaven in België* (The Matthew Effect. Unequal distribution of social policy measures in Belgium), Kluwer, Antwerpen, 379 (only available in Dutch).

Deleeck, H. (1991), *7 lessen over sociale zekerheid* (7 lessons about Social Security), Leuven, ACCO, 192 (only available in Dutch).

Gieselink, G., Peeters, H., Van GestelL, V., Berghman, J., Van Buggenhout, B. (2003), *Onzichtbare pensioenen in België (Invisible pensions in Belgium)*, Gent, Academia Press, 241 (only available in Dutch).

Kapuy, K., Pieters, D., Schoukens, P., Van Leuffel, L., (2008), Het EVRM en de sociale zekerheid (ECHR and Social Security), in Themis, afl. 45, 2007–2008, 53–72 (only available in Dutch).

Kune, J.B., (2007), Solidarities in collective pension schemes, in Steenbeek O.W., Van S.G. Der Lecq, (ed.), *Costs and benefits of collective pension systems*, Springer, 247.

Musgrave, R. (1957), 'A Multiple Theory of Budget Determination', *FinanzArchiv*. N.F.17 (1956/57), **3**, 333–343.

NBB (2006), Recente ontwikkelingen in het Belgisch financieel systeem (Recent developments of the Belgian Financial System), December, available at www.nbb.be.

NBB (2006), Recente ontwikkelingen in het Belgisch financieel systeem (Recent developments of the Belgian Financial System), December, available at www.nbb.be.

NBB (2007), Financial Stability Review 2006 and 2007, available at www.nbb.be.

Poterba, J., S. Venti, and D. Wise, (1996), 'How Retirement Saving Programs Increase Saving', *Journal of Economic Perspectives*, **10**, 4, pp. 91–112;

Van Eesbeeck, P. and Vereycken, L. (2004), *Aanvullende pensioenen voor zelfstandigen (Supplementary pensions for self-employed)*, Mechelen, Kluwer, 351 (only available in Dutch).

Van LangenDonck, J. (1994), *Handboek Socialezekerheidsrecht (Manual Social Security law)*, Kluwer rechtswetenschappen, Deurne (only available in Dutch).

Wuyts, G., Stinglhamber P.,Valenduc Ch., and Zachary M.D., (2007), 'Saving for retirement in the Third Pillar of the Belgium Pension System', *Forum Financier* 2007/2, 55–62.

10. Conflicting Objectives in Personal Pension Provision and Personal Saving in Ireland

Gerard Hughes and Jim Stewart[1]

1. INTRODUCTION

In a report published in 1998, Securing Retirement Income, the Pensions Board (1998) advised the Minister for Social, Community and Family Affairs on the future development of pensions policy in Ireland. This report argued that the problem of high rates of poverty in old age could be addressed by having a target replacement income of 50 per cent of gross pre-retirement income and a minimum income of 34 per cent of gross average industrial earnings. It recommended that these targets could be achieved by a two-pronged approach. The first would be to increase the State public pension from a quarter to a third of gross average industrial earnings. The second would be to put in place a legislative framework which would encourage private sector financial institutions to introduce a personal pension, the Personal Retirement Savings Account (PRSA), with the aim of increasing supplementary pension coverage from 54 per cent for those aged 30 and over to 70 per cent over a ten-year period. The Board therefore envisaged that the problem of pensioner poverty could be dealt with by public provision of a minimum income related to gross average industrial earnings and private provision of personal pensions which together would eventually replace half of pre-retirement income for 70 per cent of the working population aged 30 and over. The replacement rate for the remaining 30 per cent was expected to be more than half of pre-retirement income because they would be concentrated at the bottom of the income distribution.

The pensions Board envisaged that the PRSA would be a simple investment product owned by an individual which would be transferable from one pension provider to another and that could be transferred to an annuity provider when a life annuity is eventually purchased. The savings would be invested in funds held with and managed by approved PRSA providers including supermarkets and the Post Office. It was also seen as a new marketing device offering more relevant and easier access to low cost pension products for everyone. It would contain features to indicate that it met a quality standard in order to encourage those not covered by existing pension arrangements to start saving for their retirement. The PRSA was intended to offer similar tax incentives as other pension products although limits would be placed on the amount of investment qualifying for tax relief. In making its recommendations for a simple personal pension which could be bought off the shelf without the need for advice tailored to the individual the Board expected that up to one-third of those who had no pension cover would take out a personal pension.

This chapter will outline what were considered by the Pensions Board to be barriers to the extension of private pension coverage and how they could be overcome by the introduction of a low cost, quality assured and easily accessible personal pension product, the Personal Retirement Savings Account (PRSA), which would increase income during retirement. It will argue that the original idea for a simple retirement savings product was changed during negotiations with the private pensions industry into a complex product which could only be sold by traditional pension providers. It will argue that these changes have resulted in a relatively high cost product with a bewildering range of charges for the consumer which has increased the complexity of the pensions market rather than simplifying it. It will show that the take-up of PRSAs by employees has fallen well short of expectations, that they are more attractive to people outside the labour force rather than to the target group of employees without pension coverage for whom they were designed, and that the main beneficiaries of the tax incentives for PRSAs are middle and higher income groups who already have high levels of pension coverage. The chapter will argue that the relative failure of PRSAs is also partly attributable to the introduction of a short-term savings product, the Special Savings Investment Account (SSIA), which offered far more attractive terms than the PRSA. The SSIA was introduced in response to submissions to the Minister of Finance in the year 2000 by the financial services industry and the trade unions.

2. PRIVATE PENSION COVERAGE

In the mid-1990s the Pensions Board commissioned the Economic and Social Research Institute (ESRI) to undertake a survey of private pension coverage in Ireland. An overview of the results of the survey by Hughes and Whelan (1996) is given in Table 10.1. The survey showed that the coverage of the private pension system was virtually confined to those who were in employment and that coverage was much greater for those working in the public sector than for those working in the private sector or working on their own account. Over four-fifths of public sector employees were covered whereas less than two-fifths of private sector employees and just over a quarter of the self-employed were covered. The overall coverage rate for those at work was 46 per cent. Only 7 per cent of those not at work were covered and most of these were retired people who were employed before retirement.

Table 10.1 Overall private pension coverage in 1995 from ESRI survey

Economically Active	Total in Category (000)	With Pension Coverage (000)	Pension Coverage %
Private Sector Employees	640.8	246.2	38
Public Sector Employees	276.0	230.3	83
Total Employees	916.8	476.5	52
Self-Employed	265.1	72.2	27
Total At Work	1181.9	548.7	46
Not Economically Active (aged 15 or more)			
Unemployed	217.7	7.1*	3
Retired	222.9	68.4*	31
Home Duties	637.9	15.2*	2
Others Not Economically Active	410.5	8.6*	2
Total Not At Work	1,489.0	99.3	7

Note: Those with a deferred pension or in receipt of an occupational pension.

Source: Hughes and Whelan (1996, Tables 2.1, 3.1, 4.14 and 4.18).

Following the publication of the survey results the Minister for Social, Community and Family Affairs launched a National Pensions Policy Initiative in October 1996, jointly sponsored by the Pensions Board and the Department of Social, Community and Family Affairs. The purpose of was 'to facilitate a national debate on how to achieve a fully developed national pension system, to formulate a strategy and make recommendations for actions needed to achieve this system.' (Pensions Board, 1998, p. v.).

The Pensions Board (1998) issued its recommendations for the development of the national pension system in a report called Securing Retirement Income in May 1998. In order to secure adequate provision for retirement income it recommended that the basic flat-rate Old Age (Contributory) Pension (since renamed the State Pension (Contributory)) should be gradually increased from 28 per cent of gross average industrial earnings to 34 per cent to provide a minimum income in retirement, that in combination with a private pension and other sources of income would replace 50 per cent of pre-retirement income, and that the private pension system should be developed to provide easier access to pensions particularly for groups not covered by the existing arrangements such as younger people, the lower paid and atypical workers.

3. BARRIERS TO PRIVATE PENSION COVERAGE

The Pensions Board noted that significant incentives for private pension provision were provided through the exemption of employer and employee contributions and the investment income and capital gains of pension funds from taxation. However, it identified the following barriers to the expansion of the private pension system.

Access to Pension Provision

The results of the survey by Hughes and Whelan (2006) showed that access to the tax incentives for private pensions was confined to those in employment. Those not in employment were precluded from taking advantage of the tax incentives to make pension provision for their own retirement. Even those in employment could find it difficult to avail of the tax incentives particularly if they were lower paid, changed jobs frequently, or were not full-time employees. In addition the complexity surrounding access made it difficult 'for providers to access such people economically' (see Pensions Board, 1998, p. 124). Consequently, the Board argued that access to pension cover could 'be improved dramatically by breaking the formal link between employment and pension provision and by simplifying the current regime for both the individual and the provider'.

Information Gaps

The institutional and regulatory arrangements for both Defined Benefit (DB) and Defined Contribution (DC) pension schemes are complex. Non-professionals face considerable difficulties in judging what their pension target should be and how much regular savings they need to meet the target. There is a basic lack of awareness of the cost and benefit of having a private pension and non-professionals are generally unable to assess the quality of investment fund management and the probity of financial intermediaries. These information gaps create great uncertainty and inhibit many from saving for a pension.

Running Costs

The Pensions Board report did not undertake an analysis of the costs which different pension providers charge. However, it noted that the challenge of reducing costs applied to employers in providing occupational schemes, to the industry in meeting regulatory requirements and to the beneficiaries themselves.

It noted that small employers are deterred from setting up a pension scheme by the overhead costs and that individuals who cannot participate in group schemes find a large fraction of their initial pension saving is absorbed by administrative charges.

Investment and Annuity Risk

The investment performance of a pension fund can vary widely between different fund managers particularly for DC schemes where the individual bears all of the risk of under-performance. In addition stock market volatility can result in considerable changes in the accumulated value of a fund and hence the size of pension payments. In DC arrangements the individual also bears the risk of changes in the price of annuities so that the annuity that has to be purchased may cost far more than anticipated.

4. PROPOSAL FOR A PRSA

The Pensions Board recommended that the best way of addressing the barriers to the expansion of the private pension system would be to break the link with employment by introducing a new pension product, the Personal Retirement Savings Account (PRSA), which would allow individuals who move in and out of employment or self-employment to continue saving for retirement throughout their careers. The value of the PRSA at retirement would depend on the performance of the investment fund in the same way as the investment fund in a Defined Contribution pension. The Board considered that the introduction of this product would result in a major simplification of the existing regulatory and legal structures for pensions.

The Board argued that the introduction of the PRSA would address the barrier to accessing pension provision by being available to everyone irrespective of whether they are in employment or not, by being open to employers' contributions, additional voluntary contributions and to the deposit of transfer values. Portability would, therefore, be improved at low administrative cost. Simplification of the regulatory environment would be achieved by harmonising the tax rules for different types of pensions, allowing access to the pensions market for established financial institutions with wide retail networks such as building societies, credit unions and the Post Office, and by having a common regulator for occupational and personal pension plans. It gave tangible expression to its objective of increasing pension coverage by setting specific targets by employment status and gender for five and ten years after implementation of its proposals. The most important of these was that the coverage of those over the age of 30 should increase from its 1995 level of 54 per cent to 70 per cent.

The existing information gaps would be reduced by providing a certificate of reasonable expectation of the future value of PRSA and other DC pensions and guidance on the adequacy of savings being made. The PRSA would have an investment mandate that would help consumers to understand and accept an appropriate level of risk. It would have a standard minimum set of terms and conditions not available for existing occupational or personal pensions. In addition, providers whose pension products meet specified standards of flexibility, scope and information would be allowed to use a kitemark to assure customers that the product meets quality assurance standards. The kitemark would provide protection for consumers. However, the scope of the quality assurance would be clearly spelled out to ensure that the State would not have to compensate beneficiaries in the event of default or poor investment performance. As PRSAs would be contracts with individuals they would be protected by consumer legislation and measures relating to personal financial contracts.

Cost reduction would be achieved by drawing a wider range of providers into the market to increase competition and provide easier access to pensions, by the emergence of industry-wide or umbrella schemes which would provide economies of scale, by the simplification of regulations and by controlling abuse of market power. Higher investment returns would be facilitated by the introduction of standard investment mandates which would encourage individuals to take appropriate levels of risk. These mandates would ensure that fund managers would take into account the age of the beneficiaries and the annuity risk. Because Ireland was a member of the EMU it was argued that index-linked annuities could be provided by hedging against the Euro rate of inflation. The danger of abuse of market power would be reduced by requiring charges to be explicitly stated as a percentage of contributions or of asset value and by allowing the Minister for Social, Family and Community Affairs to impose controls on charges if necessary.

Existing occupational pension plans required the employer to meet at least one-sixth of the cost of the plan in order for the plan to be approved by the Revenue Commissioners. To make it possible for people who are not in employment to commence or continue making pension contributions the Board recommended that this provision should not apply to PRSAs. This meant that the only legal obligation of the employer to the employee would be to designate a PRSA provider.

5. RESPONSE OF THE GOVERNMENT AND OTHER ACTORS TO PENSION PROPOSALS

The Pensions Board's report Securing Retirement Income received a favourable response from the Government and the Minister for Social, Community and Family Affairs. In a special bulletin issued by his department in May 1998 the

Minister, Dermot Ahern (1998) set out the Government's response to the Pensions Board report. The Minister said the Government had increased the basic State pension and was committed to achieving a pension of £100 (€127) per week by the year 2002, that it welcomed the Board's target of achieving a supplementary pension coverage rate of 70 per cent for those aged 30 and over, and that it had 'in principle, decided to introduce a new simplified Personal Retirement Savings Account (PRSA) which will make it easier for people to take out their own private pensions cover.'[2] Although, the Government did not adopt the Board's proposal that the basic State pension should be increased to 34 per cent of gross average industrial earnings it said the question of increases in the rates of social welfare pensions would be considered in the light of the overall Budgetary situation and the economic climate. The Minister announced that an inter-departmental working group would be set up to advance the proposal to introduce PRSAs. He also announced that another inter-departmental group would be set up to advance the proposals relating to simplifying the tax regime for pensions and that this group would also examine further the issue of an earnings cap for tax relief on pensions even though the Pensions Board had decided not to recommend the introduction of an earnings cap.

There was also a generally favourable reception from the pensions industry, employers and trade unions (see Kirby 1998). The proposal to broaden the range of pension providers to include non-financial institutions such as the Post Office and supermarkets was welcomed. Shortly after the report was published in mid-1998 there was an expectation in the pensions industry that some of the legislative changes necessary to give effect to the Board's proposals would be included in the Budget in December 1998 and that PRSAs would replace the existing system of Additional Voluntary Contributions (AVC) which could only be made by members of occupational pension schemes. It was expected that the Pensions Board would set standards for PRSAs that would ensure they would be low cost, simple in design, easy to understand, have different investment fund options, and that all costs would be transparent and disclosed. Nevertheless, Kirby (1998) noted that the proposal to widen the distribution of personal pension products to non-financial institutions could pose a threat to the financial institutions' network of sales staff and brokers who were the main sellers of occupational and personal pensions.

6. EVOLUTION OF THE PRSA

The legislation to implement the PRSA proposal took longer to appear than expected. It was introduced in May 2001 in the Pensions Bill. While this Bill was being prepared, the Minister for Finance in the Finance Act 1999 made substantial changes to personal retirement provision by changing the rules which required those, mainly the self-employed, proprietary directors and senior executives with a personal pension to take out an annuity on retirement. He argued that as these groups were able to take decisions about their own personal pension fund while working, they should be allowed to continue doing so after retirement. Consequently he made provision in Budget 2000 for those with personal pensions to transfer their pension fund into an Approved Retirement Fund (ARF) if they had an annual pension income of £10,000 (€12,700) or into an Approved Minimum Retirement Fund (AMRF) if they did not. These funds would be invested by a recognised fund manager. Pensioners with an annual income of £10,000 are allowed to draw down their ARF as they see fit whereas those without such an income are obliged to use £50,000 (€63,500) of their pension assets to invest in an AMRF and they are obliged to leave that amount in their fund until they are 75 years of age. Thereafter they can draw down the AMRF as they see fit.

The 1999 Finance Act also introduced new limits on the amount of contributions by an individual to a personal pension that would qualify for tax relief and an earnings cap on the amount that can be used to calculate eligible individual contributions into a fund in any year. The earnings cap was set at £200,000 (€254,000) and the maximum annual contribution to a personal pension plan by an individual that would qualify for tax relief increased with age from 15 per cent for those under 30 to 30 per cent for those aged 50 and over as shown in Table 10.2.

Any income drawn out of an ARF or an AMRF is subject to tax at the individual's marginal rate. In the Finance Act 2002 the tax relief for contributions to AVCs were harmonised with the rates for personal pensions. Eventually the percentage of earnings which could be contributed to a pension scheme while being shielded from tax was harmonised for occupational pensions, personal pension plans (also known as Retirement Annuity Contracts), AVCs and PRSAs. The earnings limits for different age groups in 2006 are shown in Table 10.2.

Table 10.2 Maximum pension contribution as a percentage of earnings eligible for tax relief in 1999 and 2006

Age Band	Percentage of Net Relevant Earnings 1999–2005	Percentage of Net Relevant Earnings in 2006
Under 30	15	15
30–40	20	20
40–50	25	25
50–55	30	30
55–60	30	35
60+	30	40

The introduction of ARFs effectively transformed the favourable tax arrangements under which pensions could be provided for proprietary directors and senior executives into a savings scheme for the accumulation of wealth which they could spend or leave as a bequest to their heirs. Some years after these changes the Department of Finance (2006) revealed that because the contribution limits applied only to individuals and not their employer, highly paid proprietary directors and senior executives had benefited from significant increases in employer contributions which had allowed them to accumulate substantial retirement funds on which no tax was being paid because the ARF was not being drawn down as a pension. For example, two individuals were found to have funds exceeding €100 million. In the Finance Act 2006 the Minister for Finance introduced a lifetime limit of €5 million on the size of individual pension funds and provided for ARFs to be subject to income tax on a phased basis from 2007 to 2009 as if not less than 3 per cent of the fund were drawn down annually.

In April 2001 the new framework for personal pensions, the PRSA, was announced by the Minister for Social, Community and Family Affairs. He said (Ahern 2001) that:

> The objective of our pension policy is that all citizens will have an adequate income on retirement and the main components of this are the Social Welfare pension and an occupational/personal pension. The Personal Retirement Savings Account is a key element in our comprehensive pension plans for the twenty first century.

The Press Release setting out the framework for the PRSA lists the main features as follows.

- The PRSA will be contract based between an individual and a PRSA provider.
- There will be standard and non-standard PRSAs – Standard PRSAs will be an 'off the shelf' product with charges capped at 5 per cent of contributions paid and 1 per cent per annum of the assets.
- Charges to a PRSA cannot be expressed in cash terms.
- PRSAs will be regulated by the Pensions Board.
- Employers who do not provide an occupational pension scheme for their employees, must provide access to at least one Standard PRSA.
- Employees can take PRSAs with them when changing jobs.
- Contributors to a PRSA will be able to suspend/reactivate premium payments without penalty.
- Contributors will be able to make contributions irrespective of employment status.
- Contributors will be able to transfer between PRSAs providers without a charge being imposed.
- Contributors will be able to take benefits from a PRSA from the age of 60.
- PRSA providers will be obliged to give contributors a Statement of Reasonable Projection of the value of the PRSA on a regular basis.

The tax relief proposed for a PRSA was somewhat more generous than the tax relief for a personal pension, as a comparison of Table 10.3 with Table 10.2 will show. However, the actual age related tax reliefs eventually granted were the same as for other pension contributions. Contributions can be made to a PRSA even where the contributor is not working and the tax relief can be carried forward and claimed against future earnings on return to work.

Table 10.3 Proposed and actual tax relief on PRSA contributions

Age Band	Proposed percentage of Net Relevant Earnings Eligible for Tax Relief on PRSA Contributions	Actual percentage of Net Relevant Earnings Eligible for Tax Relief, 2002–2005	Actual percentage of Net Relevant Earnings Eligible for Tax Relief, 2006
Under 30	15	15	15
30 < 40	25	20	20
40 < 50	30	25	25
50 < 55	30	30	30
55 < 60	30	30	35
60+	30	30	40

PRSA Charges

The Pensions Board's proposal for kitemarking PRSA products was dropped in favour of standard, cloned and non-standard PRSAs which have to be jointly approved by the Board and the Revenue Commissioners. Cloned PRSAs have similar names to standard PRSAs but lower charges related to the size of the contribution. The official explanation for allowing non-standard PRSAs was that the charges for the standard product were capped whereas no cap was put on the non-standard PRSA to allow providers to recover the cost of providing advice for these products. However, the traditional pension providers had argued strongly for non-standard PRSAs because as Kirby (2001) reported:

> The pension companies lobbied hard against a kite-mark or a maximum charge (they certainly didn't want anything like the total 1% limit imposed on Stakeholder, the UK version of the PRSA). The non-standard PRSA is certainly a compromise – a way for the pension companies (who have had this market to themselves up to now) to earn higher margins and to reward their commission-paid brokers.

Kirby's (2001) report was supported by the subsequent revelation by Brady (2001b) that the Irish Insurance Federation had claimed in a letter to the Minister for Social, Community and Family Affairs, obtained under the Freedom of Information Act, that their members would not be able to live with the price controls on the PRSA while complying with a tighter regulatory environment. The Federation's letter said that 'if the eventual regime does not give sufficient scope for profitability' there is a danger that 'only a limited number of providers [will] choose to enter the market.' The decision of the

Pensions Board to allow traditional providers to market non-standard and cloned PRSAs increased the complexity of the pensions market rather than simplifying it as originally proposed and 'ensured that the PRSA market will be a jungle for the ordinary saver' as Gilhawley (2003, p. 7) pointed out.

The maximum charges that were finally agreed for the Standard PRSA are not cheap and are towards the top end of what is normally charged for personal pensions. Table 10.4 compares charges for a PRSA with charges for an Additional Voluntary Contribution (AVC) scheme for teachers operated by Cornmarket Group Financial Services, charges for an off the shelf pension marketed by the Irish Life Assurance company, and charges for existing personal pension contracts (cited by O'Quigley 2003).

Brady (2001a) argued that Cornmarket Group Financial Services, which is owned by Irish Life and Permanent, were charging 'at the top end of what is normal practice in the pensions business' for their AVC schemes for teachers. He noted that industry sources said that an individual who is not a member of a group scheme could expect to pay a flat €3.81 policy fee on each contribution and an annual management charge of 0.9 per cent. O'Quigley (2003) also noted that 'the capped charge of 5 per cent of each contribution plus 1 per cent per annum of the accumulated fund is not particularly low.' He pointed out that the usual charge for existing personal pension contracts is no more than 5 per cent 'and is frequently less' while 'the average management charge is 0.75 per cent per annum of the accumulated fund.'

Table 10.4 Comparison of maximum charges for a standard PRSA, an AVC and a personal pension contract

	PRSA Max. Charges	Cornmarket Group Charges for AVC for a Teacher	Irish Life Personal Pension	Personal Pension Contract
% of each contribution	5%	5%	€3.81	5%
% of accumulated fund	1%	1.25%	0.9%	0.75%
Once off charge	Nil	€732	Nil	Nil

Source: See text.

Table 10.5 shows the range of the lowest and highest charges on standard or cloned PRSAs levied by 8 providers in July 2007. Cloning, as Gilhawley (2003) notes 'is designed to allow the provider to pay a range of intermediary remuneration terms for the same product, including nil commission…' Eagle Star has the lowest charges of 0 per cent of the contribution and a fund charge of 0.75 per cent per annum while all of the providers except New Ireland – Corporate, charge the maximum allowed of 5 per cent of the contribution and 1 per cent per annum of the fund.

Standard PRSAs were supposed to be a simple product which would be easy for the consumer to understand. However, Table 10.5 shows that the standard

PRSA is a complex product with many confusing variations for which the highest charges differ significantly from the lowest charges. In order for the consumer to compare these charges to find the best value for money it would be necessary to calculate the effect which the charges have in reducing the yield on the PRSA fund over a fixed period of years. For example, if the gross investment return is 6 per cent per annum over a period and the reduction in yield is 1 per cent per annum, the actual return achieved by the owner of the PRSA is 5 per cent per annum. Table 10.5 shows the effect of the lowest and highest charges on a €100 per month contribution on the yield of 28 standard or cloned PRSAs offered by 8 providers in July 2007. The highest charges levied by all of the providers reduce the yield of the investment fund by 2 per cent per annum over a 10-year period compared with 0.75 per cent per annum for the lowest charges. This means that the most expensive versions of the PRSA cost twice as much as the cheapest versions of the same product as Gilhawley (2003) points out.

*Table 10.5 Number of standard PRSA clones offered in July 2007 and reduction in yield (RIY) effect over 10 years of lowest and highest charges**

Provider	no. of standard PRSA or clones offered	lowest charges (contribut. /fund)*	RIY lowest charge version over 10 years*	highest charges (contribut. /fund*	RIY highest charge version over 10 years*
Ark Life	2	5%/1%		5%/1%	2.0% p.a.
Canada Life	4	0%/1%	1.0% p.a.	5%/1%	2.0% p.a
Eagle Star	6	0%/0.75%	0.75%p.a.	5%/1%	2.0% p.a.
EBS	2	2%/1%		5%/1%	2.0% p.a.
Friends First	2	5%/1%	2.0% p.a.	5%/1%	2.0% p.a.
Hibernian	2	5%/1%	1.0% p.a.	5%/1%	2.0% p.a.
Irish Life – retail	2	0%/1%	1.0% p.a.	5%/1%	2.0% p.a.
Irish Life – corpor.	5	1%/1%	1.0% p.a.	5%/1%	2.0% p.a.
New Ireland – retail	2	0%/1%	1.0% p.a.	5%/1%	2.0% p.a.
New Ire. – corpor.	1	2%/1%		2%/1%	

Note: Charges are for a €100 per month contribution.

Source: Update of Gilhawley (2003) and Pensions Board data on PRSA Products and Charges on 11 July 2007.

The maximum charges agreed for a Standard PRSA became the minimum charge for a non-standard PRSA for more than half of the providers as Table 10.6 shows. For them the minimum contribution charge for a non-standard PRSA range from 5 per cent on the contribution and 1 per cent per annum on the fund while the maximum charges range from 15 per cent on the contribution and 1.85 per cent on the fund. Some companies such as Friends First levy a punitive contribution charge on small contributions which would dissuade low income earners from investing in a non-standard PRSA. Most companies have a graduated set of contribution charges which decline as the size of the contribution increases to encourage high income earners to take out a non-standard PRSA.

Using the reduction in yield on the investment fund over a 10-year period shows that Eagle Star has the lowest charges while Friends First has the highest with the reduction in yield for the highest charging provider being more than four times the reduction for the lowest charging provider.

Table 10.6 Number of non-standard PRSAs offered in July 2007 and reduction in yield (RIY) effect over 10 years of lowest and highest charges (in per cent)

Provider	no. of non-standard PRSAs offered	lowest charges (contribut./ fund)*	RIY lowest charge over 10 years*	highest charges (contribut./ fund*	RIY highest charge version over 10 years*
Canada Life	4	0/1	1.3 p.a.	5/1.35	3.1 p.a.
Custom House Capital	2	3.5/1		3.5/1	
Eagle Star	11	0/1	1.0 p.a.	5/2	
Friends First	4	11/1		15/1.375	4.2 p.a.
Hibernian	3	5/1	2 p.a.	13/1	3.8 p.a.
Irish Life–retail	5	5/1.35		5/1.85	2.9 p.a.
New Ireland –retail	3	5/1	2 p.a.	5/1.5	2.6 p.a.

Source: www.pensionsboard.ie.

The reduction in yield on the investment fund is inversely related to the period for which the fund is invested as Table 10.7 indicates. The Government Department responsible (Department of Social and Family Affairs, 2007, Table 12.1), estimates the reduction in yield of the Standard PRSA charges range from 3 per cent per annum for a five year period to 1.3 per cent per annum for a 25-year period. Clearly the longer the number of years for which the fund is invested the smaller is the reduction in yield. Someone who gets a 6 per cent per annum gross return on a PRSA investment but discontinues contributions after five years would receive a net return of only 3 per cent per annum. The greater reduction in yield experienced by short-term contributors is of considerable importance because figures for the UK, cited in the Green Paper, indicate that less than half of those contributing to an employer linked group personal pension are still contributing to it after five years.

It is worth noting that while the charge for a Stakeholder Pension in the UK is lower than the charges for a standard PRSA in Ireland a detailed analysis of pension charges in the UK by the Pensions Commission (2006) suggested that a target annual management charge of 0.3 per cent of assets for a personal pension account is achievable. Unfortunately, the Pensions Board has never published an analysis of pension charges in Ireland or investigated how these charges might be reduced so it is difficult to say if a target of 0.3 per cent is achievable in the smaller Irish personal pensions market.

Table 10.7 Reduction in yield of standard PRSA charges over different periods

Investment Term (Years)	RIY of Maximum Standard PRSA Charges
5	3.0 % p.a.
10	2.0 % p.a.
15	1.6 % p.a.
20	1.5 % p.a.
25	1.3 % p.a.

Source: Department of Social and Family Affairs (2007, Table 12.1).

In addition to the deterrent effect of high PRSA charges, a number of commentators noted the possibility that short-term saving in an SSIA would be more attractive than long-term saving in a PRSA, especially for younger savers. One of the reasons for this was spelled out in an article by Broxson (2001), a director of Irish Pensions Trust. He calculated that a standard rate taxpayer saving the maximum monthly amount of £200 in an SSIA would receive a net payout on the first year's savings of £3,382 whereas the net payout on the same contribution to a PRSA would be £3,470 if the growth rate averaged 8 per cent over the four years since the first year's contribution was invested. Broxson pointed out that his example shows that the standard rate taxpayer would have to take the risk of getting a high rate of return to be only marginally better off with a PRSA than with an SSIA. Taken in conjunction with the requirement that the savings in the PRSA must be locked up until the age of 60 whereas the SSIA savings would be available after five years he argued that the standard rate taxpayers for whom the PRSA was designed would be more likely to put their money into the SSIA scheme. In his opinion the initiative of the Minister for Finance in introducing the SSIA scheme to promote short-term savings had compromised the plans of the Pensions Board and the Minister for Social, Community and Family Affairs to increase long-term saving for a pension.

Another factor which inhibited the take-up of PRSAs was the late insertion of a provision into the Pensions (Amendment) Act 2002, which prohibited switching to a PRSA by employees who had been members of an occupational pension scheme for more than 15 years. It was rumoured that large occupational funds lobbied for this change as they were afraid of significant losses of parts of their assets, (noted by Schultze and Moran 2007). In addition the Revenue Commissioners were concerned that wealthy taxpayers would switch out of occupational schemes into PRSAs to shield up to 40 per cent of their income from tax from the age of 40 onwards and to avail of the opportunity to take 25 per cent of the accumulated fund as a tax free lump sum on retirement after the age of 60. There was also a general fear that unscrupulous companies might miss-sell personal pensions to employees with perfectly adequate occupational arrangements as had occurred in the UK.

Further developments that diluted the original PRSA proposal to provide easy access to pensions was the requirement in the Pensions (Amendment) Act 2002 that only banks and life assurance companies would be recognised providers of PRSAs and that any employer contribution to a PRSA would be regarded as a benefit in kind for the employee. The latter provision is inconsistent with research evidence from the United States that the take-up of personal pensions is likely to be much higher when the employer makes a matching contribution (Munnell and Sunden 2003).

In addition, the decision to allow cloned and non-standard PRSAs as a concession to the industry resulted in many of the pension providers concentrating their marketing effort on the cloned and non-standard products. The finance director of ARK Life, the life assurance wing of Allied Irish Banks, was reported in February 2003 by Slattery (2003a) to believe that the industry would 'shun the standard PRSA, where charges are capped at a low level, and promote their more lucrative non-standard versions instead.' Evidence to support this contention was provided in the same month when the Pensions Board announced the names of the first six companies it had approved to provide PRSAs. These companies offered 41 PRSA products of which 16 were Standard or clones and 25 were non-standard. In September 2006 there were 10 companies offering 59 PRSA products on the market of which 25 were Standard or clones and 34 were non-standard. Nevertheless, the majority of those who purchased a PRSA opted for the standard product.

7. TAKE-UP OF PRSA

Providers of PRSAs accredited by the Pensions Board began to market them in April 2003 in time for the deadline of 15 September 2003 set by the Board as the date by which all employers would be legally obliged to have nominated at least one provider who would supply a PRSA for their employees. Even before that date industry sources were reported to be pessimistic about the possibility of PRSAs attracting large numbers of investors. They criticised the Government for making the products more complex to sell than had been envisaged in the Pensions Board's original proposals and the failure to offer pension products through retail outlets. However, the industry itself appears to have been responsible for the exclusion of retail outlets as such a development would have threatened their control of the pensions market. The initial marketing of PRSAs was criticised because the description 'Standard PRSA' for the basic product risked confusion with the pension products of Standard Life, a pension provider which had been operating in Ireland since the 1800s, and because the name PRSA was registered by a private company rather than by the State organisations responsible for promoting or regulating PRSAs (see Hobbs 2003).

In June 2003 shortly after the PRSA products were launched, the Irish Financial Services Regulatory Authority (IFSRA), which jointly regulates PRSAs with the Pensions Board, issued instructions to pension providers about how the sale of products. Providers are obliged to spell out to prospective clients at the point of sale, the difference between standard and non-standard products. The sale is not valid without a signed declaration from both parties that all risks have been pointed out and that all relevant information has been provided. In addition the provider has to give each client a consumer fact sheet issued by the financial regulator. The director of the IFSRA consumer division said that the reason for these precautions was that 'we do not want consumers encouraged to purchase a non-standard PRSA when it is not required, simply to generate additional revenue for the financial institutions.' (quoted by Kirby 2003)

A further criticism of PRSAs was made by a number of trade union leaders. The Regional Secretary of Amicus-MSF (now retitled UNITE), which represents 30,000 Irish workers, pointed out (Slattery 2003b) that employers did not have to pay Pay Related Social Insurance (PRSI) on the PRSA contribution made by an employee. Effectively, therefore, the employer PRSI contribution was reduced without an obligation on employers to make any contribution to their employees PRSA. Irish Life, one of the largest providers of PRSAs, estimated on the basis of the average contribution by its PRSA clients that the reduction amounted to about €300 per contributing employee per year in cases where the employer was not contributing anything to the PRSA (Slattery 2003c).

In providing information about PRSAs the Pensions Board has focused on the number of employers, employees and others taking out PRSA contracts.[3] Although it collects some information about the characteristics of those taking out PRSAs this information is not in the public domain. This makes it difficult to estimate the percentage of PRSAs being bought by those at work and not at work who have no pension coverage. All of the information the Board has about the characteristics of owners of PRSAs should be made available on its website.

The information which is available is presented in the tables which follow. Table 10.8 and Figure 10.1 show the number of employers who have nominated a pension provider for their firm in each quarter from September 2003 to September 2007, the percentage of employers designating a PRSA provider and the percentage of firms whose employees were contributing to a PRSA. By December 2003, three months after the date by which all firms were required to have designated a PRSA provider, 58,770 employers had nominated a provider or just under 40 per cent of the total number of registered firms in 2003.

The response to designating a PRSA provider by the required date was so poor that in September 2004 the Pensions Board contacted 64,000 firms to remind them of their legal obligation to designate a PRSA provider. Over time

Table 10.8 Number of employers designating a PRSA provider and number of firms where contributions are being made, 2003–2007

Date	No. of emplyrs. designating a PRSA provider	No. of firms making contributions.	Percentage of emplyrs. designating a provider	Percentage of firms in which employees are contributing to a PRSA
Sep 2003	51,782	845		
Dec 2003	58,770	2,502	39.6	1.7
Mar 2004	60,505	4,050		
June 2004	61,977	5,251		
Sep 2004	66,486	5,951		
Dec 2004	70,382	6,694	44.7	4.3
Mar 2005	71,634	7,245		
June 2005	72,779	7,667		
Sep 2005	74,284	8,193		
Dec 2005	76,304	8,710	47.5	5.4
Mar 2006	77,667	9,251		
June 2006	78,590	9,680		
Sep 2006	79,494	10,168		
Dec 2006	80,463	10,647	47.1	6.2
Mar 2007	81,516	11,226		
Jun 2007	82,467	11,764		
Sep 2007	83,361	12,304		

Source: Pensions Board PRSA figures.

Note: No. of firms on Companies Register: 2003 148,303; 2004 157,502; 2005 160,707; 2006 170,719.

the number of employers designating a provider increased and by December 2006 80,463 employers, or 47 per cent of all firms, had designated a PRSA provider. As employers are not obliged to make any contributions to PRSAs the number of firms where contributions are being made is far less than the number of firms which have designated a provider. In December 2003 contributions were made by the employees of 2,502 firms or less than 2 per cent of all firms. The number increased gradually over time so that in December 2006 employees of 10,647 firms were making contributions. To date, therefore, there are just about 6 per cent of firms in which employees have availed of the opportunity to contribute to a PRSA. The average number of contributors per firm is just three and a half.

The number of those at work and those not at work making contributions to PRSAs is shown in Table 10.9 and Figure 10.2. In September 2003 2,454 people at work and 4,253 people not at work were contributing to a PRSA. The number in both categories contributing increased steadily up to September 2007 to 42,926 of those at work and 76,936 of those not at work. Relating the number of PRSA contributors to the total number of persons at work and not at work shows that the take-up rate for persons at work increased from 0.1 per cent in

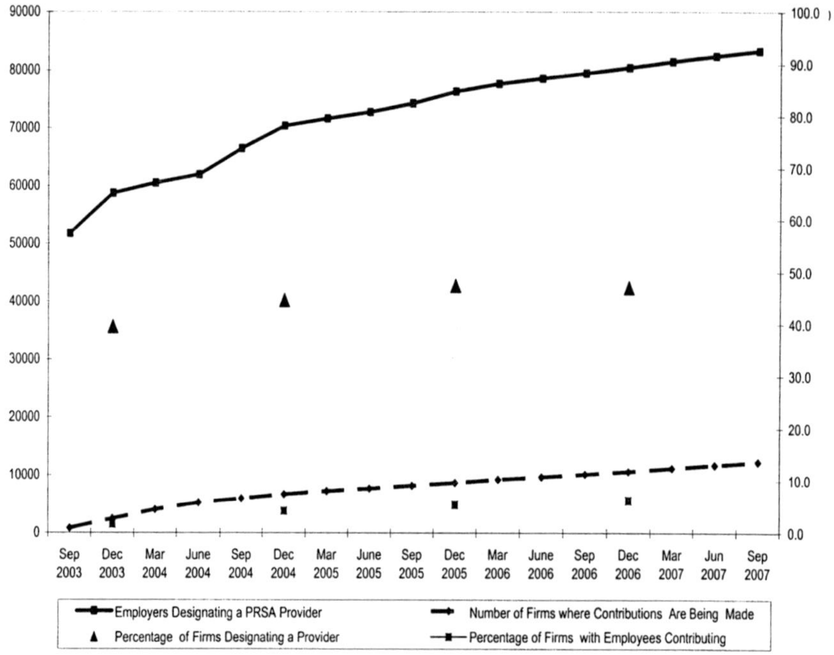

Figure 10.1 Number and percentage of firms designating a PRSA provider and number and percentage of firms whose employees are contributing to a PRSA

September 2003 to nearly 2 per cent in June 2007 while for persons not at work it increased from 0.3 per cent to 5.8 per cent. The coverage rate for employees achieved to date by PRSAs has, therefore, been very small. PRSAs have been much less successful in increasing coverage of their target group (people at work) than of people not at work for whom the Pensions Board set no coverage target.

The split between standard and non-standard PRSAs is shown in Table 10.10. Just over 71 per cent of PRSA contracts written in September 2003 were for standard PRSAs. The figure increased to a peak of 79.4 per cent in June 2004 but since then it has fallen back to its current level of 76.5 per cent These data suggest that the great majority of purchasers of a personal pension want a fixed cost, low risk, quality assured product which can be purchased without having to seek professional advice. As there is no published information on the characteristics of purchasers of the standard and non-standard products we

Table 10.9 Total number contributing to a PRSA comparing employees and others, 2003–2007

Date	No. of employees making PRSA contributions	People Not in Labour Force making PRSA contributions	Total making PRSA contributs.	% of employees making PRSA contributions	% not in labour force making PRSA contributions
Sep 2003	2,454	4,253	6,707	0.1	0.3
Dec 2003	7,499	11,523	19,022	0.4	0.9
Mar 2004	12,464	14,435	26,899	0.7	1.1
June 2004	16,048	16,872	32,920	0.8	1.4
Sep 2004	18,117	18,969	37,086	1.0	1.5
Dec 2004	20,286	25,971	46,257	1.1	2.0
Mar 2005	22,162	28,634	50,796	1.1	2.3
June 2005	23,658	31,353	55,011	1.2	2.6
Sep 2005	25,555	33,696	59,251	1.3	2.7
Dec 2005	27,381	40,876	68,257	1.4	3.2
Mar 2006	29,433	43,889	73,322	1.5	3.5
June 2006	31,154	46,889	78,043	1.5	3.8
Sep 2006	33,274	50,516	83,790	1.6	4.0
Dec 2006	35,285	59,760	95,045	1.7	4.7
Mar 2007	37,884	65,143	103,027	1.8	5.2
Jun 2007	40,411	71,421	111,832	1.9	5.8
Sep 2007	42,926	76,936	119,862		

Source: Pensions Board PRSA figures

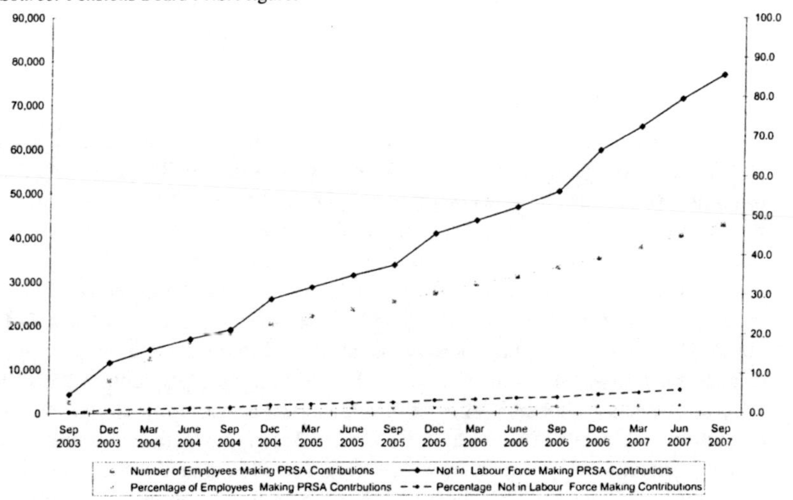

Figure 10.2 Number and percentage of employees and people not in the labour force contributing to a PRSA, 2003–2007

cannot investigate how purchasers of the standard and non-standard products differ in their attitude to risk and rate of return.

Table 10.10 Number of standard and non-standard PRSA contracts sold, 2003– 2007

	Number of PRSA Contracts Sold			
Date	Standard	Non-Standard	Total	% Standard
Sep 2003	4,764	1,943	6,707	71.0
Dec 2003	14,686	4,336	19,022	77.2
Mar 2004	21,306	5,593	26,899	79.2
June 2004	26,154	6,766	32,920	79.4
Sep 2004	29,373	7,713	37,086	79.2
Dec 2004	36,557	9,700	46,257	79.0
Mar 2005	40,102	10,694	50,796	78.9
June 2005	43,205	11,806	55,011	78.5
Sep 2005	46,359	12,892	59,251	78.2
Dec 2005	53,001	15,256	68,257	77.6
Mar 2006	56,678	16,644	73,322	77.3
June 2006	59,887	18,156	78,043	76.7
Sep 2006	64,111	19,679	83,790	76.5
Dec 2006	72,761	22,284	95,045	76.6
Mar 2007	78,926	24,101	103,027	76.6
Jun 2007	85,355	26,477	111,832	76.3
Sep 2007	91,675	28,187	119,862	76.5

Source: Pensions Board PRSA Figures.

Although the PRSA is a personal pension rater than an occupational pension it appears that nearly all of those at work contributing to a PRSA (about 2 per cent of employees) regard it as an occupational pension. Table 10.11 shows that in the first quarter of 2002, before the introduction of PRSAs, the pension coverage rate for persons at work was 51.2 per cent according to a special survey carried out by the Central Statistics Office (2004). In the firs t quarter of 2005 the coverage rate had increased to 55 per cent (see Central Statistics Office, 2006). However, all of this increase is attributed to the growth in coverage of Occupational pensions from 35.4 per cent in 2002 to 40.1 per cent in 2005.[4] The coverage rates for personal pensions and for personal and occupational pensions combined both declined between 2002 and 2005. It appears, therefore, that about half the increase in pension coverage between 2002 and 2005 is due to the introduction of PRSAs. Unfortunately, there is very little published information available on the characteristics of contributors to PRSAs so it is not possible to provide a comprehensive analysis of how those at work and those not at work differ in their PRSA contributions. However, the fact that the take-up rate for persons not at work is almost three times greater than for persons at work indicates that PRSAs are unattractive for their primary target group of people who are in employment but who have no pension cover. Data from Household Budget Survey 2004–2005 (CSO 2007) provide strong evidence that people in households which have little or no private pension cover or cover from AVC schemes are not contributing to PRSAs.

Table 10.11 Overall private pension coverage of persons in employment (ILO) aged 20 – 69 years in the first quarter of 2002 and 2005 from CSO surveys

Category	Pension Coverage 2002 Q1 (%)	Pension Coverage in 2005 Q4 (%)
Occupational pension only	35.4	40.1
Personal pension only	12.9	12.1
Both	2.9	2.8
Total	51.2	55.0

Note: Green Paper par. 12.30 shows data which suggest that almost all new registrations of occupational schemes are due to one-member schemes because of attractiveness of ARFs.

Source: Central Statistics Office (2004 and 2005).

Table 10.12 shows that virtually nobody in households in the bottom half of the income distribution is contributing to a PRSA. Virtually all of those contributing to a PRSA are in the top half of the income distribution where households already have pension cover. For households which are contributing to a PRSA, the average contribution is less than €1 per week. This suggests that households contributing to a PRSA are not saving nearly enough to ensure that the combined value of their retirement income from a PRSA and the State pension will replace 50 per cent of their pre-retirement income. An analysis in the Green Paper (2007, Tables 9.3 and 9.4) suggests that the average contributor is paying 10.5 per cent of salary and that this is not nearly enough to provide a replacement rate of 50 per cent of pay from a combination of a personal and a State pension. Benchmarking the actual against the required contribution rates for 42,109 active PRSA contributors the Green Paper shows that 80 per cent of those earning over €25,000 are not saving enough to achieve the replacement rate target.

Table 10.12 Actual and percentage private pension fund contributions, additional voluntary contributions (AVC) and PRSA contributions by income decile, 2004–2005

Gross household income deciles (€)	Private pension fund contrib -utions	AVC contrib -utions	PRSA contrib -utions	Gross av. household income (€)	Private pen. fund contrib- utions	AVC contrib -utions	PRSA contrib -utions
					Percentage of household income		
1st Decile <190.37	0.21	0.00	0.00	150.00	0.14	0.00	0.00
2nd Decile –312.23	0.06	0.00	0.00	251.30	0.02	0.00	0.00
3rd Decile –433.37	0.63	0.00	0.04	372.75	0.17	0.00	0.01
4th Decile –599.11	3.08	0.10	0.17	516.24	0.60	0.02	0.03
5th Decile –777.33	7.03	0.10	0.02	688.22	1.02	0.01	0.00
6th Decile –983.50	13.25	0.64	0.55	880.42	1.50	0.07	0.06
7th Decile –1228.62	21.92	2.03	0.50	1106.06	1.98	0.18	0.05
8th Decile –1526.39	32.58	2.71	0.71	1377.51	2.37	0.20	0.05
9th Decile –2024.14	50.98	6.18	0.56	1775.27	2.87	0.35	0.03
10th Decile >2024.14	115.75	10.18	0.91	3000.00	3.86	0.34	0.03
State	24.53	2.19	0.35				

Source: CSO (2007)

It is clear from the limited amount of information available on the take-up of PRSAs that the introduction of very generous age-related tax incentives for personal pensions has not overcome the barriers to the extension of the private pension system. The introduction of PRSAs has not resulted in the dramatic increase in pension coverage of those at work that the Pensions Board expected when it recommended that there should be easy access to low cost, low risk, off the shelf personal pensions. The most important reasons for this failure appear to be the high cost of the standard PRSA, the lack of co-operation of employers in designating providers, the lack of a matching contribution by the employer and the increased complexity which PRSAs have introduced into the pensions market. Another factor which merits further consideration is the introduction of a Special Saving Incentive Account to encourage short-term saving at a time when a major strand of Government savings policy was to encourage long-term saving for retirement. This issue is explored in the next section.

8. THE ORIGINS OF THE SPECIAL SAVINGS INCENTIVE ACCOUNTS SCHEME

In the Finance Act 2001 the Minister for Finance introduced a Special Saving Incentive Account (SSIA) to encourage short-term savings. Under this scheme individuals were allowed to save up to £200 (€254) per month to which the Government would add 25 per cent or a maximum of £50 (€63.50) per month provided the money was left on deposit with a recognised financial institution for a period of five years (see www.Revenue.ie). Individuals were given one year from May 2001 to May 2002 to decide whether to invest in the scheme

The SSIA scheme is costly in terms of tax foregone but in contrast to PRSAs was very successful in terms of the number of participants. During the year 2000 the Minister for Enterprise, Trade and Employment, Mary Harney, was reported as arguing for the introduction of tax-based incentives to increase medium to long-term saving (*Irish Times*, 19 July 2000). Prior to the 2001 Budget there were numerous submissions arguing for tax incentives for savings schemes (*Irish Times* 4 December 2000), including one from the Irish Congress of Trade Unions. However the scheme as introduced is most similar to one proposed by the EBS Building Society (*Irish Times*, 14 November 2000). The scheme as proposed and introduced was not included in the Budget statement for 2001, and hence not debated as part of the Annual Budget, but rather was introduced as an amendment to the Finance Bill and discussed at Committee Stage by the Finance and Public Service Committee.[5] Perhaps for this reason this initiative did not receive a great deal of analytic discussion. The Minister for Finance on introducing the amendment to introduce the scheme stated:

> The introduction of this scheme will encourage people, particularly younger people, to get into the habit of savings. We were all young once and, in the nature of things, it is only now that we fully appreciate that, just as it is never too early to plant a tree, it is never too early to start savings. I commend the amendment to the Committee. This amendment, which runs to 23 pages, is a major part of the Bill.

During the course of the committee debate the Minister also discussed the possible cost in terms of tax foregone as being approximately €130 million (£100 million) per annum. This turned out to be a gross underestimate. Reference is also made by the Minister to opposition to this scheme from his own officials in the Department of Finance because of possible switching from other savings schemes, for example savings in new individual pension arrangements such as the PRSA. As already noted, this had been recommended in the Pensions Board report in 1998 (Pensions Board, 1998, Chapter 6) and it was finally enacted in the Pensions (Amendment) Act, 2002.

SSIA funds could be invested in a variety of savings instruments for example equity based, or deposit based with a fixed or variable interest rate, although most SSIA contracts were for interest only based returns. Because of the subsidy, the minimum rate of return on a deposit scheme (assuming zero interest rates) is over 8 per cent compound per annum. Assuming an additional rate of return for a deposit type scheme of 4.5 per cent per annum, the rate of return after tax (23 per cent of interest earned) is just over 12.1 per cent.[6] Thus the returns were above any other comparable savings product and the numbers participating, sums saved, and costs to the exchequer were also large as shown in Table 10.13.

Table 10.13 shows that the absolute number of those with SSIA schemes has fallen over time, but annual subscriptions have increased leading to a rise in average monthly payments (Department of Finance, 2005).

Table 10.13 Subscriptions to SSIA schemes, tax cost to the exchequer and number of subscribers

Year	Subscriptions € million	Tax Cost € million	Number of Subscribers 000s
31 Dec. 2001	356.6	71	398
30 April 2002			1,170
31 Dec. 2002	1,859.3	433	1,143
31 Dec. 2003	2,187.3	532	1,114
31 Dec. 2004	2,264.8	548	1,094
31 Dec. 2005		597	1,084

Source: Pensions Board, National Pensions Review Appendix 8, Tables 3.1 and 3.2, Tax Strategy Group, Special Savings Incentive Accounts, various years.

The CSO (2003) estimate the total population aged 20 and over was 2,777,000 in 2002. The legal age to enter an SSIA contract was 18, and if it is assumed that a small number with SSIA contracts were aged 18–19, 42 per cent of the total adult population joined this scheme. It is likely that an even larger proportion of the workforce (1,801,000 in 2002) entered an SSIA contract. The success of the SSIA scheme in terms of numbers involved and absolute value of funds (€15 billion according to a Department of Finance press release dated 1 June 2006) compared with personal pension schemes (particularly PRSAs) has led to calls for similar arrangements for personal pension arrangements, in particular from financial institutions (See Department of Finance 2005 appendix 3). The National Pensions Review states (p. 78):

> ... a significant number of contributions to the NPR process have proposed that the incentive for supplementary pensions should be provided by means of a partial contribution match (as for SSIAs) rather than as tax relief. Under this proposal, pension contributions would be made from after tax income, but the Exchequer would add a matching contribution to the pension investment made each year.

The National Pensions Review Report goes on to comment (p. 74) that the success of SSIAs is due 'in large part' to the means of granting tax relief via a direct grant.

There are also proposals in the National Pensions Review to 'Capture SSIA Savings' (p. 75), via extra tax reliefs and to relax rules for contributions to pensions. The National Pensions Review states (par 7.13):

> SSIA take up was considerably higher than expected. The data about income and ages of SSIA holders show that in many cases they are from those groups with relatively low pension coverage, which seems to indicate that SSIAs have succeeded where the pensions savings message has not been effective.

Data presented in the National Pensions Review shows that SSIA saving is largely a function of income (p. 330): high income tax payers earning €50,000 or more per annum amounted to 6.1 per cent of all tax payers but they accounted for 17.1 per cent of all SSIA account holders. Most middle (earning less than €50,000) and low income earners (earning less than €20,000) are likely to have contributed less than the maximum permitted per month. At the end of 2003, 40 per cent of all accounts were for the maximum permitted amount per month. If it is assumed that all high income earners saved the maximum amount per month, then 24 per cent of all middle and low income earners made the maximum permitted saving. Most of these are likely to be middle income earners. Arguments for granting incentives to convert SSIA schemes into personal pension plans assume that those with SSIA schemes do not have adequate pension cover. However there is no evidence presented in this Report that those without pension provision constitute a significant proportion of those with SSIA accounts.

9. COSTS AND RETURNS FROM SSIA INVESTMENTS

To date, equity linked schemes may have higher gross returns, but these returns (excluding the government subsidy) are subject to tax. In addition there are management charges. These can vary from institution to institution (Barrington 2006). One institution charged 5 per cent of the monthly payment plus 1.65 per cent of the value of the investment. If it is assumed that in addition to the benefits provided by the State, returns amount to 4.5 per cent per annum, charges as described over a five-year period reduce the lump sum after tax by €1,475. Another way of considering this is to estimate the required return in an equity–based scheme which would achieve a comparable lump sum as in a savings scheme earning a fixed rate of 4.5 per cent per annum with zero charges. On this basis the required comparable compound annual return almost doubles to 8.3 per cent. It is also interesting to note that required returns are higher partly because tax payments are higher, as a greater proportion of returns consist of taxable income. A similar concept in estimating the effects of costs is to consider the reduction in yield, defined as the difference between gross returns and net returns to an investor after all charges have been met (Pensions Commission, 2nd Report, p. 437). So that in the case of a return of 4.5 per cent per annum gross of charges, net of charges returns fall to 1.22 per cent resulting in a reduction in yield of 3.28 per cent. These estimates of the reduction in yield are indicative as return calculations are sensitive to the precise way in which charges and returns are calculated, so that returns and charges may not be estimated on a monthly basis as assumed here but may be compounded quarterly and charges estimated on the value of the fund at year-end and on this basis the estimated reduction in yield would fall.

The combination of variable charges as a function of the accumulating sum, taxation on the accrued lump sum (excluding the government subsidy), but no tax relief on falls in the value of the lump sum and volatility in asset prices can result in asymmetric returns – an increase of 10 per cent in asset values in the first four years will not compensate for a 10 per cent fall in asset values the following (fifth) year. In addition because the lump sum accrues through time changes in asset values towards the end of the life of the savings scheme can have large absolute effects.

This can be illustrated using the following SSIA example. Assume the maximum permitted contribution, in an equity-based scheme in which growth is at 10.9 per cent gross of management charges, per annum compound for four years, but that in the last year growth is zero, and that charges are fixed at 5 per cent of the annual contribution and 1.65 per cent of the accumulated fund. So that the value of the fund falls by 1.65 per cent in the fifth year. On this basis an equity based fund at the end of the fifth year is slightly lower than that of a fixed interest fund earning 4.5 per cent compound per annum. This example illustrates the interaction between the charge structure, and variable rates of return, in determining the overall value of the fund. Finally because a fund is growing though time the effects of falls in asset prices in the last year have large absolute effects on the value of the fund and rates of return. So that if asset growth were 20 per cent compound per annum for the first four years and then fell 15 per cent in year 5 including charges as described previously the value of the accumulated fund is slightly lower than the no charges no risk example earning 4.5 per cent compound. In this example, returns are considerably below the arithmetic average – 15 per cent. A DC type pension fund accumulating over a 40-year period, with investments in assets whose prices may vary is likely to experience similar periodic falls in fund values with consequent adverse timing effects on the size of pension payments.

The examples illustrate the gap between investment returns and returns to the savings contract. A similar gap exists for pension contracts. The pensions commission in the UK has extensive discussion of costs (Pension Commission, First Report pp. 72–81). Costs of providing individual pensions are estimated at annual management charge of 1.5 per cent compared with a cost of 0.1 per cent for State pensions and between 0.1 and 0.3 per cent for large company schemes (Pensions Commission, Second Report, p. 70).

Such charges may partly explain the low take-up of PRSA-type schemes. Although maximum charges are set at 5 per cent of the contribution and 1 per cent of the accumulated fund on standard PRSA schemes, charges may be higher on non-standard PRSAs (see Tables 10.5 and 10.6). The same calculations were performed for a PRSA scheme over a five-year period as for an equity-based SSIA with returns of 4.5 per cent per annum, but with lower annual charges of 1 per cent, and 5 per cent of annual contributions. It was also assumed that the same gross amount is invested as in the previous examples (€317.44). If charges of 5 per cent are levelled on the gross amount contributed the actual sum invested amounts to €301.60. The lump sum amounts to Euro €19,744 after five years a reduction of €1,570 compared with a lump sum in the absence of charges. This equals a reduction in yield over a five-year period of 2 per cent. Taxation changes the net of tax returns as PRSA payments are tax deductible. This means that the higher the marginal tax rate the greater the deduction, funds accumulate tax free but 25 per cent of the accumulated fund may be withdrawn without tax. So that if it is assumed that an individual can deduct payments into a PRSA at a marginal tax rate of 42 per cent, the fund accumulates at 4.5 per cent per annum. If it is also assumed that charges are as in the previous example, and that the fund is liquidated after 5 years, the rate of return after tax is 8 per cent compound. Because taxation forms a large part of the total returns changes in future tax rates are a considerable source of uncertainty in relation to future returns. Another source of uncertainty in relation to net returns arises from changes in tax liabilities. Those who pay no tax cannot benefit from tax concessions.

The Pensions Board has published a discussion document on a possible mandatory pension system designed to increase coverage. The Report states that it is 'a technical examination of the practical issues' (p. 22, 31). Given the effect of charges and tax rates on returns it is surprising that the Pensions Board mandatory system gives such a very brief discussion of charges (p. 77). In contrast to the work of the Pensions Commission in the UK there are no estimates of reduction in yield due to management charges. Nor is there any discussion on the effects of differing assumed rates of taxation on returns.

The Finance Act 2006 included provisions to increase pension saving and pension coverage. These measures consists of granting tax and other reliefs designed to encourage those holding SSIA accounts to transfer funds into a PRSA account. Such a measure was advocated in the recently published National Pensions Review (2006 p. 15) and by the pensions industry. The reason for this initiative is low coverage of occupational pensions as discussed earlier and the relative failure of the PRSA initiative to increase coverage. Pension coverage according to CSO surveys (2002, 2006) is static at around 51 per cent despite the large sums spent on 'awareness campaigns' by the Pensions Board.

The industry wants to capture this large pool of SSIA saving because their fee income is a function of the size of assets under their control.

In terms of increasing coverage this initiative did not have much effect. The Minister noted in his Budget Statement that the current cost of tax reliefs in terms of revenue foregone is in excess of €3 billion per annum, yet occupational pension coverage appears to be falling. So it is puzzling why even more tax reliefs would increase coverage. One reason why increased tax reliefs will not increase coverage is because of complexity. The rules under which tax relief will be granted under this current initiative are complex (see Finance Act 2006). Tax relief was also restricted in various ways. For example only those with incomes in the previous year of less that €50,000 and paying tax at the lower rate are eligible. But more fundamentally the Pensions Board and the industry do not appear to understand why SSIAs were successful and PRSAs were not. The Board seem to consider that the success of SSIAs was due to 'the means of granting tax relief' and 'branding'. The reality is that these products had guaranteed rates of return (provided as in the vast bulk of cases, they were not invested in equities), these rates of return were higher than any other savings product before or since, there were no charges (unless they were equity based), they were virtually risk free (again unless they were equity based), and because they were short term there was little longevity risk (it is highly unlikely that those with SSIAs would die before they matured).

10. THE KEY ISSUES IN PENSION PROVISION

It is likely that the bulk of SSIA savings are held by those who are currently members of occupational pensions. The most recent tax changes designed to switch SSIA funds into personal pension products is a distraction from the core of the problem. There are three main issues that need to be addressed strategically in relation to pension provision. These are first, the large and growing number of those aged 65 and over. Second, the low numbers who are members of an occupational pension scheme, and the inadequacy of the pensions many have now and will have in the future. This means that large numbers now, and many more in the future, will be dependent on the State Old Age pension for retirement income. Currently the State Old Age pension is about 60 per cent of the minimum wage and about one-third of the average gross industrial wage. The third main issue is that most defined benefit pension schemes in Ireland are in serious financial difficulties

There are a number of reasons why so many people either have no pension at all or one which is not adequate for their needs. One of these is the excessive charges made by those selling pension products. The Commission on Public Service Pensions, for example, estimated the costs for one type of personal pension as varying between 12 per cent and 20 per cent of contributions and this estimate excluded certain charges.

A second reason is that there are considerable tax advantages to pension savings. But for those who are unemployed or changing jobs or for whatever reason not earning taxable income, the value of tax allowances is reduced or may be zero. For those with an atypical working career, for example many women opt out of paid work during child-rearing years, the value of pension tax reliefs for those years is zero.

A third reason is the risk people take when they establish a personal pension. The returns for them are very uncertain. This means that where average returns are expected to be positive individual returns may still be negative. There may also be variations in returns over a time period. These factors can have a considerable impact on the size of eventual pension payments.There are other risks borne by pension providers which can impact on individual pensioners. Circumstances such as when pensioners live longer than anticipated and the pension provider has not adequately provided for future pension liabilities. Just such a situation arose for those with pension and other policies with Equitable Life and remain unresolved.

It will be recalled that the Pensions Board listed a number of barriers inhibiting the expansion of the private pension system. The attempt to overcome these barriers by introducing personal pension accounts has failed to increase private pension coverage in Ireland because the Government was unable to provide easy access to private pension products through supermarkets and the Post Office because the pensions industry was able to persuade the Government to confine provision to traditional providers. The Government was unable to persuade the pensions industry to market PRSA products at low cost. The charges levied by the industry for the standard product are at the high end of the fees charged for providing personal pensions. The pensions industry successfully argued that low cost products would not be profitable and was able to charge high fees for providing the standard product and to introduce a non-standard product without any regulation of the fees to be charged.

The Government was unable to give any guarantees about the prospective rate of return on PRSAs. It is made clear to purchasers of PRSAs that the State would not compensate them in the event of poor investment performance. Purchasers of PRSAs, therefore, have no certainty about what level of income their personal pension will provide in retirement.

The introduction of SSIAs before PRSAs were launched made a short-term savings plan available to potential purchasers of PRSAs which was far more attractive than a PRSA because the Government provided an explicit matching contribution and the money invested could be withdrawn after five years rather than at the age of 60 or over. The risk attached to investment in a PRSA was higher for a standard rate taxpayer than the risk attached to investment in an SSIA. Both of these factors undoubtedly influenced some individuals to enter an SSIA type contract rather than a PRSA, but it is difficult to estimate the numbers involved.

The prohibition on older members of occupational pension schemes transferring their pension assets to a PRSA confined PRSAs to younger members of the labour force who had less disposable income with which to purchase a personal pension.

In order to safeguard the interests of consumers the Government obliged pension providers to give information about standard and non-standard PRSA products which undermined the intention of having an 'off the shelf' product which could be bought without requiring any advice from pension providers.

The failure to require employers to make some contribution towards PRSAs has undermined employees' willingness to invest in them. Munnell and Sunden (2003) cite research in the United States which indicates that the take-up of personal pensions is strongly influenced by whether the employer makes a matching contribution or not.

11. CONCLUSION

For future retirees the most efficient (and cost effective way) of increasing retirement income for those without current pension coverage is to increase the basic State pension. The cost to the State could be contained by significantly reducing tax relief for private pensions. Currently the cost of pension tax expenditure on private pensions in Ireland as a proportion of GDP is the highest in the OECD. Such a solution would have the merit of introducing a greater measure of fairness into the pension system. It would redistribute State expenditure currently devoted to tax reliefs to increasing state pensions and help redress the anomaly where those who are already well off benefit disproportionately from pension tax reliefs.

In launching the National Pensions Review, the Minister for Social, Community and Family Affairs stated 'There is a view that some form of mandatory provision is the only way of ensuring that people make adequate provision for their retirement'. Ireland already has a mandatory pension – the basic State Pension – why not use it?

NOTES

1. We would like to thank Tony Gilhawley of Technical Guidance Ltd. for providing information about the market for Personal Retirement Savings Accounts.
2. In 2002 the personal rate for the Old Age Contributory Pension amounted to €134.59, or about 30 per cent of gross average industrial earnings, so that the target of €127 was exceeded.
3. All employers except those who provide an occupational scheme for all of their employees are obliged to designate a PRSA provider. As Hughes and Whelan (1996) estimated that only 4 per cent of employers had schemes that covered all employees the percentage of employers designating PRSA providers is based on the total number of firms listed in the Companies Registration Office.

4. Membership figures from the Annual Reports of the Pensions Board suggest that coverage of occupational schemes has fallen from 40.2 per cent in 2002 to 38.1 per cent in 2005. 5.
5. See Finance Bill 2001 Committee Stage, Committee Debates, Joint Committee, Finance and the Public Service, 7 March 2001, available at http://www.gov.ie/committees.
6. These and subsequent calculations were performed using the standard excel annuity function.

REFERENCES

Ahern, D., (1998), *Action on Pensions*, Dublin: Planning Unit, Department of Social, Community and Family Affairs, 7 May.

Ahern, D., (2001). 'Dermot Ahern Publishes Framework for Personal Retirement Savings Account (PRSAs)', Department of Social, Community and Family Affairs Press Release, 12 April.

Barrington, K. (2006). 'SSIA Charges the Tip of the Iceberg', *Sunday Business Post*, 29 January.

Brady, N., (2001a) 'Teacher's Pension Lesson', *Sunday Tribune*, 24 June.

Brady, N., (2001b), 'Insurers Attack Government Charge Controls on Pensions', *Sunday Tribune*, 12 August.

Broxson, A., (2001), 'Pension Scheme Has Competition for Participants', *Irish Times*, 20 April.

Central Statistics Office, (2001), *Population by Age 2002*, Available at http://www.cso.ie/statistics/.

Central Statistics Office, (2002), *Quarterly National Household Survey: Pensions*, First Quarter 2002.

Central Statistics Office (2003), *Census 2002 Principal Socio Economic Trends*, Dublin: Stationery Office.

Central Statistics Office, (2004), Quarterly National Household Survey: Pensions Update. First Quarter 2004.

Central Statistics Office, (2006), *Quarterly National Household Survey: Pension Provision*, Fourth Quarter 2005.

Central Statistics Office, (2007), *Household Budget Survey 2004–2005.*

Department of Finance (2005), Tax Strategy Group, *Special Savings Investment Accounts*, 05/13, available at http://www.finance.gov.ie.

Department of Finance (2006), 'Internal Review of Certain Tax Schemes: Section G: Tax Relief for Pensions Provision – Sections 770-790B of the Taxes Consolidation Act 1997', available at www.finance.gov.ie

Department of Social and Family Affairs (2007, *Green Paper on Pensions*, Dublin: Department of Social and Family Affairs.

Gilhawley, T., (2003), 'PRSA's – The Real Picture Emerges, and it isn't a Pretty Sight', *Irish Pensions*, Summer 2003.

Hobbs, E., (2003), 'Cracking Up…', *Irish Examiner*, 25 June.

Hughes, G., and B. Whelan, (1996), *Occupational and Personal Pension Coverage 1995*, Dublin: The Economic and Social Research Institute.

Kirby, J., (1998) 'Proposed PRSAs Would Make Pensions More Accessible', *Irish Times*, 13 May .

Kirby, J., (2001) 'Hatching Your Own Nest Egg', *Business and Finance*, 19 April.

Kirby, J., (2003) 'Regulator Right to Target Non-Standard PRSAs', *Sunday Times*, 29 June.

McManus, J., (2001), 'Another Case of McCreevy Knows Best', *Irish Times*, 2 April.

Munnell, A., and A. Sunden, (2003), *Suspending the Employer 401(k) Match*, Issue Brief No. 12. Boston, MA: Center for Retirement Research.

O'Quigley, J., (2003), *When it Comes to PRSAs – Caveat Emptor*, Deloitte and Touche.

Pensions Board, (1998), *Securing Retirement Income: National Pensions Policy Initiative*, Report of the Pensions Board, Dublin: The Pensions Board.

Pensions Board, (2005), *National Pensions Review*, Dublin: Pensions Board.

Pensions Board (2006), *PRSA Products and Charges*, available at http://www.pensionsboard.ie/. Accessed on 22 August 2006.

Pensions Board, (2006), *Special Savings for Retirement*, Dublin: Pensions Board.

Pensions Commission (2004), *Pensions: Challenges and Choices, the Second Report of the Pensions Commission*, London: Pensions Commission.

Pensions Commission (2005), *A New Pensions Settlement for the 21st Century, the Second Report of the Pensions Commission*, London: Pensions Commission.

Pensions Commission (2006), *Implementing an Integrated Package of Pension Reforms: the Final Report of the Pensions Commission*, London: Pensions Commission.

Rapple, C., (2003), 'Pension Costs Are Too High', *Irish Examiner*, 25 June.

Schultze, I., and M. Moran, (2007), 'Ireland: Pensioning the 'Celtic Tiger' in E.M. Immergut, K., M. Anderson and I. Schultze (editors), *The Handbook of West European Pension Politics*, Oxford: Oxford University Press.

Slattery, L., (2003a), 'Pension Products Set to Start Battle Royal', *Irish Times*, 21 February.

Slattery, L., (2003b), 'Employers Urged to Contribute to Pensions', *Irish Times*, 20 September.

Slattery, L., (2003c), 'Broker Warns PRSA failing to hit target', *Irish Times*, 12 September.

PART III

Other Issues with Individual Pension Provision

11. The Annuity Market and Personal Pensions

John Turner

1. INTRODUCTION

The ultimate goal of a pension system is to provide retirement income, but individual account pension schemes accrue benefits in the form of an account balance. Participants need a flow of income to pay for their consumption expenditures in retirement. In part because of the relative newness of individual account systems, less attention has been paid to the payout phase than to the accumulation phase.

This chapter surveys the range of payout options provided in the individual account systems in Sweden, the United Kingdom, and Chile. These three countries were chosen for this policy analysis because they provide a wide range of payout options under different institutional arrangements. The Swedish system is the newest of the three, and it has been designed with an attempt to learn from the experience of other individual account systems. The British and Chilean systems have substantial experience in paying benefits, and those systems have evolved over time.

A key issue with individual pension provision is the provision of annuities. If annuities are not required an individual pension scheme is indistinguishable from a tax-favored savings account. In discussing annuity options, the chapter focuses on four issues: (1) policies to reduce workers' risks associated with annuitisation; (2) women's issues – exclusion, survivors benefits, divorced spouses benefits, credits for care giving; (3) the effect of benefit payouts on inequality and (4) whether benefits are bequeathable, to whom, and under what conditions.

Individual account pension schemes can pay old-age benefits in any, or a combination, of five basic ways: (1) a lump sum, (2) a life annuity, (3) a phased withdrawal (based on annual recalculation of life expectancy); (4) an instalment (term certain) payments; or (5) ad hoc (unscheduled) withdrawals.

A lump sum provides no insurance against the risk of outliving one's resources. An annuity is a financial instrument that converts an account balance into a stream of periodic payments. With life annuities, workers receive periodic payments that continue until death. Life annuities insure workers against the economic costs of living longer than expected. With phased withdrawal, workers receive benefits each year that are based on their remaining life expectancy and the amount in their individual accounts. The individual's retirement benefit is recomputed each year, taking into account the fund's investment performance and whether the worker's spouse or other beneficiaries have died. Thus, the benefit provided with phased withdrawal differs each year.

The chapter compares the pension outcomes for men and women in the individual accounts in Sweden, Chile and the United Kingdom. The payment options in those three countries provide examples of most of the issues arising concerning the structure of annuities in individual accounts systems. Table 11.1 summarises the analysis for these three countries.

This chapter compares how the different annuity options affect women compared to men. Women tend to have shorter job tenure and are more likely to change jobs. They are more likely to work part-time. They are more likely to have interrupted paid work careers because of care giving responsibilities. They are more likely to be economically dependent on their spouse. When working in paid employment, they tend to have lower wages than men. They tend to live longer. They are more likely to end life alone – single, divorced and not remarried, or widowed. When comparing women to men, the comparisons are made assuming these differences.

2. ANALYSIS OF THE ISSUES

First, a brief introduction is provided concerning the mandatory individual accounts in Sweden, Chile and the United Kingdom.

Sweden finances its mandatory individual accounts with a payroll tax of 2.5 per cent. That tax is levied in addition to a tax of 16 per cent of pay that is contributed to a mandatory pay-as-you-go system. Participants must annuitise their benefits, but they have a choice of a fixed annuity or a phased withdrawal.

Chile finances its mandatory individual account schemes with a tax of 10 per cent, plus an additional tax that covers disability benefits and the cost of administering the system. The individual account system has completely replaced the traditional social security program – it is the primary source of retirement income. While the Swedish individual account system provides some provides some flexibility for workers concerning the receipt of benefits, the Chilean system provides workers with more options.

Table 11.1 Features of annuities in mandatory individual account systems in Sweden, Chile and the United Kingdom

Features	Countries		
	Sweden	Chile	United Kingdom
Entitlement Conditions			
Entitlement age	61	60 women, 65 men	60
Early benefit receipt before entitlement age with more stringent requirements	no	yes, based on account balance	No
Benefit receipt while working	yes	yes	yes
Maximum age by which benefit receipt must begin	no	no	75
Annuity Acquisition			
Mandatory versus voluntary annuitisation	mandatory	voluntary	until 2006, mandatory, starting at age 75; starting in 2006, mandatory at age 75, except for those claiming a religious exemption
Annuity provider	government	life insurance companiess	life insurance companies
Factors used in determining annuity Value	age, year of birth	no restrictions	age, gender, impaired health, year of birth
Fees			
Level and structure of fees for annuitisation	uniform per cent of account balance	determined by life insurance company	determined by life insurance company
Disclosure of fees	not separately disclosed, bundled with individual account fee	not separately disclosed, incorporated in net annuity payments	not separately disclosed, incorporated in net annuity payments
Benefit Forms			
Phased or partial annuitisation	yes	no	Yes
Fixed or variable annuity	either fixed annuity with some upside variability or phased withdrawal	fixed but price indexed	price indexed, up to 5% a year
Lump sum benefit allowable	no	yes, for part of account	no

Table 11.1 (continued)

Disability benefits	provided separately	provided separately	provided separately
Pre-retirement withdrawals for medical expenses, educational expenses, or for home purchase	no	no	no
Minimum period payment guarantees	no	no	no
Minimum benefit guarantee	no	yes, for workers with 20 years of contributions	no
Benefits for Other Persons			
Spousal benefit	worker can contribute to acc. of spouse	no	no
Benefit for divorced spouses	no	no	can be negotiated as part of divorce settlement
Survivor benefit	optional	required for men who annuitize their account	yes, 50 % survivors benefit must be provided
Bequeathable benefits	no	yes, if taking phased withdrawals	yes, if taking phased withdrawal before age 75
Risk Reduction			
Reinsurance of annuities	government guarantees annuities	government guarantees annuities	no government guarantee
Inflation protection	no price indexing, option of variable annuity	fully price-indexed annuities	annuities price indexed up to 5% year
Interest rate guarantee for annuitisation	guarantee at min. of 3 %	no guarantee	no guarantee
Taxation and Income Redistribution			
Taxation	same as wage earnings	same as wage earnings	same as wage earnings
Income redistribution	no explicit redistribution, implicit redistribution through mandatory annuitisation	minimum benefit guarantee provides some redistribution; unrestricted annuity pricing limits redistribution through annuitisation	no explicit redistribution, implicit redistribution through mandatory annuitisation

Source: Author's compilation

The British individual account system differs from the mandatory systems in Sweden and Chile because it is a voluntary carve-out system rather than a mandatory system. With a voluntary carve-out system, workers voluntarily choose to reduce their participation in the mandatory social security programme in exchange for making contributions to an individual account. The relationship between the reduced benefits in the social security system and the amount of benefits in the voluntary carve-out pension can be complex as to how it varies across workers, and is not one-for-one. The British call this system 'contracting out', and the resulting individual accounts are called 'contracted-out personal accounts'.

Annuity Acquisition

Mandatory versus voluntary annuitisation

Some degree of mandatory annuitisation may be desirable to assure that workers will not outlive their retirement savings. Mandatory annuity purchases reduce annuity prices by expanding the market to cover individuals regardless of health and life expectancy. Also, mandatory annuities would be less expensive to administer, with greater economies of scale and reduced enrolment costs. Mandatory annuity purchases ensure that individuals will not spend all their resources in the early years of retirement.

Full mandatory annuitisation, however, may not be desirable in some circumstances. Mandatory annuitisation restricts the access of participants to their accumulated funds, and for this reason may weaken the argument that individual accounts foster the 'ownership society'. Annuitisation reduces flexibility in meeting unplanned expenses. Mandatory annuitisation reduces freedom of choice and may exempt small account balances because of the low level of annuity they would provide and the relatively high costs.

Annuitisation is generally a prerequisite to providing survivors with benefits. Thus, the requirement for annuitisation is related to the provision of survivors protection for widows. Annuitisation could be required to be a joint decision of husbands and wives. For example, annuitisation could be the default with other forms of benefit receipt only being allowed if the spouse signs an agreement permitting that.

Participants are at risk concerning interest rate changes that may adversely affect the value of the annuitised benefit they receive for a given account balance. For any given account balance, the annuitised benefit received is lower the lower is the interest rate at the point of annuitisation. Perhaps in part because of the interest rate risk associated with conversion of an account balance to an annuity, many countries with mandatory individual accounts do not require that workers annuitize account balances. Seven countries with mandatory individual accounts in Latin America allow their workers to choose between an annuity or phased withdrawals throughout retirement, while two countries mandate annuity purchases (Kritzer 2000). Countries that do not mandate annuitisation generally mandate that benefits be withdrawn monthly through phased withdrawals.

None of the three countries requires annuitisation – all allowing phased withdrawals as an option. In Sweden, where the mandatory individual account is a relatively small part of the mandatory benefits, workers must either fully annuitise their account balances or take the benefits as a phased withdrawal. Chile does not require workers to annuitize their account balances, but workers not annuitising must take their benefits as a phased withdrawal. British workers until 2006 were required to annuitise their account balances by the age of 75. That requirement has been dropped, but phased withdrawals must begin by that age.

None of the three countries have policies to encourage annuitisation. For example, annuitisation could be encouraged by favorable tax treatment, but none of the three countries have adopted such a policy. Mandatory annuitisation may be more favorable to women than men because women live longer and are more likely to need the income protection that annuities provide.

Annuity provider

Annuities are generally provided by private sector life insurance companies, and in some countries by banks with life insurance subsidiaries, but government agencies, functioning as life insurance companies can also provide annuities. In countries where annuities are provided by private life insurance companies, the worker generally has the choice between life insurance companies. Private life insurance companies are financial entities that generally cannot provide full assurance that they will pay benefits as promised. If the government is the provider, concern arises as to the role of the government in investment markets for the investments that back the annuities, and the role of the government as a competitor of private insurance companies.

In all countries around the world with mandatory individual account systems, only Sweden provides annuities solely through a government agency overseeing the mandatory individual account system, with that agency functioning as an insurance company (Turner 2006).

Chilean and British private insurance companies provide annuities. Workers must select a company if they wish to purchase an annuity with their account balance. The companies that manage the Chilean individual accounts do not provide annuities, so the worker must find a different company if he or she wishes to obtain an annuity. Generally British insurance companies manage individual accounts, so that the worker with individual accounts need not switch companies to obtain an annuity. Most workers, however, do not search for a better offer, and thus may pay more than they need to for the annuities they obtain.

The institution providing annuities may be important to women because life insurance companies use gender-based life tables for calculating annuities, unless prohibited from doing so by law. The annuities provided by life insurance companies in Chile and the United Kingdom are calculated using gender-based life tables. The government agency in Sweden that provides annuities, however, uses unisex life tables. Unisex life tables are also used by employer-provided pension plans in the United States, but are not used for individually purchased annuities. With gender-based life tables, men may find that they can obtain higher benefits in the individual purchase market, which uses gender-based tables, than they can obtain through the group-purchase employer-based market, which uses unisex tables.

The issue of whether gender is used for determining the value of annuities may be the single most important issue relating to annuities for women. The importance of the issue is mitigated, however, when couples choose joint and survivor annuities because those annuities involve both male and female life expectancies, and thus unisex pricing is not so disadvantageous to males or advantageous to females. The issue is also complicated by differences in the ages of the husband and wife. For example, a wife could possibly obtain a more favorable annuity in the individual purchase market than a joint and survivor annuity in the unisex market if her husband is sufficiently older than she is.

Fees

Fees have an important effect on the level of annuities. The fees are generally not disclosed, only being discernable as they affect the level of benefits provided. Thus, by comparison shopping as to level of benefit provided, an annuitant could in effect obtain information about fees. The fees for the management of account balances during the phase when accounts are being built up before retirement are disclosed in prospectuses, but generally participants are ill-informed about those fees.

Level and structure of fees for annuitisation

Private life insurance companies charge fees either explicitly or imbedded within the pricing structure for the life insurance. They charge fees to cover their expenses: for marketing and sales expenses, for determining life expectancies and converting individual accounts to annuities, for managing the investments that support the payment of annuities and for making annuity payments. These fees can substantially reduce the value of the annuity paid. The fees can be charged as a flat percentage of the assets in the individual account, or the fees may be a lower percentage for larger accounts. Often, insurance companies do not charge an explicit fee. Rather, their fee results from the difference between the rate of return they implicitly pay annuitants and the rate they earn on their investments.

A study in the UK has estimated that the costs for an annuity of the US equivalent of roughly $15,000 to $20,000 would be 0.29 per cent of assets per year (Murthi, Orszag, and Orszag 2000). That estimate is for an annuity that is fixed in nominal terms. If the annuity were price indexed, the cost would be higher.

The fees associated with annuitisation in Sweden are included in the fees charged by the government for its role in managing the individual account system. Those administrative fees are charged as a fixed proportion of the individual account balance. The portion of fees resulting from the cost of providing annuities is not separated from the total fees charged, and thus the fees associated with annuitisation are not disclosed by the Swedish government.

Because Chilean and British workers negotiate annuities individually rather than at group rates, the fees are relatively high. In Chile, insurance companies may pay fees to independent brokers who bring them clients, while the companies providing phased withdrawals are prohibited from doing so. This regulatory limitation on payment of fees favors insurance companies in acquiring customers, and may help explain the relatively high level of annuitisation of Chilean individual accounts (James, Martinez and Iglesias 2006).

Because expenses borne by annuity providers tend to be fixed costs per participant, not varying by the size of the participant's account balance, the way fees are assessed may have a differential effect on women. Because women tend to have smaller account balances than men, flat fees would generally be a higher percentage of account balances for women than men, while fees charged as a percentage of account balances would tend to cause cross-subsidisation of women's expenses by men.

Disclosure of fees

While some policy analysts view individual accounts as being more transparent than traditional defined benefit social security programs (World Bank 1994), an aspect of individual accounts that is frequently not transparent is the fees they charge for annuitisation (Gillion et al. 2000). To be transparent, the disclosure of fees should indicate the amount of all fees, to whom they are paid, the service that they are paying for, and the amount by which they reduce future account balances. Life insurance companies typically imbed fees for annuitisation in the payment of the annuity, reducing benefits paid. They do not disclose fees, either in absolute terms (such as euros) or as a percentage of assets. Sometimes it is possible to determine the commission received by the sales person selling the annuity. Once the type of annuity is specified, however, workers can compare the implicit level of fees by comparing the level of benefit payouts, with insurance companies promising higher benefit payouts having lower implicit fees.

Fees disclosed in dollars or euros actually paid by the participant may be more informative than fees disclosed as a per cent of assets. Even if fees were explicitly charged and disclosed, life insurance companies could structure their annuity pricing so that there were implicit fees. If an insurance company used a life table with high life expectancy, that would result in a lower benefit payout, and would be an implicit fee that would be charged through lower benefits paid.

In Sweden, Chile, the United Kingdom, and other countries, insurance companies do not disclose the fees they charge for annuitisation. They provide the annuitised benefit net of fees.

Benefit Forms

Phased or partial annuitisation or deferred annuitisation

Phased annuitisation offers workers the option of annuitising their account balance in stages over time. This option facilitates phased retirement, and it is a way of dealing with the interest rate and financial market risk associated with the timing of annuitisation. This option allows for receipt of partial benefits.

Sweden and the United Kingdom allow phased or partial annuitisation, while Chile does not. Because Sweden allows partial annuitisation, workers can phase in their annuitisation over time, initially annuitising only a quarter, then a half and then three-quarters of their account balance, if they wish. Once participants have claimed benefits, they can suspend payment or change the percentage of a full payment the participant receives. Chilean workers may defer annuitisation by receiving benefits as a phased withdrawal and then later annuitise the remainder of their account balance.

Phased or partial annuitisation facilitates part-time work with a part-time pension, and thus may be a favorable option for women because it provides greater flexibility for mixing paid work and family responsibilities.

Fixed or variable annuities

Annuities can provide fixed nominal or fixed real payments, or the payments can vary over time. Annuities that vary depending on the investment performance of the underlying assets are called variable annuities. The providers of variable annuities are financial service providers that pass on to the participant the underlying investment income, after charging fees. Assuming the market for variable annuities is competitive, the profit earned by providers of variable annuities is just a competitive profit. Variable annuities offer both the advantages of annuities and the advantages of investments in equities, as well as the risks of investments in equities. For workers or retirees holding variable annuities, their income from variable annuities is generally taxed as ordinary income. By comparison, their income on investments in equities may receive more favorable individual income tax treatment on capital gains and dividends.

Participants in all three countries have the option of a fixed annuity or phased withdrawal. None of the countries offer variable annuities or escalating annuities for the participants in mandatory individual accounts. Thus, in this respect voluntary annuity systems tend to provide more options than do mandatory annuity systems.

If a Swedish participant chooses a fixed annuity, Sweden guarantees a fixed monthly payment for life. The monthly amount may be increased by a bonus, however, depending on the investment experience If a worker chooses a phased withdrawal, the benefit may vary since the worker's benefit will be affected by the value of the underlying funds. If a phased withdrawal is chosen, the funds remain invested with the mutual funds the worker has chosen.

Chilean workers may take their benefit as a price-indexed annuity or as a phased withdrawal or as a combination of the two. British workers choosing annuities must take price-indexed annuities, but they have the option of a phased withdrawal.

The option of phased withdrawal does not provide longevity insurance, and for this reason it may not be a good option for many workers, especially women.

Lump sum benefits

Lump sum benefits are popular with many retirees who tend to like the liquidity and financial control that these benefits provide. However, these benefits are not popular with policy experts. Policy experts tend to favor annuities because of the insurance protection they provide against outliving one's resources due to poor planning or due to living longer than expected. The two, however, are not mutually exclusive. Lump sum benefits can be paid using a part of the funds in an individual account, with the remainder paid as an annuity or a phased withdrawal.

The three countries differ in their policies concerning lump sum benefits, with Sweden being the only one that does not allow lump sum benefits. Chile permits lump sum benefits as an option for taking a part of the account balance. Chilean workers may withdraw a lump sum benefit from their individual account if the remaining amount is sufficient so that the participants can meet one of two conditions: they purchase an annuity at least equal to 120 per cent of the minimum guaranteed pension, or they take scheduled withdrawals that are at least 70 per cent of the participant's price-indexed covered wages. Few Chilean workers have met these requirements. In Chile, however, some insurance company sales agents in companies charging high sales commissions have provided unofficial lump sum payments of part of the sales commissions, permitting workers to convert part of their individual accounts to a lump sum payment (James, Martinez, and Iglesias 2006).

In the United Kingdom until 2006, workers had to take the entire account balance of a contracted-out personal pension as an annuity. Since April 2006, it has been possible to take up to 25 per cent of the account balance as a lump sum, which is consistent with the treatment of other personal pensions.

Lump sum benefits do not provide longevity insurance, and thus may not be a good option for women.

Pre-retirement withdrawals for medical expenses, educational expenses or for home purchase

Some countries, such as Singapore, allow pre-retirement withdrawals for medical expenses, educational expenses, or for purchasing a home. Sweden, Chile, and the United Kingdom prohibit such withdrawals.

Minimum period payment guarantees

Annuities can guarantee a payment for a fixed minimum number of years (a period-certain annuity). A similar type of annuity guarantees to pay out at least as many dollars as were paid in (a cash refund annuity). Some workers prefer these guarantee features because the features eliminate the risk that they or their survivors will receive little in benefits if they die early. Annuities that provide such guarantees pay a lower benefit per year than annuities without such a guarantee. While these features are commonly offered with voluntary annuities, the Swedish, Chilean and British mandatory individual account systems do not provide these types of guarantee.

Benefits for other persons

As well as providing benefits to the workers earning them, annuities may pay benefits to related persons. Doing so, however, generally reduces the benefits received by the participant while both persons are alive because the extra benefits must be financed out of the account balance. For example, the provision of survivor benefits for a spouse generally would reduce the benefits paid while both persons were alive by 8 per cent to 20 per cent, depending on the ages of the two people (American Academy of Actuaries 2001). Spousal benefits, benefits for divorced spouses, survivors benefits and bequeathable benefits are of particular value to women because they are more likely to be economically dependent on their spouse than are men.

Spousal benefits

Traditional defined benefit social security systems, such as in the United States, sometimes provide spousal benefits. A non-working spouse, or a spouse with low earnings relative to the earnings of their partner, receives a retirement benefit while both persons are alive that is based on the earnings history of the working spouse. Spousal benefits are provided with no reduction in benefits to the participant. Individual account systems rarely provide spousal benefits.

In Sweden, however, workers can advance-fund retirement income for their spouse by having their contributions deposited into their spouse's account instead of into their own. Doing so reduces the benefits received by the worker. The Chilean and British individual accounts do not provide spousal benefits. Dependent spouses must rely on the benefits of their working spouse.

Benefits for divorced spouses

Providing benefits for a divorced spouse from an individual account is particularly difficult if the worker has remarried and has a current spouse. This situation poses problems in all pension systems except redistributional traditional social security systems. In an individual account system, any benefits provided to the divorced spouse would reduce the benefits received by the worker and current spouse.

British workers can negotiate rights to pension benefits in divorce settlements. In Chile, divorced spouses have no rights to pension benefits of their former spouse. In Sweden, divorced spouses have no benefit rights. While current spouses, same-sex partners, and dependent children are eligible for survivors' benefits if the participant elects to provide them, divorced spouses are not eligible for survivors' benefits. If a spouse is named as a beneficiary and a divorce subsequently occurs, the divorced spouse loses the right to the future survivor benefit.

Survivors' benefits

Survivors' benefits provide important economic protection for women. These benefits are more important for women than men because women are more likely than men to be the survivors in a marriage, and they are more likely than men to be economically dependent on their spouses. Survivors' benefits can be a mandated part of an individual account system, or they can be provided as an option. In the US Social Security system, survivors' benefits are provided with no reduction in benefits for the couple when both are alive. The survivors' benefit equals 100 per cent of the participant's benefit. However, in individual account systems, the provision of survivors' benefits results in lower benefits to the couple while both are alive.

In voluntary individual account systems, participants generally have a choice of level of survivors' benefits – 100 per cent, 75 per cent, 66.6 per cent, or 50 per cent. An issue when providing survivors benefits is what happens to the benefit of the participant if the dependent spouse dies first. The participant's benefit could be decreased because there would be only one person for it to support, or it could be increased because there is no longer a need to provide survivors' benefits.

Sweden does not require married workers to provide survivors' benefits for their spouses. Participants may voluntarily choose the survivor benefit, which Swedish workers primarily use as survivor protection for widows. The individual account system provides survivors' benefits separately for the pre-retirement and retirement periods. Participants pay the cost of purchasing a survivor benefit from the funds in the individual worker's account, so it is only available to workers with a sufficient account balance to cover the cost of the option. If the participant chooses to provide a survivor benefit and then dies before retirement, the survivor is paid a fixed amount (without regard to the participant's account balance) for five years. Beneficiaries of this survivor benefit include children under the age of 20, and a spouse, registered partner or cohabitant, including same-sex partners. Individuals who have selected the survivor benefit option will receive reduced benefits while alive. If a Chilean worker chooses an annuity and is a married man, he must provide a survivor's annuity for his spouse and minor children. A married woman must do so only if her husband is disabled. The survivors' benefits are 60 per cent to the wife, or 50 per cent to the wife if survivors' benefits are also paid to children, with 15 per cent for each surviving dependent child younger than age 18 (age 24, if a student). A survivor benefit of 36 per cent is paid to the surviving mother of extramarital children (30 per cent if the children are younger than age 18). If the deceased worker's account balance is too small to provide the minimum survivor benefit, life insurance proceeds supplement the survivor benefit.

The United Kingdom is the only country of the three that requires all married participants to provide survivors benefits. It requires a married participant to provide survivors' benefits equal to 50 per cent of the benefits received by the participant. Doing so reduces the benefit received while living by 10 to 15 per cent compared to that received by a single person.

A characteristic of the survivors' benefits in all three countries is that, given that survivor benefits are provided, the participant and spouse do not have a choice as to the level of survivor benefits (in Sweden, there is a choice of not providing those benefits). Thus, in this respect it appears that mandatory individual account systems offer less choice than do voluntary systems.

Bequeathable benefits

Bequeathable benefits take the form of a lump sum payment made to a surviving spouse or other surviving family member or unrelated person at the death of a pension participant. Individual account systems may distinguish between deaths that occur before the worker has started receiving retirement benefits and deaths that occur while receiving benefits. In some countries, such as the United States, the possibility to accumulate bequeathable wealth through individual account systems is considered to be a desirable feature. This possibility allows workers to accumulate wealth that they might bequeath to their heirs, but the trade-off is that annuitised benefits are reduced to below what they otherwise would be. Bequeathable benefits generally result when an individual account has not been annuitised, and are eliminated when an account has been annuitised.

If workers die before having annuitised their account balance, the Swedish pension system does not allow the bequest of their remaining account balance at death. That amount is redistributed among all the participants in the system. When Chilean or British workers die, their account balances are bequeathable to their survivors. If they die during retirement and they have not annuitised their account balance, the remaining account balance is also bequeathable.

3. RISK REDUCTION

Risk is inherent in most financial transactions. The risk associated with annuity payments can be reduced several ways.

Reinsurance of annuities

When private sector life insurance companies provide annuities, retirees face the risk that the insurance companies will go bankrupt and be unable to pay the promised benefits. For that reason, insurance protecting the annuities is desirable. The government may need to provide re-insurance in case the insurer is unable to meet its benefit commitments.

Because the Swedish government is the annuity provider, participants do not need reinsurance to guarantee the annuity payments. The Chilean government guarantees the annuities, when workers choose that option. The government provides this guarantee without charge to the participants or the insurance companies. The guarantee is for 75 per cent of the annuity, subject to a maximum amount. To prevent the need for this insurance being used, the Chilean government sets stringent regulations on insurance companies. Thus far, for the 25 years the Chilean system has operated, no claims have been made against the insurance (James, Martinez, and Iglesias 2006). The British government does not guarantee the benefits provided by insurance companies.

Because women tend to be more risk averse than men (Hinz, McCarthy and Turner 1996), the risk reduction aspect of re-insurance may be more valuable to women than to men.

Inflation protection

While the social security systems in most high-income countries provide inflation protection, mandatory individual account systems generally do not provide inflation-protected benefits. They do not provide inflation protection because few countries have well-developed markets for inflation-protected securities that could be used to provide the financial backing for inflation-indexed annuities. When inflation protection is provided, initial benefits are lower than they would be without such protection, while benefits received at older ages are higher due to the indexing of benefits.

The Swedish system does not offer an inflation-indexed benefit. Workers who choose phased withdrawal that may provide some protection from inflation, depending on the performance of asset markets.

Both Chile and the United Kingdom are unusual in providing inflation-protected annuity benefits through individual accounts. Chile has a well-developed market for price-indexed bonds. Pensioners may begin taking their benefits as a phased withdrawal and later switch to a price-indexed annuity. British annuity benefits must be price indexed up to an increase in the Retail Price Index of 5 per cent per year. For benefits accrued between April 1988 and April 1997, the maximum amount of inflation indexing is 3 per cent per year.

Inflation indexing of annuities is particularly valuable for people with long life expectancy. Otherwise, inflation can considerably erode the real value of annuity benefits during retirement. For this reason, inflation indexing is particularly valuable for women.

Interest rate guarantee for annuitisation

Variations in interest rates used to convert account balances to annuities can have a large effect on the level of annual pension benefits received. For a 65-year-old US male, a 4 per cent interest rate generates annual payments of $686 per $10,000 annuitised. This amount rises to $830 at 6 per cent and $982 at 8 per cent (Ameriks 2002). Higher interest rates produce higher annual payments because the interest income produced by the account balance invested at those interest rates will be greater.

Under a guaranteed annuity conversion option, a pension scheme guarantees to convert a worker's account balance to a life annuity at a fixed interest rate, or at an interest rate guaranteed to be no lower than a fixed minimum. A more extensive guarantee would also take into account the mortality table used. If the annuity rates provided under the guarantee are more beneficial to the participant than the prevailing rates in the market, the scheme, employer or some other entity must make up the difference in the purchase price of the annuity.

Fixed rate guarantees are vulnerable to prolonged falls in interest rates (Turner and Rajnes 2006). Alternative approaches can be used to limit the interest rate risk associated with annuity conversions. One approach is to allow workers to partially annuitise in several steps, spread over time. This approach reduces the interest rate risk associated with completely annuitising at a single point in time. Another approach is to allow workers to initially take phased withdrawals, and later take an annuity, giving workers greater flexibility in picking the point at which they annuitise.

Of the three countries, only Sweden provides an interest rate guarantee for annuity conversions. The government, as the provider of annuities in the Swedish mandatory system, limits interest rate risk for workers by providing the guarantee. The interest rate used to determine the annuity varies based on market interest rates, but with a guaranteed minimum of 3 per cent (Engström and Westerberg 2003).

4. TAXATION AND INCOME REDISTRIBUTION

Because of favorable tax treatment relative to the taxation of other forms of savings, generally pension systems are generally subsidized through the tax system. The subsidisation may cause income redistribution, particularly in a progressive tax system. Taxation affects the net annuity benefit received. Effects on income redistribution generally are not an explicit factor in the design of annuities but are an outcome of the way annuities are provided.

Taxation

The taxation of pension benefits is an important source of income tax revenue in many countries. The tax structure can be used to favor particular forms of benefit receipt. For example, taxation can be used to favor or discourage workers taking lump sum benefits as compared to annuitised benefits. The progressive taxation of benefits can cause income redistribution toward lower-income taxpayers. Sweden, Chile, and the United Kingdom tax benefits the same as wages.

Progressive taxation of pension benefits tends to favor women because they generally have lower incomes than men. However, viewed over a lifetime, progressive taxation of pensions may favor men because they receive more of a tax subsidy through the tax free accumulation of pension assets. To the extent that men and women are married and taxed as couples, these issues are attenuated.

Income Redistribution

Income redistribution could be an explicit feature of the provision of benefits, but that rarely is the case in individual account systems. Rather, income redistribution occurs as an unintended outcome of features of the system – through the way annuity providers determine annuitised benefits and the way they charge fees. It also occurs through the tax subsidies provided by the personal income tax system. The income redistribution occurring through the tax system may exceed that occurring through the way that annuities are provided.

When individual accounts annuitise benefits not taking into account the longer life expectancy associated with higher income, they redistribute income toward upper-income workers. The use of unisex life tables also causes income redistribution within the system. Since women and higher-wage workers have on average longer life expectancies than men and lower-wage workers, the system redistributes money in a complex way from men to women and from lower-wage to higher-wage workers. Thus, the criticism by some policy analysts that traditional defined benefit social security programs redistribute income in complex ways (World Bank 1994) also applies, and to some extent for the same reasons, to individual accounts that mandate annuitisation.

Most of the mandatory individual account systems allow workers to avoid the regressive effects of annuitisation by taking a phased withdrawal of benefits. Providing this option, however, increases the problem of adverse selection in the annuity market and is regressive against low-income participants. Adverse selection occurs when long-lived people are more likely to choose an annuity than short-lived people but both receive the same annual benefits for a given account balance. Thus, adverse selection arises when an annuity is a voluntary option.

Because people who expect to be long-lived are more likely to purchase annuities than people who expect to be short-lived, insurers price annuities on the assumption that their purchasers are long-lived. While these prices may be actuarially fair for upper-income workers with long life expectancies, the high price keeps low-income workers out of the annuity market and deprives them of the insurance protection traditional social insurance schemes provide against the risk of outliving one's resources. This problem can be reduced by offering annuity products that appeal to people with differing life expectancies. For example, escalating annuities or indexed annuities are more appealing to people with longer life expectancies than they are to people with shorter life expectancies. Not requiring annuitisation, however, allows low-income workers who die relatively young to bequeath some of their retirement income to their survivors.

The Swedish, Chilean and British systems do not explicitly redistribute income through the payment of benefits. In Sweden and the United Kingdom, income redistribution occurs through the use of unisex mortality to annuitise benefits, with implicit transfers occurring from men to women. It also occurs from lower-income to higher-income persons because lower-income persons tend to have shorter life expectancy.

Insurance companies in Chile, but not in most countries with mandatory individual accounts, use individual characteristics, including income and gender, in determining the level of annuity benefits provided by an account balance. Calculating annuities this way limits the regressive income transfers due to annuitisation, but at the cost of lower retirement benefits for women than would be the case if unisex life tables were used to calculate annuitised benefits.

Income redistribution can also occur through the way the annuity provider charges fees. The transactions costs to the annuity provider associated with an individual worker purchasing an annuity are largely fixed costs per participant. These costs do not depend on the size of the account balance being annuitised. Thus, these costs have a regressive effect when charged to the individual. They are a larger percentage of small account balances, and small account balances tend to be held by people with lower incomes. Vittas and Iglesias (1991) found that annuity charges in Chile were a source of inequality in benefits, with larger commissions relative to annuity payments often charged to lower-income workers.

Explicit policies of income would tend to favor women because of their lower incomes than men, but are generally lacking in systems of mandatory individual accounts. Implicit income redistribution may favor men or women because it is not designed as an outcome of the system but occurs as the result of other design decisions.

5. POLICY IMPLICATIONS AND CONCLUSIONS

Countries considering mandating individual account systems have a number of decisions to make in structuring the payout of benefits through annuities. These design decisions will affect the outcomes experienced by both men and women. While this chapter has focused on the details of the structures of annuities in these systems, a few overriding decisions determine the choices countries make concerning the details of the structure.

A basic policy decision is the extent to which participants will be free to choose from a wide range of options. A wide range of options allows participants the opportunity to structure the receipt of benefits in the way that they prefer. However, in some cases, public policy goals may take overriding importance. For example, should husbands be free to decide whether to provide survivors with benefits for their wives, or should public policy require that those benefits be provided?

Typically, the range of options provided by a mandatory system is less than the range of options provided by a voluntary system. For example, none of the systems considered allow for a guaranteed payment period or an escalating annuity, which are options commonly offered with voluntary annuities.

Another major policy decision concerns the extent to which individual account systems replicate the type of protections provided by traditional social security benefits. For example, should individual account benefits be inflation-indexed and provide survivors with benefits? In addition, countries need to decide the role of the government in the retirement income system, including its role in providing annuities.

The experiences of Sweden, Chile and the United Kingdom provide examples of many of the options available for disbursing benefits from individual accounts and some of the issues that arise. The three countries differ in how they provide benefits, indicating the range of approaches different countries have used. This chapter's framework of analysis indicates the large number of decisions that must be made in structuring the payouts from an individual account system.

Various aspects of individual accounts may result in their benefit structure being regressive, which would tend to be adverse to women because they generally have lower earnings than men. Just as mandatory annuitisation results in regressive redistribution in defined benefit schemes, the same effect applies in individual accounts. The structure of fees may also cause regressivity because of the fixed costs of managing individual accounts, though that problem can be dealt with by mandating that fees be prorated based on account balances.

While proponents of individual accounts sometimes claim that individual accounts are more transparent than traditional defined benefit social security systems, the fees charged in individual accounts are far from transparent. Generally, annuity providers provide benefits net of fees, with no clear indication of the level of fees the participant has paid.

REFERENCES

American Academy of Actuaries (2001), 'Annuitization of Social Security Individual Accounts', *Issue Brief*, November.

Ameriks, John (2002), 'Recent Trends in the Selection of Retirement Income Streams Among TIAA-CREFF Participants', *Research Dialogue*, **74** (December), 1–19.

Engström, Stefan and Anna Westerberg (2003), 'Reversed Default Behavior in a New Defined Contribution Pension System', SSE/EFI Working Paper Series in Economics and Finance, No. 527, Stockholm, Sweden: Stockholm School of Economics.

Gillion, Colin, John Turner, Clive Bailey and Denis Latulippe (eds) (2000), *Social Security, Development and Reform*, Geneva, Switzerland: International Labour Office.

Hinz, Richard P., David D. McCarthy and John Turner (1996), 'Are Women Conservative Investors? Gender Differences in Participant-Directed Pension Investments', in Michael S. Gordon, Olivia S. Mitchell and Marc M. Twinney (eds) *Positioning Pensions for the Year 2000*, Philadelphia, US: University of Pennsylvania Press.

James, Estelle, Alexandra Cox Edwards and Rebecca Wong (2003), 'How It's Done in Chile: Personal Accounts – With Strings Attached', *Washington Post*, 13 February, p. B2.

James, Estelle, Guillermo Martinez and Augusto Iglesias (2006), 'The Payout Stage in Chile: Who Annuitizes and Why?', *Journal of Pension Economics and Finance*, **5** (2), pp. 121–154.

Kritzer, Barbara (2000), 'Social Security Privatization in Latin America', *Social Security Bulletin*, **62** (2), 17–23.

Liebman, Jeffrey B. (2002), *The Role of Annuities in a Reformed U.S. Social Security System*, Washington, D.C.: AARP Public Policy Institute Issue Brief 2002–17, December.

Mackenzie, George A. (2002), *The Role of Private Sector Annuity Markets in an Individual Accounts Reform of a Public Pension Plan*, Working Paper No. 02/161. Washington, D.C.: International Monetary Fund.

McCarthy, David D. and John Turner (1993), 'Risk Classification and Sex Discrimination in Pension Plans', *Journal of Risk and Insurance*, **60** (1), 85–104.

Murthi, Mamta; J. Michael Orszag, and Peter R. Orszag (2001), 'Administrative Costs Under a Decentralized Approach to Individual Accounts: Lessons form the United Kingdom', in Robert Holzmann and Joseph E. Stiglitz (eds), *New Ideas About Old Age Security*, Washington, D.C.: World Bank.

Palmer, Edward (2000), 'The Swedish Pension Reform Model: Framework and Issues', SP Discussion Paper No. 0012, Washington, DC: World Bank.

Turner, John (2006), *Individual Accounts for Social Security Reform: International Perspectives on the U.S. Debate*, Kalamazoo, MI: W.E. Upjohn Institute.

Turner, John (2005), *Social Security Pensionable Age in OECD Countries: 1949–2035*, Washington, D.C.: AARP Public Policy Institute, 2005.

Turner, John and David Rajnes (2006), *Fixed Rate Guarantees During Economic Downturns*, Washington, DC: AARP Public Policy Institute, unpublished paper.

US Social Security Administration (2006), *Social Security Programs Throughout the World: The Americas, 2005*, March, available at http://www.ssa.gov/policy/docs/.

Vittas, Dmitri and Augusto Iglesias (1991), *The Rationale and Performance of Personal Pension Plans in Chile*, World Bank Policy Research Working Paper No. 867. Washington, D.C.: World Bank.

World Bank (1994), *Averting the Old Age Crisis*, Washington, D.C.: Oxford University Press.

12. Regulation and Personal Pensions

Dana Muir

1. INTRODUCTION

Regulation of occupational pension schemes has received significant attention in recent years as many schemes have become underfunded, employers have terminated or frozen the pension plans and scandals have occurred. In the UK, Robert Maxwell was able to call on the help of related investment management firms to loot his firm's employee pension funds. (Prokesch 1992, p. 22). In the US, the government corporation that insures defined benefit plans, the Pension Benefit Guaranty Corporation (PBGC), assumed the liabilities of-United Airlines' pension plans, which were underfunded by $9.8 billion (Carey 2005, A1). The recent financial crisis is likely to result in a large increase in the number and scale of underfunded schemes (*New York Times*, 28 October 2008). The collapse of Lehman Brothers resulted in a large deficit in the UK Lehman pension scheme (*Financial Times*, 25 September 2008), and subsequent reliance on the UK Pension Protection Fund.

The market for financial products is characterised by information asymmetries especially for long-term financial products such as pension contracts. Information asymmetries are especially acute with personal pensions. Occupational pension schemes are operated by trustees. Extensive regulation and the large economic value of those schemes operate to encourage the trustees to utilise the services of a range of professionals such as investment advisors, actuaries and auditors. In comparison the individuals who purchase personal pensions typically do not have access to those professional services or if they do, the cost may be prohibitive.

Information asymmetries have contributed to scandals in personal pensions as well to as other problems such as participation rates and coverage. This chapter briefly examines two of these scandals. In the UK, the mis-selling of personal pensions during the late 1980s and early 1990s resulted in the review of sales of pension products to almost 2 million customers and in extensive regulatory change. In the US, some personal pension plans held personal pension plans held investments heavily concentrated in the stock of the of the sponsoring employer. As a result, holders of those personal pensions lost billions of dollars after the bursting of the dot.com stock market bubble in 2000 and the corporate scandals that began to come to light in 2001.

Other factors, in addition to informational asymmetries, also contribute to the concern that personal pensions may not provide sufficient and secure retirement income. Waine notes in Chapter 7 of this book that declining investment returns and significant administrative costs may make it difficult for employees to build substantial assets in personal pension schemes (Waine this volume, p. 117). Hughes and Stewart find that high account charges in Ireland have a deterrent effect (Hughes and Stewart this volume, pp. 185–88).

In sum, the experiences of the UK and the US with personal pension schemes provide evidence to show that their regulatory approaches have not been entirely successful in encouraging take-up, contributions and the building of wealth in those schemes. States who are considering implementing personal pension schemes can expect to encounter the same types of issues. Personal pension account arrangements are so different from occupational pension schemes that a regulatory scheme developed for occupational pension schemes requires, at minimum, considerable adaptation to personal pension schemes. Even the terminology of personal pension provision is difficult, particularly in making inter-country comparisons. Henceforth this chapter will use the term 'personal pensions' to refer specifically to the UK schemes popularly designated by that nomenclature. It will refer to the broader range of personal pension schemes across all states as Individual Pension Account Arrangements (IPAAs).

The allocation of regulatory authority over IPPAs is complex because of the numerous variables among those types of pension arrangements. They may be made available through a workplace or may be independent of employment. They may be alternatives to another type of pension arrangement based in the workplace, to at least a portion of a state pension or they may be an additive scheme. They may be based in the law of trust or the law of contract. The financial markets continuously introduce new investment products that target the IPAA market.

Supplementary defined benefit (DB) plans, such as the UK's occupational pension schemes, have traditionally been linked to employment through their benefits formula, the source of plan funding and the identity of plan trustees. Employers typically relied on supplementary DB plans as a tool to manage certain workforce issues, particularly those associated with employee retention. Employers had a strong financial and workforce interest in the plans. One outcome was that employers served as intermediaries between plans and regulators as well as between plans and employees.

It follows naturally then, that institutional regulators responsible for or associated with work place oversight frequently have had at least partial authority over supplementary DB plans. The hypothesis of this chapter is that a different distribution of regulatory authority may be more appropriate for IPAAs because those schemes frequently sever or attenuate the link between the workplace and the accumulation of assets for retirement. Instead of being vehicles that provide compensation in exchange for labour, IPAAs typically share many characteristics of widely-available financial products. It becomes useful then, to consider why financial products are regulated, what the best practices are in that regulation and how those concepts and insights might be applied to personal pension schemes.

After some brief introductory material, this chapter describes the fundamentally different ways in which the UK and the US allocate regulatory responsibility for IPAAs. It then offers two case studies – one each in the UK and the US – involving large pension-related scandals. Similar controversies surround the selection of default investments and account fees in the UK and US even though both states have had IPAAs in place for a number of years. The case studies show default investment issues, and fee considerations arise in different types of IPAAs in the UK as compared to the US The similarities of the issues, though, indicate that they may be inherent in the basic characteristics shared by all IPAAs. Therefore, any state that has adopted or is considering adopting IPAAs may encounter parallel issues.

The chapter ends by identifying factors applicable to the allocation of regulatory authority in the context of investment and fee issues associated with IPAAs. It does so for two potential regulators, a financial services regulator and a workplace regulator. It categorizes the factors along the dual dimensions of risk and entity to be regulated. The comparison should be of interest to the UK, which is moving toward the introduction of personal accounts in 2012. It also should be important in the US where no significant reallocation of regulatory responsibility for pensions has occurred since 1974. The considerations on distribution of regulatory authority, however, are not limited to the UK and the US. The insights from this chapter are broadly applicable and should be of value to any state interested in IPAAs.

2. BASIC PRINCIPLES OF PERSONAL PENSION PROVISION IN THE US AND UK

Individual Pension Accounts – a Definition

Before institutional oversight of IPAAs can be analyzed it is necessary to define what, for purposes of this chapter, is encompassed within the definition of IPAAs. To begin by exclusion, state-funded benefits such as those provided under the US Social Security programme and the UK National Insurance programme, are not covered in this chapter. Nor does the chapter explicitly address the various US proposals to include individual accounts as part of the Social Security program. Finally, the chapter excludes all public sector pension arrangements.

In order to qualify as a pension account, the particular type of account being addressed must be formally recognized by legislation as a savings vehicle intended to provide retirement support. Table 12.1 shows the types of accounts available in the UK and US and the extent of their relationship to the workplace. Each of the arrangements receives favorable tax treatment. None of them are government funded unless that funding is in lieu of a governmental account. Individuals may bear all of the account fees and investment risks or those costs and risks may be shared in some way among individuals or with an employer. Portions of accounts that are paid in lump sums may then be passed on to heirs. Annuities only provide protection for survivors when they are purchased with a feature, such as surviving spouse or a guaranteed minimum number of payments, that would continue payment of some portion of the annuity after the death of the account holder.

Table 12.1 The proliferation of individual pension accounts

	Employer-based Schemes		Personal Plans
	Trust-based DC	Contract-based DC	Contract-based
US	401(K) Profit-sharing, Employee Stock Ownership Plan	Simplified Employee Plan	Individual Retirement Account
Payment	Usually lump sum	Usually lump sum or annual distributions	Lump sum or annual distributions
Portability	Yes	Yes	Yes
Contribution amount	Individual and/or employer	Individual and/or employer	Individual
Choice of Investment	Individual and/or employer	Individual and/or employer	Individual
UK	Occupational Money Purchase	Group Personal Pension	Individual Personal Pension
Payment	Annuity (25% lump sum permitted)	Stakeholder Pension Annuity (25% lump sum permitted)	Stakeholder Pension Annuity (25% lump sum permitted)
Portability	Yes	Yes	Yes
Contribution amount	Individual and/or employer	Individual and/or employer (required equivalent of offset national insurance contribution)	Individual
Choice of Investment	Employer and trustee	Individual and employer	Individual

The highly individualized nature of IPAAs raises the question of whether they belong in the same pensions category as supplementary DB plans and state pay-as-you-go plans. After all, IPAAs may permit account holders to allocate their assets among an array of investment vehicles. Account holders may be allowed to take loans against their account balances. An employee who stops working for the employer associated with a particular scheme might receive an immediate distribution of all or part of the account assets held in the scheme. One basic issue with IPAAs is the extent to which they are de-linked with employment. A second is whether they bear more resemblance to traditional investment accounts – albeit with a tax-favoured status – than to devices traditionally intended for the accumulation of pension wealth.

The declines in the number of DB arrangements in the US and UK are widely known. In the UK, between 2000 and 2006, the number of open private sector occupational DB plans with only one section fell from 18,350 to 3,470. During the same period, membership in those plans also fell dramatically, from 4.1 million to 1.6 million (Daffin 2006, p. 8 and p. 16). In the US, participation in DB plans fell to approximately 18.5 per cent of workers in 2003 from 22.9 per cent in 1995. Much of the drop in US DB coverage occurred earlier than in the UK; one has to go back to 1980 to find a 35 per cent coverage rate (Pension Benefit Guarantee Corporation 2005, p. 60).

Over approximately the last 25 years, work-based IPAAs in the UK and US have increased in size both in terms of numbers and in assets held. In the UK, approximately 97 per cent of the open private sector occupational DC plans were founded after 1979. In recent years, though, the number of those plans has fallen from a peak of 46,730 in 2004 to 33,770 in 2006. Membership however has remained at about 1 million (Daffin 2006, pp. 8–9, p. 16). In the US, 401(k) plans have grown from essentially zero in 1981 (Muir 2006, p. 6) to having more participants and assets than any other type of DC plan in the US. At year-end 2006, approximately 50 million US workers participated in 401(k) plans with assets totaling an estimated $2.7 trillion or about 66 per cent of all DC assets (Holden et al. 2007, p. 2).

Beginning in 1998 the UK expanded the population eligible to open a type of IPAA designated as personal pensions. The expansion permitted employees to open personal pensions, which had long been available to the self-employed. (Waine this volume, p. 117). At the same time, workers received the right to opt out of a portion of the public pension system (then known as SERP) or their current or former employer-sponsored occupational pension scheme (Tedrow 2006, p. 48). The UK estimated that about half a million workers would establish a personal pension in lieu of SERP or an occupational pension scheme. The actual take-up rate was dramatically higher. By 1994–95, approximately 5.6 million people had established personal pensions (Black and Nobles 1998, p. 797).

Stakeholder pensions were made available in 2001. They were intended to operate at low cost while meeting minimum scheme requirements to protect scheme holders. Most employers that do not offer a pension plan meeting minimum standards must designate a stakeholder scheme. As of 2004 approximately 1 million individuals had contributed to a stakeholder plan. About the same number are members of open private sector occupational DC plans. But, 82 per cent of the stakeholder schemes designated by employers had not attracted any contributions as of 2004 (Waine 2006, p. 324, pp. 328–29).

The US and UK both make provision for individualized pension accounts initiated outside the workplace. In the UK, individuals can establish personal pensions as well as versions that qualify as stakeholder pensions. In the US, Individual Retirement Account (IRA) assets have risen from $1.1 trillion in 1994 to $4.2 trillion in 2006 (Brady and Holden 2007, p. 4).

To complicate matters further, these categories of IPAAs are more complex than they may seem on the surface and are not perfectly compartmentalized. For example, about one-half of the assets held in IRAs originated in work-based plans (Brady and Holden 2007, p. 6). The UK also plans significant changes to its IPAA schemes with the introduction of a new personal accounts scheme, which is planned for 2012 (Waine, this volume, pp. 116–9).

General Division of Institutional Authority for Pension Oversight

Once government-provided pensions are excluded, the primary participants in establishing, operating or benefiting from individual pensions are employers, individuals and providers of financial products or services (PFPS). Considering the actors to be regulated, natural choices for regulators of IPAAs would be the entities responsible for oversight of PFPSs and of workplace relationships. To the extent that IPAAs receive favorable tax treatment or other state funding, the state's taxing authority would also have an interest in ensuring the state expenditure achieves its objectives and is not subject to misuse.

The institutional oversight regimes that have developed in the UK and US are quite complex. Both states have established entities that provide a safety net in limited circumstances for underfunded DB plans. In the UK, three different ombudsman services and The Pensions Advisory Service share responsibility for assisting individuals with pension-related questions, disputes and compensatory rights. The US leaves dispute resolution primarily to its federal court system. In spite of the authority assigned to these and other regulatory entities, in the UK and the US two institutional entities have emerged as the central entities with responsibility for oversight of pension-related matters. The foundational nature of the primary institutional entities, however, differs between the two states and the two states rely on distinct conceptual approaches to the division of authority.

In the UK the entities with primary regulatory responsibility for pensions are the Financial Services Authority (FSA) and The Pensions Regulator (TPR). They have entered into a detailed memorandum of understanding that allocates authority between the two entities. At the conceptual level, the memorandum divides authority according to the entities subject to oversight. In general TPR has responsibility for oversight of and providing advice to employers and to trustees of work-based pension plans. TPR is a public body accountable to the Department for Work and Pensions (DWP). Although DPW, not TPR, develops pension policy and law in the UK, TPR is widely-recognized as a regulatory body. The FSA regulates the PFPS that advise on the marketing, sale and provision of personal pensions and annuities. The FSA also has responsibility for improving investor knowledge and understanding of financial products and markets.

In the US most of the regulatory authority over DC plans is split between the Internal Revenue Service (IRS) and the Employee Benefits Security Administration (EBSA), which is an agency within the Department of Labour (DOL). In part this division of authority may exist because US pension policy has long reflected the tension between balancing tax and other incentives for employer sponsorship of pension plans with provisions that protect employees from malfeasance and unfairness. The interests of each agency led to battles between the two agencies and the supporters of each in Congress during the debates prior to the passage of the Employee Retirement Income Security Act of 1974 (ERISA). ERISA is the primary law in the US regulating retirement and other employee benefit schemes. When the statute was finally passed, many of its provisions were duplicated in the labour and in the tax sections of the US Code (Wooten 2004, p. 232). As a result the agencies agreed to cede each other authority over specific types of regulation. The IRS received responsibility for funding, eligibility to participate in plans, and ensuring entitlement to plan funds. The DOL received authority over fiduciary issues, proper disclosure, and claims procedures. The anomalous approach to duplicated legislative provisions continues as does the division of responsibility (Stanley 2000, p. 39).

At a high level of generality, both the UK and the US have empowered an entity accountable to the state's primary regulator of workplace issues, to act vis-à-vis workplace pensions including IPAAs. The more detailed contextual examination that follows, however, reveals significant differences between the scope of authority of those workplace regulators. In addition the regulator with which the workplace regulator shares responsibility differs significantly between the states. In the UK the other regulator is the FSA, which generally has responsibility for financial market integrity and oversight of financial market firms. In the US the other regulator is the IRS, which at an institutional level is charged with collecting federal taxes and enforcing federal tax law. The differences create very different levels of direct involvement by each state's primary regulator of PFPS.

3. ISSUES ASSOCIATED WITH IPAAS

The US and the UK both have sufficient experience with IPAAs to enable identification of specific types of issues that pose challenges for the institutional oversight of those types of accounts. The next subsections delineate the nature of three of the critical decisions that need to be made for individual accounts. The first discusses two case studies of widespread scandals that have occurred in each country and draws some parallels between the two situations. Subsections following on from these explain two ongoing problems related to IPAAs.

Case Studies on the Selection of Investment Schemes and Vehicles

The first case study, from the UK, examines the mis-selling scandal from the period 1988–1994. The second, from the US, examines the more recent account losses due to individual account investments in employer stock.

Pension Mis-selling in the UK

In 1988 individuals were first permitted to choose personal pensions in lieu of SERPs or occupational pensions. Due to reports of noncompliance with regulatory standards in the sale of personal pensions in lieu of occupational pension schemes, in 1992 the Securities and Investment Board (SIB) reviewed a sample of the records associated with personal pension sales and found that only nine per cent substantially complied with regulatory rules (Nobles and Black 1998, p. 939). The SIB was one of a number of entities later combined to form the FSA. As a result of its concern, the SIB commissioned a study of industry practices. That study found 'widespread regulatory compliance failure' (Milner and Syrett 2000, p. 142).

The concern with mis-selling focused on the sale of personal pensions by insurance companies and on selling techniques by independent financial advisors to employees who then opted out of an occupational pension scheme. The investigations found that existing records were insufficient to demonstrate compliance with customer rules. Those customer rules required sales people to understand the financial position and risk tolerance of customers and to provide advice appropriate to the customer's situation. It also appeared that numerous employees who had bought a personal pension would clearly and unambiguously have been better off in the offered occupational pension scheme. Two factors caused occupational pension schemes to be more lucrative than personal pensions for most individuals. First, employers typically contribute to occupational pension schemes but not to personal pensions. Second, the benefits formula of an occupational pension typically is more generous than the investment growth in a personal pension (Select Committee on Treasury 1998, pp. 1–2).

Nobles and Black attribute pensions mis-selling to failures on the part of both the responsible regulators and by the firms involved in mis-selling. Focusing on the potentially problematic actions of the regulators, one allegation by PFPSs was that the regulators retrospectively changed the standards for suitability and 'know your customer' requirements after the selling had occurred. Nobles and Black challenge that view. They explain firstly, that although additional guidance was eventually given by a regulator, it represented a more thorough explanation rather than a change in standards. Second, Nobles and Black argue that until the 1992 SIB audit, regulators failed to focus their efforts on personal pensions as a product line. Instead the regulators suffered from a lack of expertise with personal pensions, which were a new line of products and too little industry experience. The regulators established review processes that tended to focus at the firm level and on the activities of the internal firm monitors. In a government inquiry into the cause of mis-selling, the FSA indicated that the multiple regulators experienced coordination problems.

Regulatory change expanding eligibility for personal pensions from just the self-employed to all employees presented PFPSs with a temporary opportunity. Firms responded by incentivizing new, untrained sales forces to capture market share. Furthermore those incentives were given in the context of direct sales of financial products to consumers who were entirely unfamiliar with those financial products. These factors established an environment in which aggressive sales practices thrived (Nobles and Black 1998, pp. 947–51; Select Committee on Treasury 1998, p. 3).

Ultimately regulators required sellers of personal pensions and independent financial advisors who provided advice to purchasers to undertake a two-part review process intended to identify mis-selling that occurred between April 1988 and June 1994. The priority phase covered older purchasers who were at or near retirement. Phase two extended to younger purchasers who typically were under the age of 50. As of June 2002, FSA estimated that the pensions industry would pay out £11.8 billion after reviewing the records of 1.7 million customers (FSA 2002).

Use of Employer Stock in DC plans in the US

In the US, issues arising from the investment of DB and DC pension assets in the stock of the plan's sponsoring employer pre-date the enactment of ERISA in 1974. The issues were largely dormant though, other than in the context of potential corporate takeovers and Employee Stock Ownership Plans, until two events converged, resulting in large losses in employee 401(k) accounts across a number of companies. The first event was the dramatic drop in the US stock markets after the bursting of the technology bubble in early 2000. The second event was the collapse of Enron Corporation in 2001, which was followed by a surge in governance and accounting scandals at other US companies.

Estimates of the amount lost by employees who participated in the Enron 401(k) plan range from \$1 to \$2 billion. WorldCom employees allegedly lost more than \$1 billion (Muir and Schipani 2005, p. 314; Stein et al. 2003, p. 241). Nor were these types of losses limited to the companies that appeared at the top of news stories about corporate malfeasance. An accurate count of the number of companies that faced claims by employees associated with use of their stock in DC plans is not available. Data do show that between 2003 and early 2005, US courts issued opinions involving at least 31 different employers. Legal commentators in the US are of the unanimous view that the claims are widespread and of substantial importance (Casciari and Morrison 2006, p. 637; Martin, Renaud and Akbar 2006, p. 605).

Employees alleged wrongdoing in the employer stock cases against an array of individuals and institutions including the companies sponsoring the plans, individual plan fiduciaries, company directors, and trustees that held plan assets and administered investment directions. The legal claims brought under ERISA can generally be divided into three categories, all based in fiduciary obligation. One typical allegation was that plan fiduciaries continued to permit the use of employer stock in the plan even after they knew or should have known that the stock had become an imprudent investment. Second, plan fiduciaries allegedly made material omissions or misstatements in their direct or indirect communications with employees about the employer stock. Third, plaintiffs claimed that high level plan fiduciaries failed to properly appoint or monitor the lower level fiduciaries with responsibility for communications or plan use of employer stock (Muir and Schipani 2006, pp. 459–60).

The responses to these lawsuits have varied by claim as well as by the type of defendant. Some cases involved disputed factual situations but the early court decisions addressed the viability of the alleged legal claims. One important category of responses pointed out that the claims brought by employees who had lost money in their 401(k) plan typically overlapped with claims brought under the US federal securities laws by the company's larger shareholder population. In other instances, defendants claimed that the duties allegedly imposed by ERISA were inconsistent with the federal securities laws.

The 401(k) plans involved in litigation varied significantly in the source of contributions and the available investment choices. Those plans may be funded exclusively through employer contributions, exclusively through employee contributions or though some combination of the two. Plans often provide employer contributions in the form of a 'match' for employee contributions at least up to a set amount per employee. Some employers required some or all of the plan contributions to be held in employer stock. At the other end of the spectrum, some plans provided an open brokerage account that facilitated investments in any publicly traded security.

Unlike the UK situation with pension mis-selling, the employer stock controversy remains largely unresolved. Some cases have settled. Others have been dismissed for various reasons including the lack of available relief. Most, however, continue to remain active in the court system.

For this chapter, the important subset of issues relating to investing employer stock in employee pension plans are those centered on the allegedly conflicting obligations imposed by ERISA and the US federal securities laws. The possible conflicts arise in two circumstances. One question is whether ERISA's general fiduciary provisions require more frequent or more extensive disclosure to employees holding stock in 401(k) plans than the Securities and Exchange Commission (SEC) has established, based upon federal securities laws for general public shareholders. This is related to the second problem. If employees holding stock in 401(k) plans are entitled to superior disclosure as compared to general public shareholders then compliance with the ERISA fiduciary obligations would violate the SEC prohibition on tipping and insider trading.

The US courts have not been uniform in their decisions on these arguments. One court agreed with the defendants, suggesting that disclosing otherwise non-public information about a company to employees holding employer stock in their 401(k)s would violate securities laws. The majority of courts, however, have accepted the position advocated by the Department of Labor, that the ERISA and SEC obligations can be reconciled. Companies should accomplish that by making public disclosures at the earliest time and to the highest standard of disclosure required by ERISA and the SEC (Muir and Schipani 2005, p. 340).

Gordon has questioned whether employees should have the right to invest in an undiversified manner in company stock in their 401(k) plan accounts. His concern is that the tax incentives provided to 401(k) plans are intended to support the accumulation of retirement assets, not to facilitate investments with a high risk profile (Gordon 2002, pp. 1248–9). Much has been written on why employees over invested in employer securities. Hirshleifer attributes the phenomena to employees' perception that employer stock is low risk (Hirschleifer 2001, p. 1562). Research during the period in question, though, indicated that employees were more likely to choose to invest their discretionary contributions in employer stock if the employer made a matching contribution in employer stock (Stabile 2004, p. 403). This could imply that employees used the employer investment decision as a proxy for their own decisions. Also, it was not unusual for employers to make matching or other contributions in employer stock and to require that the account assets remain in employer stock at least until employees reached a specified age. In those situations the investment in employer stock had no relation to the employees' perception of risk. The employees simply had no choice regarding the investment in employer stock.

The US Congress has considered capping employee account holdings of employer stock but to date has refused to do so. Instead it enacted legislation in 2006 that grants 401(k) plan participants certain rights to diversify out of employer stock and into alternative investments. Those rights depend on whether the employer stock was purchased through employer or employee contributions (Stanley 2006, pp. 208–9).

Comparing the Case Studies

The technical differences between the IPAAs in the two case studies are significant. First, in the UK the individuals had the ability to choose among tax-favoured pension products while the individuals in the US scandal typically had no such choice. In the UK, pension mis-selling scandal, the nature of the personal pension products enabled firms to sell directly to individuals who had the right to choose a personal pension scheme or to remain or become part of an occupational scheme. In the US, an employee's choice at the scheme level was whether to participate in a 401(k) plan or to opt out entirely of tax-favoured pension plans other than the social security scheme. Nor were individuals in the US the subject of direct selling by a firm providing pension products. The UK personal pension products were typically based in contracts between the employee and the PFPS. In the US, 401(k)s are trust-based and employers had substantial roles in establishing the trusts.

Second, the US scandal resulted from specific decisions on contribution or asset allocation whereas in the UK once an individual made a decision in favour of a specific scheme there typically was no further need for the individual to designate investment vehicles. In a number of instances in the US the investment option, company stock, was alleged to be inappropriate for any pension account. In contrast whether an employee was mis-sold a personal pension scheme in the UK depended on a variety of individualized circumstances. Those include whether the particular employee had access to alternative pension schemes and the rate of employer contributions.

In spite of the differences between them, the case studies provide important insights for the division of regulatory authority with respect to IPAAs. In each instance employees were delegated choices that would be determinative of the ultimate value of their IPAAs. Whether those choices are at the scheme level or the investment vehicle level, the mis-selling and employer stock scandals warn that delegation of decisions that determine investment returns poses serious risks for accumulation of wealth in IPAAs.

Both of the current UK regulators with primary responsibility for IPAAs, TPR and FSA, were formed after the mis-selling scandal. The establishment of the FSA as a 'super-regulator' included the merger of ten different agencies. Such a fundamental change in regulatory authority cannot be ascribed to a single scandal or set of problems. But commentators have noted that the mis-selling of personal pensions was a consideration in the formation of the FSA. The US reaction to the employer–stock scandal was more muted. In 2006 broad ranging pension legislation established the diversification rights discussed here. There has not been any change however in agency structure or in the allocation of authority over IPAAs.

The case studies prompt the question of what type of regulatory institution is best suited to anticipate, avoid and respond to risks associated with participant decisions that have direct relevance for wealth accumulation in IPAAs. In this context the difference between the UK and US approaches become particularly stark. The UK's division of authority is based on the type of entity to be regulated. As a result the FSA has responsibility for overseeing the PFPSs that are responsible for marketing, selling and paying out individual pensions. It also has responsibility to improve employees' understanding of individual pension products through education and disclosure. TPR concentrates primarily on problems and potential problems at the employer level. In the US, EBSA has regulatory and enforcement authority over all IPAA fiduciaries to the extent that the accounts in question are regulated by ERISA. If an advisor provides investment advice to either a private sector employer as plan sponsor or to an individual employee regarding 401(k) assets, the investment advisor must meet ERISA's fiduciary standards. If the IPAA is not sponsored by a private sector employer then the provision of investment advice to either a sponsoring employer or to an employee is regulated by securities regulators.

Two Current Issues with IPAAs

Two issues related to IPAAs have recently received attention from regulators in the UK and the US. The first issue is with the selection of default investments, while the second issue relates to the effect and appropriateness of account fees.

Default Investments

There are a variety of routes through which individuals with IPAAs may have their account assets allocated to a default investment. For example, in the US, a 401(k) plan may adopt an automatic enrollment provision. New employees are then enrolled automatically in the 401(k) plan unless they affirmatively opt out of the plan. Research and experience indicates that such automatic enrollment features help overcome employee inertia and thereby increase the take-up rate for 401(k) plans. Plans with automatic enrollment though need to determine a default investment for the contributions of those employees who are enrolled under the automatic feature. Similarly where an employee enrolls in a 401(k) plan or transfers funds from another plan but does not select among available investment options, the plan must default contributions to an investment vehicle. An example of the use of default investments in the UK occurs in employer-selected stakeholder schemes. In order to meet the minimum requirements of a stakeholder scheme, the employer must designate a default investment vehicle.

A recent study of the stakeholder pension plan schemes registered with TPR as of December 2006 found that the default funds offered are less uniform than one might expect. The study reviewed default funds selected by PFPSs that registered stakeholder schemes. When an employer chooses a particular stakeholder scheme, that employer has the option of designating a different default fund. Industry experience however indicates that most employers accept the default option suggested by the financial firm that packaged the stakeholder plan (Byrne et al. 2007, p. 42).

Among the registered schemes the default funds were almost evenly split between actively and passively managed funds. A few default funds are styled as UK equity funds but the majority were evenly divided between global equity funds and balanced funds. It is difficult to rationalize these significant differences in the types of funds chosen by PFPSs as default funds. A PFPS marketing a given stakeholder scheme typically markets that scheme to a wide variety of employers with various employee demographics. Perhaps the PFPSs do not agree on the appropriate type of default fund for the average individual who opens a stakeholder pension account. Or the PFPSs may not be in agreement over the typical earnings, additional investment holdings, risk tolerances and other characteristics of the average individual account holder (Byrne et al. 2007, p. 42 and 43). In any event, the requirement that stakeholder schemes must designate a default fund will be less than optimally implemented to the extent that the default funds are inappropriate for purchasers of stakeholder schemes.

In addition to its requirement that stakeholder schemes establish a default fund, in 2005 the UK began to require that every stakeholder default fund utilize a life-cycle profile. As a result of ensuring that years remaining to retirement age is a consideration in the structure of a default portfolio, the requirement addresses some of the concern over the variance in default funds. Implementation of the life-cycle requirement is not totally uniform across stakeholder schemes. The vast majority of the schemes though, begin increasing the percentage of bonds and cash held in a portfolio between five and 10 years prior to retirement (Byrne et al. 2007, pp. 42–5).

A 2006 survey of 401(k) plans in the US found that more than a third of plans with default investment funds designated lifecycle funds as the default. However 45 per cent of the plans provided for a stable-value fund or money-market fund as the default (Watson Wyatt 2006, Table 5). The goal of those types of default funds tends primarily to be the preservation of capital as opposed to investment growth. Such conservative default investments have been heavily criticized particularly for younger investors.

Although issues associated with default investments had been observable in 401(k) plans since they became popular plans, the US did not issue guidance on default fund selection until October 2007. The guidance, in the form of regulations issued by EBSA, establishes a safe harbour for liability if an employer selects a fund that has the characteristics of what EBSA terms a Qualified Default Investment Alternative (QDIA). An employer may however at its own risk designate as a default fund a fund that is not a QDIA. With the exception of investments that pre-date the regulation and investments during the first 120 days of an employee's participation in a 401(k) plan, a QDIA must consist of a mix of investments that take into account either the characteristics of the individual account holder or of a group of employees.

Account Fees

Along with the rate of contributions and return on investment, account fees have a fundamental impact on the accumulation of assets in IPAAs. The UK anticipated the issue of account fees when it established stakeholder pensions. When first offered in 2001, stakeholder scheme charges were capped at 1 per cent per year. Effective in 2005 the cap was increased to 1.5 per cent a year for the first 10 years of a customer account. Thereafter the account fee cap drops back to 1 per cent (Byrne et al. 2007, p. 48).

A recent study of fees charged by stakeholder plan default funds implies that the legal caps have had a significant impact on account fees. Based on general fee data, the expectation would be that the default funds which utilize a passive investment style would have lower fees than the default funds that consist of actively managed funds. The actual modal investment fee however is 1 per cent across both active and passive default funds. Effectively it appears that the fee cap has been established as a floor for stakeholder scheme fees. The mean charge of passive default funds is 20 basis points lower than the mean for active default funds, which is somewhat more in accordance with expectations. And a number of other factors may impact the fees charged, including the level of services provided by the scheme and the size of the employee population at a particular workplace (Byrne et al. 2007, p. 48).

To date the US has failed to adopt legislation or regulation limiting the amount of 401(k) account fees. This author was a member of the 2004 EBSA Advisory Council working group that studied the disclosure of account fees in 401(k) accounts. The working group published a report, which included both factual findings and recommendations intended to enhance fee disclosure.

No significant action was taken in the US until 2006 when a number of lawsuits were filed alleging that 401(k) plan fee structures violated ERISA's general fiduciary requirements. The claims vary depending on complexities such as the payment of 'hard dollar' fees and 'revenue sharing'. Subsequent to the filing of the fees cases EBSA and the Congress have shown an increased interest in the issues surrounding plan account fees. Legislation has been proposed in Congress. However the Assistant Secretary of EBSA recently requested in congressional testimony that Congress leave the oversight of fees and the disclosure of fees to the EBSA. In July 2008 EBSA issued proposed regulations mandating some fee disclosure.

4. WHO SHOULD REGULATE IPAAS?

The case studies and discussion of issues pertaining to the selection of default funds and account fees show that the UK and the US have faced similar problems with IPAAs. This is true even though the type of IPAAs that underlie these comparisons are quite different in each country. Rather than being specific to a particular type of IPAA scheme, the challenges encountered in the UK and the US have arisen from some of the basic characteristics of IPAAs. As compared to traditional workplace DB plans, IPAAs decrease the role of employers as mediators. At the same time the relationships between PFPSs and the individuals who hold IPAAs become stronger. Employees not only take on additional risks, they typically must make decisions which impact those risks.

On a more foundational level, there is the question about why financial products and in particular pension products should be regulated at all. In the context of banking regulation, Stewart discusses two roles for regulators. The first role is to address issues relating to conduct of business, including efforts to increase the fairness of business practices and to ensure that appropriate disclosures are made. The second role ensures the fiscal soundness of the institutional actors as well as the trustworthiness of the financial system (Stewart 2001, pp. 44–5).

Of the regulatory roles discussed by Stewart, both the conduct of business role and the system-wide soundness have application in the IPAA realm. Black identifies the specific risks to consumers associated with various types of pension products. For example, governance risk includes account charges that are not clearly disclosed or that are excessive (Black 2002, pp. 10–12). Such charges implicate the conduct of business of those selling and administering personal pensions. As noted by Hughes and Stewart, unreasonable charges and those that are not transparent also may have a deterrent effect (Hughes and Stewart, this volume, pp. 184–89). Similarly, Stewart explains that the nature of financial products as trust goods implies a need for greater regulation than is necessary for non-financial goods (Stewart 2005, p. 80).

One result of the risks and unique characteristics of IPAAs is that the proper distribution of regulatory oversight becomes a challenge for states that established their pension regulatory systems to oversee DB plans. IPAAs pose different regulatory challenges. In addition states that have little experience with supplementary pension schemes can expect to see similar issues arise as they implement IPAAs.

The UK and US have taken different approaches, at a fundamental level, to the regulation of IPAAs. The UK completely reformed its system in recent years whereas the US has not made any significant changes in either the structure of the relevant regulatory entities or in the division of authority among them. The difference is particularly stark in relation to investment and fee issues, which are discussed above and have led to problems in each country. For the most part the UK has allocated authority for those issues to the FSA, a relatively new entity charged with regulating PFPSs. The US has left authority for those issues with EBSA, the workplace-related agency that is generally responsible for the oversight of fiduciary issues, proper disclosure and claims procedures. This section examines the decisions made by the UK and the US to compare the implications of regulating IPPAs through a financial services regulator as compared to a workplace regulator. It does so by unpacking considerations in the allocation of that regulatory authority according to the conceptual approaches used by the UK and the US; that is by type of risk posed and by type of entity to be regulated.

Financial Services Regulator – a Risk Analysis

Nobles and Black argue that one factor in the pensions mis-selling scandal was the inability of regulators to understand the dynamic market for personal pensions. The regulators did not evaluate the risks created by the structure of sales commissions and other factors in the marketing of personal pensions. Nor did they focus attention on personal pensions as posing a particular set of risks to investors (Nobles and Black 1998, pp. 948–9).

The Nobles and Black critique applies to the actions of the Securities and Investment Board (SIB), which was a predecessor of the FSA. Therefore the critique could be understood to imply that a financial services regulator such as the FSA cannot be expected to bring relevant expertise to the regulation of IPAAs. Actually though their argument resonates with the benefits that could be expected to result from the choice of an experienced financial services regulator. Nobles and Black explain that the SIB was a newly formed agency at the time personal pensions were introduced. Its inexperience with private pension products and the industry prevented the SIB from successfully overseeing and identifying problems with new products in an industry undergoing a complete restructuring (Nobles and Black 1998, pp. 948–9).

One implication of Nobles and Black's analysis is that the mis-selling problem illustrates the value a regulator with experience in financial services can bring to the oversight of IPAAs. In contrast to the situation of the SIB at the time of the mis-selling, an established regulator with authority over a wide variety of financial products and PFPSs, such as the FSA, should develop a broad expertise on risks posed to investors. That broad perspective and experience should have relevance to the investment and fee issues which occur across investment products and accounts regardless of their status as IPAAs. In sum, a financial services regulator should have substantive expertise with the risks posed to IPAAs by investment and fee issues.

The risk of insolvency or nonpayment represents a different concern common across all types of pension plans as well as across all types of investment products. In traditional DB plans the first insurer against the risk that a benefit will not be paid is the employer that sponsors the plan. Both the UK and the US have established institutional guarantors that provide a second tier insurance against plan insolvency. In IPAAs though the risk of institutional insolvency is with the PFPSs, there is no reason to believe that the evaluation of financial reserves and other mechanisms to offset insolvency risk is substantially different in the context of IPAAs than it is with respect to other long term investment and insurance products. Thus the expertise developed by the financial services regulator with respect to those products should be applicable to addressing institutional insolvency risk in IPAAs.

Financial Services Regulator – an Entity Analysis

Regulatory consistency may result in increased efficiency in the regulation of IPAAs. If regulatory authority over IPAAs is allocated according to the entity to be regulated, that decision has implications for consistency of regulation. Some financial services and products cross all types of individually held investment accounts, regardless of whether the account is tax-favored or funded through payroll deductions. PFPSs do not typically limit the sale of their financial products to IPAAs, let alone to a particular type of IPAA. Consider the example of a mutual fund, which can be purchased in a traditional investment account that does not receive any tax-favored treatment. That same mutual fund might be utilized in a personal pension, in a stakeholder pension and in an occupational DC plan.

If a financial services regulator has primary oversight of the mutual fund regardless of the formal structure of the account in which the fund is being held then the mutual fund has one touch point with a regulator. A contrasting approach might allocate responsibility for IPAAs, or a segment of IPAAs, to a workplace regulator instead of to a financial services regulator. The mutual fund will then face not just two sets of regulators but also the possibility that the two regulatory entities will have different basic goals. For example the financial services regulator may place a high priority on maintaining market efficiency. A workplace regulator may be more interested in preventing and addressing fraud than with market efficiency. Or a workplace regulator may believe that holders of IPAAs require a particular type of protection not needed by the general investing population.

Consistency in disclosure regimes may be another benefit from assigning oversight of IPAAs to a single financial services regulator. Consider again the example of account fees. A regulatory regime where there would not be a financial services regulator charged with oversight of fees and fee-related disclosures in non-tax favored investment accounts would be generally regarded as being at variance with the concept of 'proper rergulation'. The existence of such authority does not presume the nature or extent of direct regulation. It only presumes that a financial services regulator will have responsibility for determining the need for such regulation. The starting point in considering fee-related disclosures in such a context should cross the boundaries of all investment products.

It is possible that policy makers would decide that individuals with IPAAs need different disclosures than those provided to individuals with standard investment accounts. If so, the deep understanding a financial services regulator would have of the nature and complexity of fees as well as its experience with investor education should be valuable in determining the extent to which the disclosures should differ. Assigning the disclosure oversight to a single financial services regulator should avoid the need for inter-agency coordination. It also provides for one agency touch-point for PFPSs subject to the disclosure requirements.

Another consistency-related benefit that may result from regulation of IPAAs by a financial services regulator is consistency and integration of investment advice across an individual's IPAA and non-IPAA investment accounts, savings products and any other type of investment vehicle. In the US investment advisors are subject to EBSA regulation for advice given in 401(k) accounts and to regulation by the SEC for advice provided on non-employment based investment accounts. As a result of the harsher ERISA regulatory standards, it is a frequent practice for investment advisors to provide advice across the entire spectrum of an individual's financial planning needs except for 401(k) accounts and any other ERISA-covered IPAAs. The lack of integrated advice limits the value of such advice.

The problem in the US remains, though perhaps to a lesser extent, even after statutory changes in 2006, which were intended to expand 401(k) participants' access to investment advice. Rather than eliminate differences in the standards governing advice or allocating authority to a single regulator, the changes authorized advice to 401(k) plan account holders if the advisors meet specific standards. Of particular importance under the legislation is the structure of advisory fees and disclosure of conflicts of interest. The US division of authority between EBSA and the SEC and the resulting differing standards governing the provision of investment advice still results in a lack of integrated advice over all of an individual's investment accounts. As such it serves as an example of the lack of consistency that can result from the involvement of multiple agencies and legislative approaches.

Workplace Regulator – a Risk Analysis

From a risk perspective certain of the risks associated with IPAAs are related to the workplace. For example in both UK stakeholder plans and US 401(k) plans the employer must withhold contributions from an employee's paycheck and transmit the funds to a PFPS. The resulting risk is that an employer may fail to transmit the withheld funds, at least on a timely basis, to the PFPS.

A workplace regulator would be expected to have expertise that would be relevant to the risk associated with contribution withholding and transmittal. For example in the US the DOL oversees regulation of overtime and minimum hourly wages and EBSA oversees the withholding and transmittal of employee contributions to the cost of health care coverage. The issues that arise under these areas would seem to have relevance for the oversight of 401(k) contributions.

Workplace oversight may not, however, be unified under a single regulator. In the UK, HM Revenue and Customs is charged with enforcement of the national minimum wage. In the US oversight of the timely payment of wages and over the withholding of some charges such as 'garnishments'[1] by creditors occurs at the state level rather than by the DOL. The lack of a single workplace regulator decreases the expected expertise that such a regulator would bring to bear on oversight of IPAA contributions.

A second question on risk is whether certain types of risks are unique to pension accounts. Stabile has argued that pension accounts require a different type of regulation than typical investment accounts. Pension accounts are intended (and enjoy considerable tax benefits) for the single goal of providing income after retirement. The investments selected for an account, the account fees, account statements and other disclosures should all support the goal of providing retirement income. In the US these concerns are evidenced in ERISA's fiduciary standards, which are more rigorous than those imposed under securities law (Stabile 2005, p. 403).

Similarly as discussed above, Nobles and Black argue that one factor in the mis-selling scandal in the UK was the failure of the relevant regulators, all of whom had responsibility for aspects of investments and financial services firms, to focus on the unique issues associated with personal pensions (Nobles and Black 1998, pp. 948–9). A state that considers its IPAAs to be highly differentiated from other investment alternatives may determine that the expertise of a general financial services regulator is of limited value in the oversight of IPAAs. In that context a workplace-related agency with experience in overseeing compensation and relationships between employees and employers may be best equipped to provide appropriate oversight over such accounts.

Workplace Regulator – an Entity Analysis

The preferred approach to achieving consistency in the regulation of IPAAs may depend upon the type of consistency a particular state values. As discussed above a financial services regulator may be best positioned to achieve consistent oversight across account fees, financial products, services and disclosure. Those issues arise with respect to all investment products, not just IPAAs.

IPAAs that are based in the workplace though, may benefit from consistency across workplace dimensions. Employers are less involved in the offering, administration and funding of IPAAs than they were in occupational DB schemes. But some states, such as the UK and US, have traditions of pension programs being embedded in the workplace. In that context the employer's IPAA-related actions are a dimension of the employer–employee relationship. An employer communication about its compensation and benefits programmes might logically categorize its IPAA activities as a part of those programs. Similarly employees, because of both historic experience and the wage-related nature of workplace IPAAs may view them as part of the compensation and benefits package.

These employer and employee expectations point to values associated with consistency of regulation across matters such as payroll withholding and communications about withholding and workplace benefits. Employers may prefer to deal with a single regulator for all of their workplace responsibilities. Multiple regulators may impose additional costs due to coordination, conflicting requirements, and multiple reporting. Particularly where workplace pensions are voluntary, those increased costs and employer preferences may discourage employers from providing IPAAs. Even in the case of a state such as the UK where employers must offer at least a minimum stakeholder pension scheme, the complexity and costs of dealing with multiple regulators could discourage employers from sponsoring more generous IPAA plans or from contributing to stakeholder plans.

Employees may also prefer to interact with a single regulator for all compensation-related matters. For example, employees with concerns that their IPAA contributions are not being properly forwarded to the scheme provider may have concerns with other employer pay practices as well. Conferring authority over all workplace issues on one regulator simplifies the complaint mechanisms for employees. It also permits that single regulator to investigate across all workplace-related issues.

In states, such as the UK and US, where employers have an established history of providing workplace-based pension schemes, employers utilized the schemes as workplace management tools. In industries where workforce stability was important, DB plans were adopted to increase employee retention. When workforce reductions were required, those same DB plans could provide early retirement programs to ease the impact of the reduction in the workforce.

IPAAs provide fewer workplace management tools because they belong to employees. Thus they are not effective in discouraging labor movement. However employers may still view IPAAs as beneficial in their relationships with employees. For example a generous employer contribution to an IPAA may be attractive in a competitive job market. The nature of IPAAs as workplace management tools may favour the designation of a workplace regulator that can coordinate regulation across all of an employer's compensation-related activities.

5. CONCLUSION

The chapters in this book describe the differences among states in the extent to which they currently permit, structure and incentivize IPAAs. Interest in IPAAs is increasing as states confront the cost of pay-as-you-go state plans and employers with DB plans seek alternative pension arrangements. Regardless of the structure of IPAAs in a particular state, inherent in the accounts are issues associated with investments and plan fees. Some type of regulatory regime is required to oversee these and other IPAA issues.

Analysis of the differences between how the UK and US allocate regulatory authority for IPAAs provides a number of insights for division of regulatory authority for IPAAs. The mis-selling and employer stock scandals illustrate the risks for capital accumulation when decision making is delegated to individuals. The continuing concern in both states regarding the selection of default investments and account fees shows the persistence of complex issues years after the authorization of IPAAs.

The ultimate allocation of regulatory authority by any state will be embedded within the values of the particular state. The paths taken by the UK and the US illustrate two approaches to the division of authority among regulators. This chapter considered the allocation of regulatory authority for investment and fee issues associated with IPAAs. It compared as alternatives a financial services regulator and a workplace regulator along the dimensions of risk and entity to be regulated.

A state's decision on allocation of regulatory authority may vary depending on the value placed on considerations such as consistency, the types of consistency that are most valued and regulatory expertise. Within those general considerations, specific concerns may favor a particular choice. If a state's goal is to minimize costs and increase the efficiency of regulation of financial services and products, it may place a high value on the consistency expected from a financial services regulator. A state that, as an example, wants to provide employees with a single point of regulatory contact for investigation and resolution of workplace or compensation-related matters may decide to allocate oversight of those aspects of IPAAs to a workplace regulator.

NOTE

1. This is a legal concept where a court order may be issued directing a third party who holds money or property belonging to a defendant to withhold it and appear in court to answer inquiries or transmit the money or property to a party designated by the court.

REFERENCES

Black, J. (2002), 'Risk, Trust and Regulation: The Case of Pensions', working chapter for the National Consumers Council.

Black, J. and R. Nobles (1998), 'Personal Pensions Misselling: The Causes and Lessons of Regulatory Failure', *The Modern Law Review*, **61** (6), 789–820.

Brady, P. and S. Holden (2007), 'The U.S. Retirement Market, 2006', *ICI Research Fundamentals*, **16** (3), 1–12.

Brooks A. (ed.) (1950), *The Complete Essays and Other Writings of Ralph Waldo Emerson*, New York, US, The Modern Library.

Byrne, H. et al. (2007), 'Default Funds in UK Defined-Contribution Plans', *Financial Analysts Journal*, **63** (4), 40-50.

Carey, S. (2005), 'Judge Clear Sway for Record Pension Default by UAL', *The Wall Street Journal*, 5 November, A1.

Casciari, M. and I. Morrison (2006), 'Should the Securities Exchange Act be the Sole Federal Remedy for an ERISA Fiduciary Misrepresentation of the Value of Public Employer Stock?', *John Marshall Law Review*, **39**, 637–66.

Daffin, C. (ed.) (2006), *Occupational Pension Schemes Annual Report,* 14, UK Office for National Statistics.

FSA (2002), '11.8 billion compensation for pensions and FSAVC reviews', Press Release, 27 June.

Gordon, J. (2002), 'What Enron Means for the Management and Control of the Modern Business Corporation: Some Initial Reflections', *University of Chicago Law Review*, **69**, 1233–50.

Hirshleifer, D. (2001), 'Investor Psychology and Asset Pricing', *The Journal of Finance*, **56** (4), 1533–97.

Holden S., J. VanDerhei, L. Alonso, and C. Copeland (2007), '401(k) Plan Asset Allocation, Account Balances, and Loan Activity in 2006', *ICI Research Perspective*, **13** (1) 1–39.

Karmel, R. (2003), 'The SEC at 70: Mutual Funds, Pension Funds, Hedge Funds and Stock Market Volatility – What Regulation by the Securities and Exchange Commission is Appropriate?', *Notre Dame Law Review,* **80,** 909–49.

Martin, C., M. Renaud and O. Akbar (2006), 'What's Up On Stock-Drops? Moench Revisited', *John Marshall Law Review*, **39**, 605–636.

Milner, M. and K. Syrett (2000), 'Personal Pensions and the Financial Services Authority: New Chapter or Same Old Story?', *Northern Ireland Legal Quarterly*, **51** (2), 141–63.

Muir, D. and C. Schipani (2006), 'The Challenge of Company Stock Transactions for Directors' Duties of Loyalty', *Harvard Journal on Legislation*, **43** (2), 437–85.

Muir, D. and C. Schipani (2005), 'New Standards of Director Loyalty and Care in the Post-Enron Era: Are Some Shareholders More Equal Than Others?' *New York University Journal of Legislation and Public Policy*, **8** (2), 279–58.

Muir, D. (2002), 'The Dichotomy Between Investment Advice and Investment Education: Is No Advice Really the Best Advice?', *Berkeley Journal of Employment and Labor Law*, **23** (1), 1–55.

Nobles, R. and J. Black, (1998), 'The Privatization Process: Pensions Mis-selling – The Lessons for Regulating Privatised Social Security', *Brooklyn Law Review*, **64**, 933–54.

Pension Benefit Guarantee Corporation (PBGC) (2006), *Pension Insurance Data Book 2005.*

Prokesch, S. (1992), 'Pension Changes Urged After Maxwell Scandal', *The New York Times*, 10 March, p. 22.

Select Committee on Treasury (1998), 'Ninth Report: The Mis-selling of Personal Pensions', UK: House of Commons.

Stabile, S. (2004), 'I Believed My Employer and Didn't Sell My Company Stock: Is There an ERISA (or 34 Act) Remedy for Me?', *Connecticut Law Review*, **36**, 385–24.

Stanley, J. (ed.) (2006), *2006 Cumulative Supplement to Employee Benefits Law*, Washington, D.C.: BNA Books.

Stanley, J. (ed.) (2000), *Employee Benefits Law*, Washington D.C.: BNA Books.

Stein, N. and P. Dilley, (2003), 'Employee Stock Ownership After Enron: Proceedings of the 2003 Annual Meeting, Association of American Law Schools section on Employee Benefits', *Employee Rights and Employment Policy Journal*, **7**, 213–51.

Stewart, J. (2005), 'Private Sector Pension Provision: Funding, Risk and Costs', in J. Stewart, (ed.), *For Richer, For Poorer*, Dublin, Ireland: New Island Press, pp. 56–89.

Stewart, J. (2001), 'Financial Regulation in Ireland: Should the Regulator be the Central Bank?', *Journal of Financial Regulation and Compliance*, **9** (1), 42–55.
Tedrow, E. (2006), 'Social Security Privatization in Other Countries – What Lessons Can Be Learned for the United States?', *Elder Law Journal*, **14**, 35–59.
Treasury Select Committee (1998), *Ninth Report: The Mis-selling of Personal Pensions*, pp. 1–9.
Waine, B. (2006), 'Ownership and Security: Individualised Pensions and Pension Policy in the United Kingdom and the United States', *Competition and Change*, **10** (3), 321–37.
Watson Wyatt (2006), 'Watson Wyatt's Survey on Default Investments and the DOL's Proposed Regulations', *Insider*.
Wooten, J. (2004), *The Employee Retirement Income Security Act of 1974: A Political History*, Berkeley and Los Angeles, US, London, UK: University of California Press, New York, US: Milbank Memorial Fund, Washington, D.C.: Employee Benefit Research Institute.

13. Talking about Pensions: An Analysis of Language Used to Discuss Pensions[1]

Bryn Davies

1. INTRODUCTION

The then Secretary of State for Work and Pensions in the UK, John Hutton, stated in 2006: 'Today's White Paper seeks to entrench a new pensions savings culture, whereby future generations can take increasing personal responsibility for building their retirement savings' (John Hutton, 2006 p. 6).

A future was presented for pension provision in the United Kingdom in terms of saving (Department for Work and Pensions, 2006). This chapter examines the use of the term 'saving', together with terms that might be used to describe alternative methods of financing pension provision, as examples of the language used in current debates on the future of pensions.

The underlying hypothesis is that much of the current discourse on pension reform is subjective and value-laden, being based on 'socially constructed stories and myths' (Lens, 2002), that serve to support a dominant attitude towards pension provision. Given such a hypothesis, the null hypothesis that needed to be tested is that discourse on pensions avoids such pitfalls and the terms that are employed, such as 'saving', are entirely neutral in their impact.

The main focus for discussion on pension provision is that which arose following the publication of the second report of the Pensions Commission, A New Pension Settlement for the Twenty-First Century, on 30 November 2005 (Pensions Commission, 2005). The publication of the report led to considerable discussion in the national media; a response from many policy orientated organisations; as well as much political debate, which culminated in the publication of the government's white paper (Department for Work and Pensions, 2006) on 25 May 2006.

The Pensions Commission's report was a substantial piece of work, with 472 pages in the main report and 40 pages for the executive summary. However, the Commission said that the two key elements of the reforms that it proposed were:

1. the creation of a low cost, national funded pension savings scheme into which individuals will be automatically enrolled, but with the right to opt out, with a modest level of compulsory matching employer contributions, and delivering the opportunity to save for a pension at a low annual management charge;
2. reforms to make the state system less means-tested and closer to universal than it would be if current indexation arrangements were continued indefinitely. In order to achieve this while maintaining the standard of living of the poorest pensioners it will need to be more generous on average. In the long-term this implies some mix of both an increase in taxes devoted to pensions expenditure and an increase in State Pension Ages (Pensions Commission, 2005 p. 6).

A selection of the textual material that followed the publication of the Pensions Commission report was looked at, up to the date the white paper was published; neither the report of the Pensions Commission or the white paper itself was analysed. It is important to emphasise that the analysis was not intended to be quantitative but, rather, a qualitative study of the way that language is used by participants in the public discourse on pensions.

In the event, the research looked at the discourse to the extent that it is about the two principle methods of pension provision, that is, 'savings' and 'promises' (Barr, 2001). As a result, it could only be a partial picture of the current discourse on pensions. However, it was clear from my successive readings of the source material that the concept of saving constituted an important and interesting theme in the great majority of contributions to the discourse and, as such, is a worthwhile basis for the analysis.

The concepts of 'saving' and 'promises' are important because a crucial question that underlies much of current debate about pensions is the best way to finance a reasonable income in retirement? Thus, 'saving', is where each individual sets aside part of their income while they are at work, so that they have the resources available when, because of their age, they are no longer gainfully employed; 'promises' is where individuals obtain commitments of support in their retirement from the economically active population.

This dichotomy of concepts surrounding pension provision is given practical effect by the choice between funded and pay-as-you-go (PAYG) arrangements (Barr, 2001) and the distinction is well understood at this level. What is not so clear is the extent to which the outcome of such debates is influenced by the language through which it is conducted. For example, Edelman argues that 'linguistic cues evoke prestructured beliefs regarding the nature and causes of public problems' (1998 p.131). He goes on to suggest that because such beliefs are not based on rigorous analysis, they typically fail to analyse problems adequately and rarely provide satisfactory solutions. If these are the consequences of an unquestioned acceptance of particular concepts, then an analysis along the lines undertaken in this essay might serve to advance future pension debates.

With this is mind, the following sections of this chapter provide the following.

- A short summary of the research method that was adopted, that is, discourse analysis.
- A review of the concepts of pension provision that might be adopted within the discourse.
- A description of the data that was analysed.
- The results of the analysis.
- Some conclusions about the language used in current debates on pensions.

2. DISCOURSE AND FRAMEWORKS

There are two elements to the research method used. First, a qualitative approach that falls within the description of discourse analysis and secondly, this approach was used to identify concepts that might influence, if not determine, the outcome of the discourse on pensions. A useful definition of discourse analysis is provided by Gill. 'Discourse analysts are interested in texts in their own right, rather than seeing them as a means of getting at some reality that is assumed to lie behind the discourse, …' (Gill, 1996).

Discourse Analysis

Discourse analysis involves the study of the texts through which policy debates are undertaken. Gill (2000; 1996) explains that, strictly speaking, there is no single 'discourse analysis' but many different styles of analysis that all lay claim to the name, having developed from different theoretical traditions and disciplines. Hollway (1989) comments that '… the primacy of language and text …' as a way of investigating social issues is almost the only thing that the many variants of discourse analysis have in common.

However, Gill (2000; 1996) suggests that these different approaches share four main themes in that they all:

- make the discourse itself the topic of study, as opposed to the true nature of society;
- take language to be constructive in that it can, for example, make a particular version of the world seem to be unproblematic (Potter, 1996 p.131);
- are orientated towards action or function, that is they share an interest in understanding how the discourse identified in the analysis is linked to actions and practices; and

- treat texts as being organised rhetorically, that is '... establishing one version of the world in the face of competing versions' (Gill, 2000 p. 176)

What these approaches suggest is that it is as important to study the significance of the terms in which a debate on social policy is undertaken, as it is to study the policies themselves.

The overall objective of this type of research is to produce novel and plausible interpretations of social phenomena (Howarth, 2000). It is not capable of producing, nor is it intended to produce, broad empirical laws (Billig, 1988), although there is a growing awareness of the way in which qualitative research in general can complement quantitative approaches to research (see Flick 2002).

In summary, the end result of discourse analysis is an interpretation of a particular social phenomenon that should be judged in terms of whether it:

- presents a coherent account that deals with apparent contradictions and alternative readings;
- provides the evidence that would enable the reader to form their own judgements;
- permits an independent audit of the chain of reasoning that led to the researcher's conclusions; and
- demonstrates to the reader an awareness of the consequences of the researcher's own presence in the research project.

Potter (1996) comments 'Perhaps the most important and distinctive feature in the validation of discourse analysis is the presentation of rich and extended materials in a way that allows the readers of discourse studies to evaluate their adequacy'. In the same vein, Howarth (2000 p. 130) says that '... discourse theory ...can be evaluated by the degree to which it makes possible new and meaningful interpretations of the social and political phenomena it investigates'. In some ways this might be regarded as a tougher target than required for the validation of quantitative analysis.

Ideas about Dominant Paradigms

The second element of the theoretical background to this analysis is an understanding of the ways in which particular frameworks of thinking about social issues acquire and retain general acceptance. This is a substantial subject in itself that can only be touched upon in this paper. However, a number of authors have provided useful descriptions of the sort of phenomena that might be found through the use of discourse analysis.

One concept that is important in this context is that of 'commonsense', that is 'the general sense, feeling, or judgement of mankind, or of a community' (OED Online, 2006). The importance of commonsense in this context is explained by Fairclough (1989), who pointed out that texts are produced and interpreted against a background of commonsense assumptions and that '... the aim [of the analyst] is to ... develop self-consciousness about the rootedness of discourse in commonsense assumptions' (Fairclough, 1989 p. 167). There is, of course, no reason to consider in this context whether such commonsense is or is not correct. What is of interest is whether there are other frameworks of thinking on the same topic that, for one reason or another, play little part in popular discourse.

Lakoff refines this approach with the concept of 'metaphorical commonsense reasoning' (Lakoff, 1996; Lakoff and Johnson, 1980). He points out that metaphor is pervasive in everyday life but this is not something we are normally aware of and is by no means obvious. He also explains that such metaphors do not need to be poetic, fanciful or rhetorical but are simply a way of understanding and experiencing one kind of thing in terms of another.

The tacit nature of the different theories we hold about society has been explored by O'Brien and Penna (1998), who point out that most often we are not consciously aware of their details. We also accept, reject and modify these theories as a matter of routine, without reflection on either how they are put together or which theories are useful in accounting for different situations and experiences. (O'Brien and Penna, 1998 p. 3).

The importance of this type of discourse is also emphasised by Schram (1995; 2006). He refers, in particular, to the importance of examining the power of discourse to invoke contexts that make some actions seem appropriate and others not. He comments that 'the power of discourse is represented in iterated discursive practices that reinforce themselves to the point that we can say they 'make themselves real' privileging their way of saying and doing things, while marginalizing others (Schram, 2006 p. xi).

Another way to understand how some ideas 'resonate more than others' is that of 'policy narratives' (Roe, 1994 p. 34). These are what Roe describes as 'stories ... which underwrite and stabilize the assumptions for policymaking in situations that persist with many unknowns, a high degree of interdependence, and little, if any, agreement.' Roe uses as an example of such a policy narrative 'The Tragedy of the Commons',[2] which is told as a story having all the classic properties of a beginning, middle and an end. But when probed empirically, Roe says that it is found that reality and story coincide imperfectly, with the data turning out to be much more ambiguous or downright contradictory. He also argues that such policy narratives are not displaced by negative findings that seem to refute it. Rather, it can only be displaced by '...an equally straightforward narrative that tells a better story' (Roe, 1994 p. 40).

A relevant description of how such narratives work in practice, with reference to how policy actors at international level have constructed the pension policy issue, is provided by Ney (2000). His paper reviews what he describes as 'policy stories' about pension reform with, he argues, each of the three different stories starting from differing assumptions, producing contradictory prognoses of the pension problem, and prescribing diverging policy solutions. Thus, while policy stories provide templates for producing plausible policy arguments in political debates they do so by '... weaving scientific knowledge, 'objective' fact and normative convictions about social welfare systems into a seamless rhetorical fabric' (Ney, 2000 p. 341).

Given the background described in this section, I have used a form of discourse analysis to search for what, if any, commonsense assumptions, metaphors and policy narratives are used in current debates on pensions. The following section therefore outlines possible frameworks of thinking on the finance of pensions.

3. PENSION FINANCE

The belief that people who want to provide for their retirement need to set aside part of their income while they are at work – in other words, that they undertake the process of saving – might appear to be no more than common sense. The problem is that while this may be correct for an individual, it is not necessarily correct for a society as a whole. This is because society, as compared to an individual, has some choice about how to secure pensions.

This choice is described by Barr (2001 p. 90) as being between:

- Saving part of each week's wages and building up a pile of money that can be exchanged for goods produced by younger people; or
- Obtaining a promise from the government to provide goods produced by others after retirement.

Barr (2001 p. 90) goes on to explain that the two most common ways of organising pensions, which parallel these different types of claim on future output, are for example, funded schemes, based on accumulation of financial assets, that is saving and pay-as-you-go (PAYG) schemes, based on the accumulation of promises.

The Pensions Commission (2004, Appendices p. 23) similarly explains that a crucial choice in pension system design is whether to rely on an unfunded pay-as-you-go (PAYG) system, or to fund pensions via investments in marketable assets. The same sort of distinction is made by the World Bank in its seminal report 'Averting the old age crisis: policies to protect the old and promote growth' (1994 p. 76).

The existence of these two approaches to pension provision is therefore clear. What is not so clear, however, are the implications of adopting one approach, as compared to the other.

The Implications of Saving versus Promises

When considering the implications of the choice of method of financing pensions there is what Barr describes as 'a large, complex and controversial literature' (2001 p. 104). At the heart of the controversy is the issue of whether one approach to the provision of pensions, that is funding, has intrinsic advantages over the other approach, that is pay-as-you-go. There is no easy resolution to this debate, but Minns (2001) has argued that while the proponents of funding suggest a range of advantages, their case depends on the argument that funding leads to greater saving and investment; which leads in turn to more economic growth; resulting in an enhanced ability to pay higher pensions in future. He supports this by drawing attention to the comment by Martin Feldstein, a major advocate of the privatisation and funding of pensions who states: 'Without extra savings and an increase in the nation's capital stock, nothing would be gained by shifting some of the existing trust fund [Federal Government Social Security] from government bonds to private stocks or bonds' (Feldstein, 1997).

His general conclusion has been supported by some later research. For example, Hemming (1999 p. 3) concluded that 'theoretical arguments tend to be consistent with the view that funding will be associated with higher saving than pay-as-you-go', although he went on to say that 'convincing empirical support is missing'.

Other commentators have taken a contrary view, however. For example, Hughes (2000) concluded that 'the balance of the evidence ... does not show that pay-as-you-go state pensions significantly reduce saving or that funded occupational or personal pensions significantly increase it'. Similarly, Orszag and Stiglitz (2001) included the idea that (funded) individual accounts raise national saving as one of their ten myths about (pay-as-you-go) social security systems.

Barr (2001 p. 104) concludes that 'the magnitude of the impact of funding on growth is controversial. Though there is some empirical evidence that funding contributes to higher savings in the USA, there is no robust evidence of a similar affect elsewhere'. Barr (Barr and Diamond 2006) also reminds us of the point made by Atkinson (1999), that any analysis which ignores the benefits of the welfare state, while considering its cost, is deficient.

Another issue to be considered is whether additional wealth is created, even if savings do increase. The standard macro-economic view is that they do, but perhaps not in the way that common sense might suggest, because of what Blanchard (2005) describes as the 'paradox of saving'. This is the theory that if people attempt to save more at a given level of income, their income decreases by an amount such that their saving is unchanged. Blanchard goes on to explain that this is only relevant in the short run and that other mechanisms come into play over time such that '... an increase in the saving rate is likely to lead over time to higher saving and higher income' (2005 p. 60). The important words to be noted here are 'likely over time'.

Despite the controversial nature of the debate on the impact of saving for pensions, the suggestion that saving does lead to economic growth has played a large part in the development of what Müller has described as a 'new pensions orthodoxy' (Müller, 2003). Adopting the phrase from the original in Spanish (Lo Vuolo, 1996), it refers to the savings orientated approach to pension provision promoted most notably by the World Bank (1994), which has become a 'dominant new policy paradigm' (Orenstein, 2003 p.172). This is despite Barr's conclusion that there is no robust evidence in support of the link between greater pension saving and growth and that even if there is such a link, there is no guarantee about the timing or the extent of any effect.

The Data

The data used for our analysis were drawn from publicly available sources and were intended to be sufficient for the purposes of the analysis that has been undertaken. As it was a qualitative study the issues of sampling and randomness did not arise when selecting data; instead the objective is to satisfy the reader that sufficient data has been used to justify the conclusions that have been drawn. As David and Sutton state 'when these [tentative] predictions are continually confirmed the researcher can conclude that enough data has been collected' (David and Sutton, 2004 p. 361)

The subject of this analysis is the public discourse on pensions that took place between 30 November 2005 and 25 May 2006. There are many potential sources of material that would reflect that debate but, in the event, I have focused on discussion in the national press and on commentaries from policy-orientated organisations. The limited scale of the project made it necessary, in any event, to make some choice of material and I concluded during the progress of the analysis that these sources were, by themselves, of sufficient interest.

The choices that have been made mean that much material of potential interest has been excluded. For example, no strictly academic work has been considered, nor has what might be described as 'popular' discourse, that is, discussion by the woman or man in the street. This is not to say that such sources are of no interest, although I would argue that neither plays as direct a role in current debates. In addition, consideration of popular discourse would certainly require radically different techniques of data collection, such as focus groups and questionnaires from either primary or secondary sources, plus a significantly more arduous process of analysis.

One source of material to which I gave more consideration was political debates during the relevant period, for example those that took place in Parliament, and, initially, I intended to include such material. In the event I have not done so, mainly due to the additional analysis that would have been required and the conclusion, reached after some initial readings, that it added little to the evidence as it broadly reflected what was already being said in the material that was included.

Table 13.1 lists the 17 newspapers that were included. Only one article was looked at from each paper; typically the main leader column or a main article in the editorial pages.

Table 13.1 Newspapers included in the analysis

Daily Mail	*Sunday Times*
Daily Star	*The Express*
Daily Telegraph	*The Guardian*
Financial Times	*The Independent*
Independent on Sunday	*The Mirror*
Mail on Sunday	*The Observer*
Morning Star	*The Sun*
Sunday Express	*The Times*
Sunday Mirror	

The 21 policy-orientated organisations concerned are listed in Table 13.2 together, where relevant, with the abbreviation that is used to identify them in the following sections. Only one paper was used from each organisation, with the most substantial piece of work being chosen from the relevant period.

Results of the Analysis

The approach adopted for the research involved looking at the discourse with reference to methods of financing pensions and looking for similarities and the differences as they relate to saving and to promises. The purpose is not to produce a representative sample, in quantitative terms, but simply to illustrate how the discourse worked. Given this approach, one feature that became clear was that while the use of the concept of saving as a means of financing pensions was widespread in the discourse, for example a commonly expressed view is as follows:- 'It seems we've all got to work longer, save more money and pay more tax.' *Daily Star* (1 December 2005). The concept of pensions being financed by promises was, by contrast, absent, except by implication, as discussed below. Given this difference in treatment, Table 13.3 lists the different terms that were coded as referring to the concept of saving as a method of financing pensions, with a count of the number of newspapers and organisations respectively that employed that concept in its different forms.

Given the absence of any direct reference in the discourse to promises as a means of financing pensions, there is no equivalent table for that concept.

Table 13.2 Organisations included in the analysis

Full Name	Abbreviation Used
Association of British Insurers	ABI
Actuarial Profession	
Age Concern	
The Association of Retired and Persons Over 50	ARP
British Banking Association	BBA
Carers UK	
Confederation of British Industry	CBI
Citizens Advice	
Consumers' Association	
Centre for Policy on Ageing	CPA
Engineering Employers' Federation	EEF
Equal Opportunities Commission	EOC
Fawcett Society	
Help the Aged	
Investment Managers' Association	IMA
Institute of Directors	IoD
National Pensioners' Convention	NPC
Pension Reform Group	PRG
Pensions Management Institute	PMI
Pensions Policy Institute	PPI
Tomorrow's Company	
Trades Union Congress	TUC

The Commission's Approach

As might be expected, much of the debate on pensions that took place during the period of analysis was framed by the conclusions of the Pensions Commission in its second report (Pensions Commission, 2005). This might be considered to be a problem in trying to undertake the analysis, in that most contributions to the discourse might be simply a reflection of the Commission's approach. In quantitative terms it might be considered to be a 'confounding variable' (Meltzoff, 1998), which masks what is really going on in the discourse. This is a real danger but not necessarily a problem, providing it is appropriately recognised when undertaking the analysis.

Table 13.3 Number of texts coded as using concepts related to saving as a means of financing pension provision

	Newspaper	Organisations
Discourage saving	1	0
Saving process	14	13
Individual ownership	2	3
Provide for retirement	1	1
Invest	3	3
Saving structures	9	10
Self-reliance	1	0
Defer consumption	1	1
NPSS	5	5
Personal pension saving	1	1
Encourage saving	4	5
Any of the above	15	17
Total texts	17	21

The Commission's third and final report (Pensions Commission, 2006), which was written and published towards the end of the chosen period, noted that the debate that had taken place had 'revealed a high degree of consensus on the direction of policy reform now required'. In particular, emphasising a theme of all three of its reports, it said, with reference to its conclusion in its second report (Pensions Commission, 2005) that the UK's pension system was not 'fit for purpose', that: 'There is a significant degree of consensus that the solution must and should entail some combination of higher private pension saving, higher average retirement ages, and an increased percentage of national income spent on state pensions.' (p. 10)

Of the Commission's three options for improving the pension system, that of higher average retirement ages is neutral as between saving and promises. Thus, an increase in the retirement age is equally effective in increasing the benefits paid by an approach based on promises, because fewer people will be entitled to share the funds available, as it is in increasing the benefits paid by an approach based on saving, because the accumulated fund accrues further interest and needs to purchase an annuity for a shorter period. Given this neutrality, I did not analyse the discourse on pension age.

Both of the Commission's other two options, that is, higher private pension saving and an increased percentage of national income spent on state pensions, relate to the issue of how pensions are financed, with the former based on the 'saving' and the latter based on 'promises'. The suggestion that they constitute different options is interesting in itself, given the extent to which it can be argued that there can be limited differences in practice. The objective of the research, however, was simply to explore differences in the way they were treated within the discourse on pensions.

There was certainly little or no explicit rejection within the discourse of the Commission's analysis of possible solutions, with a number of contributions providing specific support. There was one contribution that represented an implicit rejection of the Commission's approach, however, with the National Pensioners' Convention seeing its desired solution solely in terms of increased spending on State pensions

Given the extent of the support for saving as a means of financing pensions, as compared to the absence of support for promises as a means of financing pensions, I looked for what differences there were in the way that savings and promises were treated in the discourse.

Saving

There was widespread discussion of a solution to the problems identified by the Pensions Commission based on greater saving, with the overwhelming majority indicating some degree of support and no explicit rejection. It was found that 15 out of 17 newspapers and 17 out of 21 organisations made reference to the concept of saving as a means of financing pensions. And, of those newspapers and organisations that did not employ the concept, in all cases but one, it was because they did not address the issue of how pensions were to be financed, rather than because they employed the concept of promises instead. The one exception to this rule was, as mentioned above, the NPC.

Despite this widespread acceptance of an important role for saving in pension provision, the approach was not seen as problem free. Some participants identified specific drawbacks in the savings approach, that is, the fact that some people find it tough to save; or that saving might have an adverse effect on economic growth. Nevertheless, despite the recognition of these drawbacks, they did not lead anyone to reject an approach based on saving.

Promises

The discourse included almost as many references to pensions provided on the basis of promises as it did to pensions based on saving. Thus, 11 out of the 17 newspapers and 15 out of the 21 organisations made such references.

Thus, the concept of pensions based on promises was an important element in the discourse. However, there are two important differences between such contributions, as compared to those made about saving, that is, first, the concept of making promises as a method of pension provision was never referred to explicitly, unlike saving which was referred to throughout, usually in favourable terms; and secondly, the references to promised based pensions focused almost entirely on the desired or anticipated outcome, rather than the method by which these outcomes were to be financed.

The second point is particularly important in this analysis. Thus, in the limited number of references to how improved state pensions were to be financed, they were, without exception, expressed in terms of higher taxation. These illustrations also indicate how paying more tax was seen consistently in a negative light, associated mainly with the use of words like 'pain' and 'sacrifice'. For example, there were no contributions to the discourse which illustrated the need for additional saving by employing a metaphor such as 'grasping the nettle', although, as far as the individual is concerned, the impact on their current income is the same, whether pensions are financed through increased saving or increased taxation.

Another feature of the discourse, where it related to pensions based on promises, is that the main function of such provision was perceived to be in support of savings-based provision.

Summary of Analysis

The twin options of pensions based on saving and pensions based on promises were both discussed widely in the discourse. There was a significant difference, however, in that the term 'saving' was used widely and explicitly as description of how pensions were to be financed, whereas the term 'promises', or synonyms such as 'solidarity' or 'sharing' were effectively absent from the discourse.

To the extent that reference was made in the discourse to the finance of promise based pensions, there was almost total uniformity in the use of the word 'tax' and the presentation of such an option in a negative light or, at best, politically infeasible. At the same time, the main role of promised-based pensions was seen as being to facilitate savings-based pensions.

5. CONCLUSIONS

The main conclusion of the analysis is that while saving is extensively referred to as a means of financing pensions, the other option of promises is conspicuous by its absence. Instead, it appears by means of a proxy which, in the terms used by the Pensions Commission, is 'increased spending' (Pensions Commission, 2005 p. 10), but in the discourse itself was referred to invariably as 'more tax'. In other words, the discourse is essentially presented in terms of 'more saving' or 'more tax'. For example, while *the Mirror* (a mass circulation newspaper) says 'WHY IT'S FAR BETTER WE ALL SAVE FOR OUR RETIREMENT' (their capitals), *the Sunday Mirror* says 'Significantly more taxation or higher retirement age for the state pension'.

Validation

It is ultimately for the reader to decide whether this analysis provides a coherent account of the relevant discourse on pensions and if the conclusions that have been reached provide a novel and meaningful interpretation of what took place. For this purpose the full dissertation, which includes a large number of direct quotations is available from the author or, ultimately, it is possible to access all the original material via the Internet. In this way it is possible to undertake an independent audit of my conclusions.

Implications for debates on pensions

Given these conclusions about the terms in which the choice between methods of financing pensions is discussed, it is important to consider whether saving and taxation can be regarded as concepts that are neutral in their impact. A useful starting point in such consideration is their respective dictionary definitions. Table 13.4 provides a dictionary definition of saving (Chambers, 2003).

'Saving' clearly has a number of different shades of meaning but, other than hoarding, they would probably all be regarded as 'a good thing'. In essence, saving is seen as an ideal, with both private and public benefits. As Mann (2006 p. 80) has pointed out, albeit somewhat critically, 'Working and saving are portrayed as unequivocally good for the individual, good for the economy and, in so far as they promote prudent habits more generally, good for society.'

Table 13.4 Dictionary definition of saving

v.t.	to rescue; to bring or keep out of danger; to bring safely out of evil; to protect; to preserve; to prevent or avoid the loss, expenditure, or performance of, or the gain of by an opponent; to reserve; to spare; to deliver from the power of sin and from its consequences; to be economical in the use of; to hoard; to (enter an instruction to) store (data) on a tape or disk (comput.); to prevent (a goal) from being scored; to obviate.
v.i.	to be economical; to reserve esp. money for future use; to act as a saviour;
n.	an act of saving

It is clear that the definition of tax shown in Table 13.5, is of a very different nature to that of saving and while it is possible to argue that taxation is a good thing, in that it makes possible the range of public services that people demand including, in particular, decent pensions, the underlying perception that is created by the use of the term is that it represents a burden. Saving, on the other hand, will be perceived as a virtue. This is certainly a perception that is reinforced by reading the data.

Table 13.5 Dictionary definition of 'tax' (Chambers, 2003)

v. t.	to lay a tax on: to burden: to accuse, censure: to assess: to examine (accounts) in order to allow or disallow items.
n.	a contribution exacted by the state: anything imposed, exacted, or burdensome.

There is, of course, no reason to assume that the outcome of the discourse will be determined by dictionary definitions or even by the discourse that takes place in newspapers and publications from policy-orientated organisations. It is of interest therefore to contrast the attitudes demonstrated in the data with the public's attitude to both saving and taxation as reported in the latest edition of the British Social Attitudes survey (Park et al. 2005).

As far as saving is concerned, the survey reports that 'The suggestion that people should save more is ... popular in principle, with most of the British public being in favour of people saving for their own retirement (and from a relatively early age)' (Phillips and Hancock, 2005 p. 188). For example, the survey found that around 80 per cent of the sample was in favour of the government encouraging people to provide something for their own retirement, instead of relying only on the state pension. However, the report goes on to point out that actual savings behaviour is not so clear-cut. Nevertheless, it is clear that saving is widely seen in a positive light.

By contrast, there is much less support for additional taxation as a means of financing pensions. Thus, the survey found that while there was a clear majority of the sample who favoured higher state pensions (73 per cent), only around half of those (that is 38 per cent of the total sample) were in favour of doing so by means of tax increases (Phillips and Hancock, 2005 p. 174). What the survey also found, however, was that there was strong support for redistribution of incomes as a by-product of spending and taxing in the ways that people want, even though redistribution was not seen to be a primary objective of the system (Sefton 2005 p. 27).

Impact on Pension Debates

It does not require a profound analysis to suggest that there might be some impact on the outcome of the discourse on pensions, as a result of using these different terms for the two possible approaches to financing pension provision. An obvious response to this suggestion is that it is simply a reflection of the true nature of the choice that has to be made but it would not be unreasonable to conclude that the use of a term other than 'tax' to describe the method of financing pensions based on promises might have some impact on the debate. This suggestion is given some support by the value that successive Government's have seen in retaining the term 'National Insurance Contributions' for what is now, in reality, just another tax (Hills, 2003).

It would seem reasonable to conclude, therefore, in the words of Potter (1996 p. 131), that a solution based on saving will be seen as less problematic that one based on promises, simply through the choice of words that are used to describe the alternatives. It might also seem no more than common sense to assume that pensions will be provided through more saving, even when the outcome is more complex. There is even an extent to which saving acts as a sort of generalised metaphor or policy narrative for pension provision, where people can have a picture in mind of what is involved. On the other hand, promises, particularly when expressed in the form of taxation, will not offer such an easy or such an attractive image. Ultimately, to use the approach suggested by Roe (1994 p. 34), saving is an idea that is bound to resonate more favourably than taxation. It is not necessarily the case that taxation is bound to be unpopular; but it is the case that saving appears to be inherently attractive.

NOTES

1. This is a shortened version of the dissertation I submitted in August 2006 as part of my M.Sc. course on Social Policy (Research) at the London School of Economics. Copies of the full paper are available on request from the author.
2. *The Tragedy of the Commons* is a parable written by William Forster Lloyd (1833) that was intended to demonstrate how common access to pasture inevitably ruined the resource because the benefits accrued to individuals, whereas the costs were paid collectively.

REFERENCES

Atkinson, A.B. (1999), *The Economic Consequences of Rolling Back the Welfare State*, Cambridge, MA: MIT Press.

Barr, N.A. (2001), *The welfare state as piggy bank: information, risk, uncertainty, and the role of the state*, Oxford: Oxford University Press.

Barr, N.A., and Diamond, P. (2006), 'The Economics of Pensions', Oxford Review Economic Policy, **22**, 15–39.

Billig, M. (1988), 'Methodology and scholarship in understanding ideological explanation', In C. Antaki (ed.), *Analysing everyday explanation: a casebook of methods* (pp. vii, 232). London: Sage.

Blanchard, O. (2005), *Macroeconomics* (4th ed.), Upper Saddle River, N.J.: Pearson and Prentice Hall Publications.

Chambers (2003), *The Chambers Dictionary*, Edinburgh: Chambers Harrap.

Coffey, A., and P. Atkinson, (1996), *Making sense of qualitative data: complementary research strategies*, Thousand Oaks, London: Sage Publications.

David, M., and C.D. Sutton, (2004), *Social Research: The Basics*, London: Sage Publications.

Department for Work and Pensions, (2006), *Security in Retirement: Towards a New Pensions System*, Cmd. 6841. London: HMSO.

Edelman, M. (1975, 1998), 'Language, Myths and Rhetoric', *Society*, **35** (2), 131–9.

Fairclough, N. (1989), *Language and power*, Harlow: Longman.

Feldstein, M. (1997), *The Case for Privatisation*, Foreign Affairs, **76** (4).

Flick, U. (2002), *An Introduction to Qualitative Research*, London: Sage.

Forster Lloyd William (1833), *Two Lectures on the Checks to Population*, Oxford: S. Collingwood.

Gill, R. (1996), 'Discourse analysis: practical implementation', in J.T.E. Richardson (ed.), *Handbook of Qualitative Research Methods for Psychology and the Social Sciences*, Leicester: BPS Books.

Gill, R. (2000), 'Discourse Analysis', In M.W. Bauer and G. Gaskell (eds), *Qualitative researching with text, image and sound: a practical handbook for social research*, London: Sage Publications.

Hemming, R. (1999), 'Should Public Pensions be Funded?' *International Social Security Review*, **52** (2) Apr.–June, 3–29.

Hills, J. (2003), *Inclusion or Insurance? National Insurance and the future of the contributory principle*, (CASE paper 68), London: Centre for the Analysis of Social Exclusion.

Hollway, W. (1989), *Subjectivity and method in psychology: gender, meaning and science*, London: Sage Publications.

Howarth, D. (2000), *Discourse*, Buckinghamshire, England: Open University Press.

Hughes, G. (2000), 'Pension Financing, the Substitution Effect and National Savings', G. Hughes and J. Stewart (eds), *Pensions in the European Union: Adapting to Economic and Social Change*, Amsterdam: Kluwer Academic Publishers.

Hutton, J. (2006), 'Statement on Pensions Reform. Commons Hansard Debates', **446** (158), Col. 1649.

Lakoff, G. (1996), *Moral politics: what conservatives know that liberals don't*, Chicago and London: University of Chicago Press.

Lakoff, G., and M. Johnson, (1980), *Metaphors we live by*, Chicago and London: University of Chicago Press.

Lens, V. (2002), 'Public voices and public policy: changing the societal discourse on 'welfare', *Journal of Sociology and Social Welfare*, March.

Lo Vuolo, R. M. (1996). 'Reformas previsionales en América Latina: el caso Argentino', *Comercio Exterior*, **46** (9), 692–702.

Mann, K. (2006), 'Three Steps to Heaven? Tensions in the Management of Welfare: Retirement Pensions and Active Consumers', *Journal of Social Policy*, **35** (1), 77–96.

Meltzoff, J. (1998), *Critical thinking about research: psychology and related fields*, Washington, D.C.: American Psychological Association.

Minns, R. (2001), *The cold war in welfare: stock markets versus pensions*, New York: VERSO.

Müller, K. (2003), 'The Making of Pension Privatization in Latin America and Eastern Europe', in R. Holzmann, M.A. Orenstein and M. Rutkowski (eds), *Pension reform in Europe: Process and Progress* (pp. viii, 202). Washington, D.C.: The World Bank.

Ney, S. (2000), 'Are You Sitting Comfortably… Then We'll Begin: Three Gripping Policy Stories About Pension Reform', *Innovation*, **13** (4), 341–371.

O'Brien, M., and Penna, S. (1998), *Theorising Welfare: Enlightenment and Modern Society*, London: Thousand Oaks, Ca.: Sage publications.

OED Online (2006), *The Oxford English Dictionary*, 2nd ed., from http://dictionary .oed. com /cgi/entry/00181778

Orenstein, M. A. (2003), 'Mapping the Diffusion of Pension Innovation', in R. Holzmann, M.A. Orenstein and M. Rutkowski (eds), *Pension reform in Europe: process and progress* (pp. viii, 202). Washington, D.C.: The World Bank.

Orszag, P.R., and J.E. Stiglitz, (2001), 'Rethinking Pension Reform: Ten Myths About Social Security Systems', in R. Holman and J.E. Stiglitz (eds), *New Ideas About Old Age Security*, Washington, D.C.: World Bank.

Park, A., J. Curtice, K. Thomson, C. Bromley, M. Phillips, and M. Johnson, (2005), *British Social Attutudes – the 22nd Report*, London: Sage Publications.

Pensions Commission (2004), *Pensions: Challenges and Choices: The First Report of the Pensions Commission*, London: The Stationary Office.

Pensions Commission (2005), *A New Pension Settlement for the Twenty-First Century: The Second Report of the Pensions Commission*, London: The Stationary Office.

Pensions Commission (2006). *Implementing an Integrated Package of Pension Reforms: The Final Report of the Pensions Commission* London: The Stationary Office.

Phillips, M., and R. Hancock, (2005), 'Planning for retirement: realism or denial?' in A. Park (ed.), *British Social Attitudes: the 22nd report* (pp. xx, 350). London: Sage Publications.

Potter, J. (1996), 'Discourse analysis and constructionist approaches: theoretical background', In J.T.E. Richardson (ed.), *Handbook of qualitative research methods for psychology and the social sciences* (pp. ix, 225) Leicester: BPS Books.

Roe, E. (1994), *Narrative Policy Analysis: Theory and Practice*, Durham: Duke University Press.

Schram, S. F. (1995), *Words of Welfare: the Poverty of Social Science and the Social Science of Poverty*, Minneapolis: University of Minnesota Press.

Schram, S.F. (2006), *Welfare Discipline*, Philadelphia: Temple University Press.

Sefton, T. (2005), 'Give and take: attitudes to redistribution', in A. Park (ed.), *British Social Attitudes*: the 22nd report (pp. xx, 350). London: Sage Publicatiopns.

World Bank (1994), *Averting the old age crisis*, Oxford UK, Published for the World Bank [by] Oxford University Press.

Index

open funds 40–41, 43–4, 47, 51, 53, 56, 60
Optional Employee Partnership 25
optional employee retirement savings plans 2

promises 11, 80, 264, 269, 272–3, 275–7, 279–80
providers of financial products or services (PFPS) 234–5, 240–41, 241, 247
public good 152–3